MARXISM AND RELIGION

WITHDRAWN FROM
THE LIBRARY
UNIVERSITY OF
WINCHESTER

A
T

D1425900

Also by David McLellan

ENGELS
KARL MARX: Early Texts
*KARL MARX: His Life and Thought
KARL MARX: Selected Writings
KARL MARX: The Legacy
MARX
*KARL MARX: Interviews and Recollections (*editor*)
MARX: The First 100 Years
IDEOLOGY
*MARXISM AFTER MARX
*MARX BEFORE MARXISM
*MARX'S GRUNDRISSE
*THE THOUGHT OF KARL MARX
*THE YOUNG HEGELIANS AND KARL MARX

*Also published by Macmillan

Marxism and Religion

A Description and Assessment of the
Marxist Critique of Christianity

David McLellan
Professor of Political Theory
University of Kent at Canterbury

MACMILLAN
PRESS

© David McLellan 1987

All rights reserved. No reproduction, copy or transmission
of this publication may be made without written permission.

No paragraph of this publication may be reproduced, copied
or transmitted save with written permission or in accordance
with the provisions of the Copyright Act 1956 (as amended),
or under the terms of any licence permitting limited copying
issued by the Copyright Licensing Agency, 33–4 Alfred Place,
London WC1E 7DP

Any person who does any unauthorised act in relation to
this publication may be liable to criminal prosecution and
civil claims for damages.

First published 1987

Published by
THE MACMILLAN PRESS LTD
Houndmills, Basingstoke, Hampshire RG21 2XS
and London
Companies and representatives
throughout the world

Typeset by Wessex Typesetters
(Division of The Eastern Press Ltd)
Frome, Somerset

Printed in Great Britain by
Anchor Brendon Ltd
Tiptree, Essex

British Library Cataloguing in Publication Data
McLellan, David
Marxism and religion: a description and
assessment of the Marxist critique of
Christianity.
1. Communism and Christianity—History
I. Title
201   HX536
ISBN 0–333–44629–1 (hardcover)
ISBN 0–333–44630–5 (paperback)

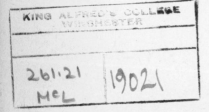

KING ALFRED'S COLLEGE
WINCHESTER

261.21
MeL   19021

For Deborah

Contents

Preface

This book is (I hope) academic, but it is also personal. The two subjects under discussion – Marxism and religion – have long been of interest to me. I became a Roman Catholic while an undergraduate student at Oxford; I even aspired to enter the Society of Jesus and spent some time in the Jesuit noviciate – an experience for which I shall always be grateful. Meanwhile, my attention had been drawn to Marxism by a fortuitous short visit to the Soviet Union. I pursued this interest on entering academic life and have continued to do so for the last twenty years. The Marxist critique of religion seemed to me the most powerful available – certainly more powerful than the anaemic dissections produced by variants of logical positivist analysis or the narcissistic discussions of some disciples of Freud or Nietzsche – and I was determined to get to the bottom of it; the following pages are the result. Of course, I have not succeeded in plumbing the depths. But what I have tried to do is to set out as fairly as I can the accounts of religion available in the main Marxist tradition with some commentary as to their consistency and historical accuracy, and then, in a substantial conclusion, change tone by offering some thoughts on the wider import of these Marxist accounts. The subject is vast and my treatment necessarily superficial and so, as a palliative, I have added a largish critical bibliography for those who wish to pursue particular aspects. Lastly, it should be noted that the 'religion' of the title refers almost exclusively to Christianity. This is not out of disrespect for other world religions or Marxist accounts of them; it is because the elision of the two terms is inherent in the Western and Soviet Marxist tradition that I am examining and also because Christianity is the only religion of which, through adherence, I have had much experience.

DAVID McLELLAN

Introduction: Religion and Marxism

In the autumn of 1843 a deputation of progressive German intellectuals visited Paris. These Young Hegelians wished to unite the radical humanist theory that they had acquired through Feuerbach's critique of Hegel with practical progressive politics. The repressive political climate in their own country and the knowledge that socialism was a French invention led them inevitably to Paris. Their leading members were Arnold Ruge, Moses Hess and Karl Marx. Ruge's diary amusingly records their consternation at finding as they traipsed from one socialist salon to another, that their intended crusaders-in-arms agreed with most of their ideas but that the one thing they could not stomach was their apparent atheism. Lammenais, Blanc, Cabet were all believers and held to Robespierre's anathema of godless philosophy. The dominant, if rather simple, view was that communism was just Christianity in practice and that Jesus Christ was the first Communist.

This happy marriage did not last for long. The Christian Churches grew increasingly conservative as the nineteenth century progressed, a high point being reached with the condemnation in Pius IX's *Syllabus Errorum* of liberalism, progress and democracy. With, on the other hand, socialism's acquiring a progressively rigid Marxist form and thereby, in the 1890s, a materialist metaphysic, a divorce between religion and socialism became unavoidable. This applies, of course, much more to the continent of Europe than to Britain where the pluralism of religious tradition, allied perhaps to a native distrust of overly systematic thought, has permitted a more fruitful relationship between some sorts of religion and politics.

In general, however, it was only the changed climate of recent decades that allowed a re-emergence of what came to be known, in the vernacular of the time, as a Marxist–Christian 'dialogue'. The coincidence of the 20th Congress of the Communist Party of the Soviet Union and the Second Vatican Council lessened the attraction of dogma for its own sake. The enthusiasm for dialogue came mainly from the Christian side, and in particular from energetic German Protestant theologians: many of the Communist protagonists simply abandoned their positions: Kolakowski left Poland and Garaudy was expelled from the French Communist Party. This dialogue was also a product of the relatively untrammelled expansion of post-war capitalism in the 1950s and 1960s. With the consequent alleged demise of ideology many Christian theologians felt obliged to embrace secularisation and, in the manner of Harvey Cox, actually celebrate it as an at least partial realisation of the Gospel.

It is against this background that I wish to re-examine this dialogue from the point of view of Marxism. Given that Christianity has informed Western culture for almost two millennia it is inevitable that Marxism should, in some sense, be a Christian heresy. And if Marxism is a child of Christianity I wish to enquire what Marxist approach inside the heresy could best bridge, if no more, the generation gap.

Marxism, too, has its orthodoxy. This orthodoxy proclaims that Marxism is a science. And such a science had been held to be incompatible with religious belief on two grounds. The first, and more straightforward one, is that Marxism contains a materialist metaphysic. If, as alleged by Engels, 'the unity of the world consists in its materiality', then all statements, including religious ones, are ultimately reducible to statements about the movement of matter. Secondly, religion can be dismissed not in metaphysical, but in functional terms: religion is an instrument of class rule, an ideological bulwark of the dominant class. This view, too, contains a covert ontology, both in its simplistic equation of the origin of a belief with its truth value and its assumption that religious assertions must always be a cloak for something else – obviously so in the case of conservative religion but equally so in the case of radical religious movements (Anabaptists, Cargo Cults) which must be cloaks for political demands. The traditional Marxist metaphor from heavy engineering – that of base and superstructure – tends to put religion on the tip-top of the superstructure and thus as the furthest remove from 'reality'. It is this approach which explains why so much Marxist writing on religion is so bad. Marx has often been taken, along with Weber and Durkheim, to be one of the three founding fathers of sociology. As far as religion is concerned, the contributions of Marxists to our understanding of religion seems, often in contrast to those writing in a Weberian or Durkheimian tradition, to be usually very poor. This is not always for lack of interest – it is just that many Marxists could not take religion

seriously. Marx himself devoted little time to a study of ｝
indeed his famous pregnant aphorisms on religion are little more, as
he himself says, than a repetition of Feuerbach.

Although the orthodox Communist view has been that Marxism
as a science implies that religion is some sort of an illusion, there is
another view of Marxism as a science that does allow room for
legitimate religious belief. Marxism, it is said, is the science of
society, a description of how society works: for normative
judgements about society we shall have to go elsewhere. This has a
respectable Marxist pedigree and indeed became the dominant
interpretation of Marxism during the two decades preceding the
First World War. With the growing prestige of natural science,
Marxism came to be seen as a similar 'science' of society and Marx's
method was seen as akin to that of Darwin. It was Engels himself
who declared at Marx's graveside: 'Just as Darwin discovered the
law of development of organic nature, so Marx discovered the law of
development of human nature.' The growth of mass Marxist
movements, too, particularly in Germany, called forth an exposition
of Marxism that was clear, simple and comprehensive. And the
neo-Darwinian interpretation of Marx seemed to fit the bill
admirably – all the more so as it seemed to bring the added
psychological advantage of an assured eventual victory.
Nevertheless, like nature, you can pitchfork values out but they will
come rushing back. And indeed they did with a revival of
Kantianism inside Marxism. Faced with the apparent autonomy of
the material world, Kant had embraced the divorce of facts from
values and attempted to construct a moral system that was justified
in its own terms, and without reference to the world. As such, it was
obviously compatible with a neo-Darwinian Marxism reduced to an
allegedly scientific account of the laws of motion of society. Kantian
morality could be laid on top of Marxist science and socialism could
have both its facts and its values, a position most fully worked out
by the Austromarxists. Moreover if, as came very slowly to be
concluded, Darwinism in one shape or form was not necessarily
incompatible with the Christian religion – then why should neo-
Darwinian Marxism be incompatible? What harm could religion see
in a mere science of society? Or Marxism in a religion that was
irrelevant to scientific socialism?

But I am unhappy with this neat – over-neat – solution to our
problem. This is no dialogue, let alone any dialectic. It is simply a
division of labour. One of the most depressing aspects of some

contemporary intellectual life is the compartmentalisation of
knowledge. The cobbler should stick to the last, it is said. We all
have our 'fields'. No politics is sport. Leave nuclear power to the
experts, etc. But it seems to me that much of the most interesting
work is done, certainly in the social sciences, on the borderlines or
'interface', as the contemporary expression has it, between two
disciplines; where, instead of sleeping peacefully side by side,
disciplines engage in fruitful intercourse. Of course, it may well be
safer to stick to one's last and one can obviously see why, under
certain circumstances, party and church have adopted the 'safe'
option of carving a piece of ideological territory which is exclusively
theirs to till as they will without outside and alien interference. But
the very roots of the Marxist and Christian traditions preclude this
option – to be true to themselves they have to live dangerously.

For Christianity this may seem obvious: only the most perverse
fixation on such statements as 'render unto Caesar' or 'my kingdom
is not of this world' could lead to the view that Christianity is only
concerned with disembodied values and essentially an 'other-
worldly' religion. But what of Marxism? I wish to suggest that in the
relationship of Marxism to religion a dialectical Marxism which takes
its debt to Hegel seriously – as opposed to those versions outlined
above – is capable of a more fruitful approach. The only approaches
open to 'scientific' Marxism are either negation or exclusion, saying
of religion either 'it is false' or 'it has nothing to do with me'. And we
can see that this is borne out by a glance at the classical Marxist
thinkers. Although Marx said little about religion, most of what he
did say – connected with the subject of alienation, for example – has
provided much food for Christian thought. Engels, on the other
hand, is rather more sparse when it comes to material for dialogue –
except in his early period, which is of course precisely the time when
he was busy secularising his Young Hegelian views. Kautsky and
the Second International Marxists have no time for Hegel and –
correspondingly, so I am arguing – no interest in the content of
religion. Lenin's views of religion as 'mediaeval mildew' or 'one of
the most odious things on earth' and of the idea of God as a concept
of 'inexpressible foulness' go hand in hand with the simplistic
materialism of *Materialism and Empiriocriticism*: Lenin's views are
much more muted after his serious study of Hegel in the war years.
Stalin reinforced, in philosophy at least, the worst aspects of
Leninism and had as little time for religion as he did for Hegel –
except as an added support for Russian patriotism during Hitler's

war. Certain sections of the Frankfurt School, Gramsci, the later Sartre, have all conserved something of the legacy of Hegel and thus talk, in some respects, the same language as Christianity. It is significant that one of the factors leading to a loss of interest in Marxist–Christian dialogue in France was the growing popularity of the anti-humanist, anti-Hegelian, anti-religious Marxism of structuralist inspiration *à la* Althusser. After so much muddying of the waters by such as Roger Garaudy when it was difficult to spot the difference between progressive Communists and left-wing Catholics, many a Party member must have breathed a very heavy sigh of relief when at last there arose an intellectual leader whose version of Marxist doctrine was of a rigour and rigidity that precluded any sort of conversation with wayward Christians, existentialists and the like. Though, curiously enough, Althusser is more explicit than any other Marxist on the likelihood of religion persisting under communism as the masses will need some sort of ideology – science, of course, being necessarily the preserve of the Party intellectuals such as himself. The following chapters, therefore, are not just an academic exercise in the history of ideas. I believe that it matters which kind of Marxism or socialism is adopted by those who are inclined to espouse such ideas. It would be a mistake for those on the left to fail to leave some space for religion in their approach to society and politics. Religion in some shape or form has been a deep and enduring aspect of human activity – and there is every reason to think that this will continue to be so for at least the near future. Benign neglect or outright rejection by the left will mean that the immense power of religion can be captured by the ideologies of the right. Consider here the dangerous role of the so-called 'moral majority' in America and the way in which, almost by default, a whole string of repressive social measures, let alone aggressive nuclear stances, appear to many to have behind them the weight of the whole Judeao-Christian tradition.

For the religious side, though, too, the consideration is appropriate that the Marxist attitude to religion is a function of the kind of religion they see. Marx's idea of God as a projection of alienated human beings whereby God becomes rich in proportion as humanity becomes poor does indeed apply to a lot of the extreme Lutheranism of the time with its belief in the utter corruption of human nature, unbridgeable gulf between God and humanity, salvation therefore *fide sola*, etc. And Engels's views are undoubtedly coloured by the appalling Pietism of his Wuppertal background. Lenin's extreme views on religion are rendered entirely intelligible by the even more appalling mixture of other-worldly spirituality and this worldly subordination to Tsarist autocracy that characterised the Russian Orthodox Church of his time. The question therefore confronting religious believers with progressive social and political views is whether, without prejudicing their faith, they can present a face in which Marxists can see reflected much of their own aspirations for humanity. As a contribution to this whole process what I try to do in the following chapters is to describe what the mainstream Marxist thinkers have said about religion together with some intellectual and historical background to supply a context; to assess, where possible, the coherence and empirical accuracy of these views; and finally, to offer some thoughts about the general significance of the Marxist critique of religion.

1

Marx

1. INTRODUCTION

Marx's best-known statement about religion is that religion is the opium of the people. But the various interpretations to which this apparently simple description has been subject strikingly demonstrates the possible ambivalence of Marx's attitude. The central Marxist tradition, as in, for example, Lenin, has seen the opium analogy as entirely negative.[1] It has, on the other hand, been claimed that the target of Marx's criticism is limited to a peculiarly other-worldly sort of Protestant Christianity, that the uses to which opium were put at the time meant that it had a far less pejorative connotation than it does today, that in the same passage Marx speaks of religion as 'protest', and so on.[2] Still others have claimed that, however much the metaphyiscal claims of Marx's early humanism may militate against religious belief, this is not true of his later 'scientific' work whose flavour is – as regards religion at least – more neutral.[3]

This chapter will attempt to shed some light on these controversies by describing Marx's comments on religion, firstly in his early work where they are numerous and then in his later writings where they are much rarer. There follows an evaluation of Marx's more empirically oriented comments on the role of religion in particular historical conjunctures. Finally, Marx's prognostications for the future of religion will be discussed together with the difficulties inherent in his overall account.

2. THE GENESIS OF MARX'S ATHEISM

Unlike his friend and colleague Engels, Marx has been called a natural atheist.[4] This may be too definite, given the sparsity of evidence on Marx's early life, but it is clear that whereas Engels came from a strongly Christian household, the prevailing religious atmosphere in Marx's house was the anaemic rational religion of the

Englightenment. Although it would be difficult to find anyone with a more Jewish ancestry than Marx and although this undoubtedly contributed to his rather rootless cosmopolitanism and the critical attitude he was thus able to develop towards society, there is no evidence that Marx's Jewishness directly influenced his views of religion.[5] Marx's father was a reluctant convert (for reasons of job security) from Judaism to Protestantism and a follower of Voltaire and Rousseau. He was a 'Protestant *à la* Lessing'[6] whose shallow, moralising deism is reflected in his advice to his son that 'a good support for morality is a simple faith in God. You know I am the last person to be a fanatic. But sooner or later a man has real need of this faith. . . . Everyone should submit to what was the faith of Newton, Locke or Leibniz.'[7] And these sentiments are echoed – as one might expect – in Marx's set essay on religion for his school-leaving exam which, for all its pious expressions, has a basically rationalist structure explaining how the advent of Christianity was necessary for the full moral development of humanity.[8]

Such formal expression of piety, however, did not long survive Marx's entrance into the Universities of Bonn and Berlin. The conception of a distant God who served as the guarantor of human aspirations was overtaken by the indelible impression made upon Marx by the philosophy of Hegel which then dominated the University of Berlin. Hegel took very seriously the historical function of religion. He remained a practising Lutheran all his life and considered Protestant Christianity to be the highest and final form of religion. But Hegel strongly historicised and thereby relativised religion which he saw as one form among many of the manifestations of spirit. Religion did apprehend truth, but only in the imagination and in symbols. This religious imagination was a necessary stage in the development of Absolute Spirit but one which was inferior to the conceptual grasp that a philosophical interpretation of religion could afford.[9] What impressed Marx here was Hegel's picture of a self-contained interlocking intellectual enterprise which, while capable of self-transcendence, left no room for supernatural entities. As he wrote excitedly to his father on reading Hegel:

A curtain had fallen, my holy of holies was rent asunder, and new gods had to be installed. I left behind the idealism which, by the way, I had nourished with that of Kant and Fichte, and came to seek the idea in the real itself. If the gods had before dwelt above the earth, they had now become its centre.[10]

And this feeling for an immanent naturalism was to stay with him all his life.

But Marx soon gave his enthusiasm for Hegel a marked anti-religious twist. In this he was strongly influenced by the Young Hegelians. On Hegel's death in 1831, his followers split into two camps. The Old Hegelians propounded a version of the Master's thought which was religiously and politically conservative. The Young Hegelians, by contrast, turned Hegel in a radical humanist direction: David Strauss's *Life of Jesus* saw the Gospel narratives as myths originating in the early Christian Communities while Marx's close friend and mentor Bruno Bauer saw the Gospels as the quasi-artistic creation of individual authors.[11] Bauer, in particular, became a virulent opponent of Christianity and Marx followed him in the doctoral thesis that he submitted in 1841. The subject of Marx's thesis – ancient Greek atomic theory – was rather obscure. But it clearly had two heroes. The first was Epicurus whom Marx later described as 'the true radical Enlightener of antiquity'[12] in that his emphasis on the absolute autonomy of the human spirit had freed men from all superstitious belief in transcendant objects. The second was Prometheus whom Marx invoked in the Preface to his thesis: 'Philosophy makes no secret of it. The proclamation of Prometheus – "in a word, I detest all the gods" – is her own profession, her own slogan against all the gods of heaven and earth who do not recognize man's self-consciousness as the highest divinity. There shall be none other beside it.'[13]

Following the acceptance of his thesis, Marx was forced by the increasingly conservative atmosphere prevailing in Prussia to give up his aim of a university teaching post and to turn to journalism. He planned to edit, with Bauer, a review to be entitled *Atheistic Archives* and wrote a long article criticising Christian art.[14] Neither of these projects saw publication and Marx rapidly became involved in the liberal newspaper *Rheinische Zeitung*, of which he soon became editor. In his articles he attacked the alliance of throne and altar in Prussia that prevented criticism of religion (Bruno Bauer had recently been dismissed from his post for unorthodoxy) and insisted that 'the state must be built on the basis of free reason not of religion'.[15] If Christianity was consonant with scientific enquiry, then it was odd that it should need police protection. In particular Marx was concerned to refute the idea that religion contained the essential backbone of any society and that religious decline meant secular decline: on the contrary, 'it was not the downfall of the old religions that caused the downfall of the ancient states, but the downfall of the ancient states that caused the downfall of the old religions.'[16] His involvement in journalism made Marx increasingly impatient of the empty stridency of a lot of Young Hegelian comment and wrote to a friend concerning his former colleagues:

> I asked that religion be criticised more through a criticism of the political situation, than the political situation be criticised through religion. For this approach is more suited to the manner of a newspaper and the education of the public, because religion has no content of its own, and lives not from heaven but from earth, and falls of itself with the dissolution of the inverted reality whose theory it is.[17]

Marx himself began to turn to more empirical matters such as exploring the causes of poverty among winegrowers in the Moselle region and the economic interests behind the recent abrogation of traditional rights to pick up fallen timber. But one of the results was that the government closed his paper and Marx was at liberty to turn his mind to wider issues.

For the next six months Marx retired, as he put it, into his study. He worked at an extensive critique of Hegel's political philosophy, became interested in French socialist ideas, and moved from Bauer to Feuerbach as his mentor in the critique of religion. For Bruno Bauer, religion contained the worst of humanity in that it was a distorted creation of the human mind which came to possess its own malign influence; for Feuerbach, on the other hand, religion represented the best in humanity but in an alienated form in that the attributes of humanity itself were projected onto an alien, imaginary entity.[18] During 1843, with his distancing himself from Bruno Bauer and his growing interest in politics and economics, Marx abandoned for ever religion as a topic of central interest. Henceforth, his comments on religion were always to be peripheral to political or economic interest.

Marx distilled much of his 1843 meditations into two articles published in the *German–French Yearbooks* early in 1844. Marx had now settled in Paris, the birthplace of socialism, and the *Yearbooks*, of which he was an editor, were designed to effect a synthesis between German philosophy and French socialism. They also contained some of his best-known comments on religion. The first article, entitled *On the Jewish Question*, signalled Marx's break with Bauer in that he took issue with Bauer's views on Jewish emancipation. Marx's main theme was that, as cited above, 'religion has no content of its own and lives not from heaven but from earth, and falls of itself with the dissolution of the inverted reality whose theory it is.'[19] Bauer's solution to the problem of Jewish emancipation was to propose a thorough-going secularisation of the German state which would thus recognise neither Jews nor Christians. For Marx, this merely political emancipation from religion was not radical enough. For Bauer's proposals had been implemented in the United States which, nevertheless, all observers agreed to be the land of religiosity *par excellence*. Marx continued:

But since the existence of religion is the existence of a defect, the source of this defect can only be sought in the nature of the state itself. Religion for us no longer has the force of a basis for secular deficiencies but only that of a phenomenon. Therefore we explain the religious prejudice of free citizens by their secular prejudice. We do not insist that they must abolish their religious limitation in order to abolish secular limitations. We insist that they abolish their religious limitations as soon as they abolish their secular limitations. We do not change secular questions into theological ones. We change theological questions into secular ones. History has for long enough been resolved into superstition: we now resolve superstition into history. The question of the relationship of political emancipation to religion becomes for us a question of the relationship of political emancipation to human emancipation.[20]

This purely political emancipation implied the recognition of the State and this itself implied an alienation parallel to that of religion.[21]

Just as, in religion, heaven was separate from earth, so the emancipation political state was separate from civil society: in the heaven of the state, human beings were valued as citizens, as communal beings, as species-beings and were imaginary participants in an imaginary sovereignty; in earthly civil society they were atomised individuals whose separate economic interest resulted in a war of all against all. In the bourgeois society of North America which accorded religion the status of a private arbitrary right, 'religion has become the spirit of civil society, the sphere of egoism, the *bellum omnium contra omnes.* Its essence is no longer in community, but in difference.'[22] What, according to Marx, explained the flourishing of religion in North America was precisely this separation of ideal and reality.[23]

Thus with the application of liberal principles 'man was not freed from religion; he received freedom of religion'.[24] In the second, and inferior, part of his article Marx claimed that the Jews had already emancipated themselves in a Jewish way. This had been possible because the Christian world had become impregnated with the practical Jewish spirit. Their deprivation of theoretical political rights mattered little to Jews, who in practice wielded great financial power. Although Judaism could not develop further as a religion, it had succeeded in installing itself in practice in the heart of civil society and the Christian world. Thus Christianity, which arose out of Judaism, had now dissolved itself back into Judaism.[25] Marx's general conclusion was that the only solution to society's problems was a *human* emancipation in which human beings reclaimed their species-being by repudiating religious and political alienations and organised their social powers communally.

As sociology with any claim to empirical reference, Marx's treatment of the Jewish question is very thin. Large and quite undifferentiated entities such as 'Christianity' and 'Judaism' are manipulated with brilliant legerdemain. The sketch of the role of religion in the United States, following such writers as de Toqueville, is certainly striking, but it remains, for the most part, rather abstract polemical journalism (which was, after all, its original intent) rather than the genuine conversion of theological questions into secular ones. It should, finally, be noted that although Marx declared that he found the Jewish religion 'repulsive',[26] there is little evidence that he was personally anti-semitic – however much some of his careless expressions can be, and have been, used in this direction.[27]

But how was such a 'human' emancipation to be achieved? After a few brief weeks in Paris, Marx thought himself to have found the answer and proclaimed it triumphantly in his second article for the *German–French Yearbooks* cumbersomely entitled 'Introduction to a critique of Hegel's "Philosophy of Right"'. Marx began by summarising his views on religion. As far as Germany was concerned, he said, the criticism of religion was complete. Marx is here referring to the achievement of Feuerbach.[28] In a famous passage he summarised this achievement while at the same time giving it a socio-political dimension not found in Feuerbach:

> The foundation of irreligious criticism is this: man makes religion, religion does not make man. Religion is indeed the self-consciousness and self-awareness of man who either has not yet attained to himself or has already lost himself again. But man is no abstract being squatting outside the world. Man is the world of man, the state, society. This state, this society, produces religion's inverted attitude to the world, because they are an inverted world themselves. Religion is the general theory of this world, its encyclopaedic compendium, its logic in popular form, its spiritual *point d'honneur*, its enthusiasm, its moral sanction, its solemn complement, its universal basis for consolation and justification. It is the imaginary realization of the human essence, because the human essence possesses no true reality. Thus, the struggle against religion is indirectly the struggle against the world whose spiritual aroma is religion.
>
> Religious suffering is at the same time an expression of real suffering and a protest against real suffering. Religion is the sigh of the oppressed creature, the feeling of a heartless world, and the soul of soulless circumstances. It is the opium of the people.[29]

Marx's comments here have often been read as containing a positive evaluation of religion as a vehicle of protest.[30] But, if so, then it was an extremely backhanded compliment. Religion may well represent humanity's feeble aspirations under adverse circumstances, but the whole tenor of the passage is that religion is metaphysically and sociologically misguided and that its disappearance is the necessary pre-condition for any radical amelioration of social conditions.

The very completion of the critique of religion by Feuerbach meant that attention was now turned in other directions. Religious alienation was alienation at one remove and now the point was to turn attention to its roots.

> The criticism of religion [he wrote] 'is therefore the germ of the criticism of the valley of tears whose halo is religion. . . . The criticism of heaven is thus transformed into the criticism of earth,

the criticism of religion into the criticism of law, and the criticism of theology into the criticism of politics'.[31]

The difficulty was that Germany, compared with France and Britain, was backward both economically and politically; it was only in philosophy that Germany was advanced. Here the way had been paved by Luther who

> removed the servitude of devotion by replacing it by the servitude of conviction. He destroyed faith in authority by restoring the authority of faith. He turned priests into laymen by turning laymen into priests. He liberated man from exterior religiosity by making man's inner conscience religious. He emancipated the body from chains by enchaining the heart.[32]

Although Luther did not provide the solution, at least he asked the right questions and Marx saw a distinct parallel between his own ideas and those of Luther.[33]

In order to accomplish its task, philosophical theory had to ally itself with a material base, with practical activity to achieve that unity of theory and practice which Marx called *praxis*. In Marx's view, theory could turn into a practical force through a radical humanism that would seize the masses:

> To be radical is to grasp the matter by the root. But for man the root is man himself. The manifest proof of the radicalism of German theory and its practical energy is that it starts from the decisive and positive abolition of religion. The criticism of religion ends with the doctrine that man is the highest being for man, that is, with the categorical imperative to overthrow all circumstances in which man is humiliated, enslaved, abandoned, and despised.[34]

At first sight, however, there seemed to be no room for this kind of revolution in autocratic, backward, conservative Germany. But just as Trotsky sixty years later saw in Russia's backwardness the opportunity – indeed necessity – for a thorough-going socialist revolution, so Marx thought a similar situation in Germany could lead to a more profound transformation than that so far accomplished in France or England. The agent of this transformation would be the proletariat. Although very small as yet in Germany, Marx extrapolated present tendencies into the future. To the question of where the real possibility for German emancipation lay, he answered in a famous passage:

> in the formation of a class with radical chains, a class in civil society that is not a class of civil society, of a social group that is the dissolution of all social groups, of a sphere that has a universal character because of its universal sufferings and lays claim to no particular right, because it is the object of no particular injustice but of injustice in general. This class can no longer lay claim to a historical status, but only to a human one. It is not in a one-sided opposition to the consequences of the German political regime, it is in total opposition to its presuppositions. It is, finally, a sphere that cannot emancipate itself without emancipating itself from all other spheres of society and thereby emancipating these other spheres themselves. In a word, it is the complete loss of humanity and thus can only recover itself by a complete redemption of humanity. This dissolution of society, as a particular class, is the proletariat.[35]

This passage is the main source for those who have sought to find a religious inspiration in Marx's work.[36] It is, of course, true that there are echoes of both the Old and the New Testaments in such a passage: Marx was familiar with the Bible and borrowed many of its resonances, as he did those of Shakespeare or the Greek classics. And Marx was certainly much influenced by Hegel whose thought was heavily imbued with Protestant Christianity. But claims such as 'the universality of the proletariat echoes the claims of the universal Christ is confirmed by Marx's insistence that the proletariat will exist, precisely at the point when it becomes universal, in a scourged and emptied condition – and this, of course is Marx's variant of the divine *kenosis*'[37] are surely to overstate the case. It is clear from the rest of the article that Marx's view of proletarian potential was a direct outcome of his extensive studies of the French revolution: just as the French bourgeoisie claimed in 1789, in words often attributed to Sieyès,[38] 'I am nothing and I should be everything', now Marx saw the proletariat as moving into that position. And his enthusiasm for the proletariat can be directly attributed to his first-hand contact with socialist intellectuals in France. Instead of editing a paper for the Rhenish bourgeoisie or sitting in his study in Kreuznach, he was now at the heart of socialist thought and action.

From October 1843 Marx was breathing a socialist atmosphere and even living in the same house as Germain Maurer, one of the leaders of the League of the Just whose meetings Marx frequented. It is not surprising that his surroundings made a swift impact on Marx.

The intellectual assimilation of this sudden impact was a series of notebooks written in the summer of 1844 and only published some fifty years after Marx's death under the title *Economic and Philosophical Manuscripts*. In these manuscripts – the most important of his writings before he developed fully his materialist conception of history – Marx applied his interpretation of Feuerbach's theory of religious alienation to the field of political economy: any attempt to come to terms with political economy had to be based on the discoveries of Feuerbach whose work had a 'sure, deep, lasting and comprehensive effect.[39] Central to the manuscripts are the twin poles of an extended description of the mechanism by which the worker in capitalist society is alienated and the contrasting vision of human potential under a communist organisation of society.

When describing the way in which in capitalist society workers were alienated from the product of their labour, from work itself, from their species-being, and from their fellow human-beings, Marx repeatedly drew parallels with religious alienation:

> The more [he wrote] the worker externalizes himself in his work, the more powerful becomes the alien, objective world that he creates opposite himself, the poorer he becomes himself in his inner life and the less he can call his own. It is just the same in religion. The more man puts into God, the less he retains in himself.[40]

Marx was insistent that it was alienated labour that was the fundamental social process rather than the existence of private property which was really its consequence although it appeared to be its cause 'just as the gods are originally not the cause but the effect of the aberration of the human mind, although later this relationship reverses itself'.[41] The whole idea of alienated labour presupposed a picture of humankind as *causa sui*. With the abolition of private property and with co-operative production human beings would be able to objectify themselves without alienating themselves. History was the process of the genesis of human beings in their essential relationship to nature; society 'completes the essential unity of man and nature, it is the genuine resurrection of nature, the accomplished naturalism of men and the accomplished humanism of nature.'[42]

Nature seemed to mean to Marx what was opposed to human beings, what afforded them scope for their activities and satisfied their needs. It was these needs and drives that made up the nature of human beings. Marx called his view 'naturalism' both because human beings were orientated towards nature and fulfilled their needs in and through nature and also, more fundamentally, because human beings were a part of nature. Thus human beings as active natural beings were endowed with certain natural capacities, powers and drives. This paeon to naturalism led necessarily to atheism, and atheism was thus part of Communist pre-history.[43]

The last part of Marx's manuscript consisted of a rather uncharacteristic digression on the question of whether the world was created or not. One of the key ideas in Marx's picture of human beings was that human beings were their own creators; any being that lived by the favour of another was a dependent being. Accordingly, Marx rejected the idea that the world was created: although the notion of creation was a difficult one to dispel, it had been practically refuted by the science of geogeny which taught that the world was generated spontaneously. Marx then rehearsed Aristotle's argument about individuals owing their existence to their parents and they to their parents and so forth. To this he replied, relying on his conception of human beings as species-beings: 'You must also grasp the circular movement observable in that progression whereby human beings renew themselves by procreation and thereby always remain the subject.'[44] Marx's imaginary opponent then asks who created the first human being and nature as a whole. Marx replied:

When you enquire about the creation of the world and human beings, then you abstract from human beings and the world. You suppose them non-existent and yet require me to prove to you that they exist. I say to you: give up your abstraction and you will give up your question, or if you wish to stick to your abstraction then be consistent, and if you think of human beings and the world as non-existent then think of yourself as non-existent, also, for you too are a part of the world and human beings. Do not think, do not ask me questions, for immediately you think and ask, your abstraction from the being of nature and human beings has no meaning. Or are you such an egoist that you suppose everything to be nothing and yet wish to exist yourself?

Marx's argument is plainly rather stilted and when his opponent replied that he did not want to assert the nothingness of nature but only to ask about its genesis, as he might ask an anatomist about the formation of bones, Marx broke off the argument and continued in a much more characteristic vein: 'Since for socialist human beings what is called world history is nothing but the creation of human beings by human labour and the development of nature for human beings, they have the observable and irrefutable proof of their self-creation and the process of their origin.'[45] Thus for socialist human beings the question of an alien being beyond human beings and nature whose existence would imply their unreality had become impossible. For them the mutual interdependence of human beings and nature was what was essential and anything else seemed unreal. 'Atheism, as a denial of this unreality, has no longer any meaning, for atheism is a denial of God and tries to assert through this negation the existence of man; but socialism as such no longer needs this mediation; it starts from the theoretical and practical sense-perception of man and nature as the true reality.'[46] This perception, once established, no longer required the overcoming of religion, just as the life of human beings, once rid of alienation, no longer needed the overcoming of private property, no longer needed communism.

This atheism did not, in the last analysis, form part of the communist programme. Since the fundamental alienation was an economic one, the positive (i.e. real, effective) suppression of private property would work its way through to other subsidiary alienations:

> Religion, family, state, law, morality, science, and art are only particular forms of production and fall under its general law. The positive abolition of private property and the appropriation of human life is therefore the positive abolition of all alienation, thus the return of man out of religion, family, state, etc. into his human, i.e. social being. Religious alienation as such occurs only in man's interior consciousness, but economic alienation is that of real life, and its abolition therefore covers both aspects.[47]

The detour via atheism would no longer be necessary.

3. RELIGION AS REFLECTION IN MARX'S MATURE WRITING

With his move from Paris to Brussels and the elaboration there of his materialist conception of history, Marx's thought underwent a decisive shift. Whereas before the key concept was alienation, now it is ideology, and Marx's comments on religion are usually in a historical or ethnographical context. This does not mean that the concept of alienation was abandoned: only that Marx was now interested in accounting for different forms of religious alienation by referring them to their changing historical contexts. This change of emphasis is best illustrated by the critical attitude now adopted towards Feuerbach. In the fourth of his famous *Theses on Feuerbach*, Marx summarised the deficiencies he saw in Feuerbach's view of religion:

> Feuerbach starts out from the fact of religious self-alienation, of the duplication of the world into a religious world and a secular one. His work consists in resolving the religious world into its secular basis. But that the secular basis detaches itself from itself and establishes itself as an independent realm in the clouds can only be explained by the cleavages and self-contradictions within this secular basis.[48]

And it was to investigating these contradictions in the secular basis of society and the consequent possibilities of revolutionising it in practice that Marx (in collaboration with Engels) devoted himself.

The first major result of the collaboration of Marx and Engels was a manuscript entitled *The German Ideology* which was a lengthy critique of their former Young Hegelian colleagues. The first hundred or so pages, devoted to an elaboration of the *Theses on Feuerbach*, was Marx's most extended account of what came to be known as historical materialism – the thesis that the nature of individuals and society ultimately depended on the material conditions which determined their production. Echoing his words in *The Jewish Question* Marx declared that his premises were strictly empirical.[49]

Thus the task of the Marxist historian and critic of religion was to display the connexion of religion with the developing productive forces in society, the increasing division of labour and the consequent class struggle. For, as he remarked, religion was 'from the outset consciousness of the transcendental arising from actually existing forces'.[50] In this respect religion was just like other forms of ideology, only more so. And thus it had even less of an autonomous history than did other forms of ideology. Largely because he was writing in opposition to former Young Hegelian colleagues who in one way or another emphasised the importance of the evolution of religious ideas, Marx returns again and again to the statement that religion has no autonomy. He insisted that '"Christianity" has no history whatsoever' and continued 'all the different forms at various times were not "self -determinations" and "further developments" "of the religious spirit", but were brought about by wholly empirical causes in no way dependent on any influence of the religious spirit.'[51] Later in his famous summary of historical materialism in 1859, Marx reiterated his view that 'a distinction should always be made between the material transformation of the economic conditions of production, which can be determined with the precision of natural science, and the legal, political, religious, aesthetic, or philosophic – in short, ideological forms in which men become conscious of this conflict and fight it out.'[52] In *Capital*, in response to the criticism that religion was more or less influential at different times, e.g. during the Middle Ages, just as politics had been in Greco-Roman society, Marx insisted that 'the Middle Ages could not live on Catholicism, nor could the ancient world on politics. On the contrary, it is the manner in which they gained their livelihood which explains why in one case politics, in the other case Catholicism, played the chief part.[53]

Although Marx is very strong on the 'wholly empirical' nature of the causes of religion, he did not go into the sort of detail that might be expected. The origins of religion, he said, lay in the fact that nature in primitive societies 'confronts man as a completely alien, all-powerful and unassailable force . . . by which they are overawed like beasts'.[54] With the appearance of the division between mental and manual labour,

> consciousness is in a position to emancipate itself from the world and to proceed to the formation of 'pure' theory, theology, philosophy, morality, etc. But even if this theory, theology, philosophy, morality, etc., came into contradiction with the

existing relations, this can only occur because existing social
relations have come into contradiction with existing productive
forces.[55]

Marx's very sketchy account of the evolution of religious belief does
not differ from that of contemporary nineteenth-century accounts
such as that of Herbert Spencer.

What does distinguish Marx is that these rather sparse facts about
the history of religion are placed in a context which includes both a
very specific idea of what is real, in which 'the religious production
of fancies' is contrasted with 'the real production of the means of
subsistence'[56] and also a concept of human nature in which the
concept of alienation continues to play a role – though Marx insisted
that this alienation be analysed in its 'actual empirical relations'.[57]
His view, moreover, that 'in religion people make their empirical
world into an entity that is only conceived, imagined, that confronts
them as something foreign',[58] led him to over-optimistic and
sometimes straightforwardly false estimations of the present and
future state of religious belief as when, for example, after blithely
equating the proletariat with 'the mass of men', he claimed that their
religious ideas 'had long been dissolved by circumstances'.[59]

Having, in *The German Ideology*, worked out his materialist
conception of history and thereby the place of religion in his scheme
of things, Marx found that he had to come to terms, in the late 1840s,
with an influential body of opinion on the left which thought that
some sort of religious belief was not only perfectly compatible with
socialism, but also an encitement to it. This was a battle on two
fronts: firstly, there was a relatively small number of Christians who
were interested in social questions and preached a form of socialist
Christianity.[60] Secondly, and more importantly, Marx vigorously
opposed those numerous socialists who claimed to find inspiration
for their views in the basic tenets of Christianity.[61] This tendency
was firmly embedded in the French socialist tradition from Saint-
Simon's *New Christianity*, through the influential writings of the
communist priest Lammenais, to contemporary socialists such as
Cabet and Leroux. Engels remarked:

> It is curious that whilst the English Socialists are generally opposed
> to Christianity, and have to suffer all the religious prejudices of a
> really Christian people, the French Communists, being a part of a
> nation celebrated for its infidelity, are themselves Christian.

One of their favourite axioms is that *le Christianisme c'est le communisme*.[62]

And the same views were widespread among German emigré workers as, for example, in the messianic communism preached by the itinerant tailor Wilhelm Weitling.

The first working-men's organisation that Marx joined – the League of the Just, renamed in 1847 the Communist League – was at the time much influenced by the ideas of Weitling. Indicative of the effect that Marx and Engels had on the League was the change of its campaigning slogan from 'All men are brothers' to 'Proletarians of all countries, unite!'. Marx was living in Brussels at the time and used the Communist Correspondence Committee there, which he controlled, to force the dispute with Weitling to a head. It was in this context that the Committee issued a circular (drawn up by Marx) to all its members condemning what it saw as the 'religious' communism propagated by Hermann Kriege, a disciple of Weitling recently emigrated to the United States. Kriege, according to the circular, 'is preaching in the name of communism the old fantasy of religion . . . which is the direct antithesis of communism'.[63] Kriege's view of communism as trying to make real the 'long yearned-for community of the blessed denizens of heaven' merely 'overlooks the fact that these obsessions of Christianity are only the fantastic expression of the existing world and that their "reality" therefore *already* exists in the evil conditions of this existing world'.[64] In particular, Marx mocked Kriege for his frequent use of the word 'love', his penchant for using biblical images when referring to the proletariat, and, in general, diminishing the revolutionary vigour of communism by constantly presenting it in sentimental religious terms. The *Circular* is strong evidence of Marx's completely uncompromising attitude to any attempt to combine socialism and religion.[65]

Marx's denunciation of Christianity was equally vehement when it concerned not the use of Christian concepts and phraseology by socialists but Christians giving their religion a socialist slant. The following year Marx took to task the newspaper *Der Rheinischer Beobachter* for claiming that the bourgeoisie was incapable of resolving the social question but that a Christian state such as Prussia could do so provided it put into practice the social principles of Christianity. Marx summed up his contempt for the latter as follows:

The social principles of Christianity justified the slavery of antiquity, glorified the serfdom of the Middle Ages and are capable, in case of need, of defending the oppression of the proletariat, even if with somewhat doleful grimaces.

The social principles of Christianity preach the necessity of a ruling and an oppressed class, and for the latter all they have to offer is the pious wish that the former may be charitable.

The social principles of Christianity place the Consistorial Counsellor's compensation for all infamies in heaven, and thereby justify the continuation of these infamies on earth.

The social principles of Christianity declare all the vile acts of the oppressors against the oppressed to be either a just punishment for original sin and other sins, or trials which the Lord, in his infinite wisdom, ordains for the redeemed.

The social principles of Christianity preach cowardice, self-contempt, abasement, submissiveness and humbleness, in short, all the qualities of the rabble, and the proletariat, which will not permit itself to be treated as rabble, needs its courage, its self-confidence, its pride and its sense of independence even more than its bread.

The social principles of Christianity are sneaking and hypocritical, and the proletariat is revolutionary.[66]

However questionable these statements may be as historical generalisations, they give a good impression of Marx's scorn for Christian 'charity' given its record of oppression, his view that Christianity constantly displaced problems to a 'heavenly' sphere, and his Nietzschean theme that Christianity inculcated servility and cowardice.[67]

Marx pithily summarised his opinion of Christian socialism in *The Communist Manifesto*. Christianity was essentially reactionary and thus used by the declining feudal aristocracy to combat the bourgeoisie:

As the parson has ever gone hand in hand with the landlord, so has Clerical Socialism with Feudal Socialism.

Nothing is easier than to give Christian asceticism a Socialist tinge. Has not Christianity declaimed against private property, against marriage, against the State? Has it not preached in the place of these, charity and poverty, celibacy and mortification of the flesh, monastic life and Mother Church? Christian Socialism is but the holy water with which the priest consecrates the heart-burnings of the aristocrat.[68]

In Marx's strongly determinist view in which 'intellectual production changes its character in proportion as material production is changed',[69] religion was seen as a mere reflection:

> When the ancient world was in its last throes, the ancient religions were overcome by Christianity. When Christian ideas succumbed in the 18th century to rationalist ideas, feudal society fought its death battle with the then revolutionary bourgeoisie. The ideas of religious liberty and freedom of conscience merely gave expression to the sway of free competition within the domain of knowledge.[70]

It was therefore quite accurate to say that the communist revolution involved the abolition of religion and morality rather than reconstituting them on a new basis; for the communist revolution implied 'the most radical rupture with traditional ideas'.[71] The demise of religion was written in the laws of historical development and any attempt to combine communism with religion was simply evidence of ignorance of these laws.

In the aftermath of the 1848 revolutions Marx settled in London to compose his definitive work on political economy. His comments on religion become less frequent but remarks in *Capital* in particular show that he had not abandoned his previous conceptions. The well-known passage on the fetishism of commodities at the end of the first chapter drew an analogy with religion. 'A commodity', said Marx, 'is therefore a mysterious thing . . . because the relation of the producers to the sum total of their own labour is presented to them as a social relation, existing not between themselves, but between the products of their labour.'[72] In other words, 'a definite social relation between men . . . assumes, in their eyes, the fantastic form of a relation between things.' And it was here that Marx found the parallel with religion:

> In order to find an analogy, we must have recourse to the mist-enveloped regions of the religious world. In that world the productions of the human brain appear as independent beings endowed with life, and entering into relation both with one

another and the human race. So it is in the world of commodities with the products of men's hands.[73]

There is, of course, a difference between this account and the opium analogy of Marx's earlier writings: in religion as opium there is contained an (illusory) protest against the actual conditions of life; whereas in the fetishism account religion only too faithfully mirrors the real world. Nevertheless, both accounts view religion as the fantasy of alienated human beings and repeat the Feuerbachian theme of the inversion of subject and object. This comes out very clearly in the so-called 'Sixth' chapter of Volume 1 of *Capital* which was omitted from the final version for unknown reasons. Here Marx discussed 'the domination of the thing over man, of dead over living labour, of the product over the producer' and claimed that 'at the level of material production . . . we find the same relationship as obtains at the level of ideology, in religion: the subject is transformed into object and vice versa.'[74] More strikingly, Marx allowed a positive role to religion in the historical process as being as necessary a preliminary to socialism as was capitalism:

> From the historical point of view, this inversion represents a transitional phase which is necessary in order to force the majority of humanity to produce wealth for itself by inexorably developing the productive forces of social labour which alone can constitute the material basis for a free human society. It is necessary to go through this antagonistic form, just as it is necessary at first to give man's spiritual forces a religious form by erecting them into autonomous power over against him.[75]

But however much Marx insisted on the parallel that 'just as man is governed, in religion, by the products of his own hand', he maintained his critical stance towards Feuerbach's simplistic method as lacking any historical materialistic basis. This is clear in a later passage where Marx was discussing the development of machinery and emphasised the historical importance of technology which 'reveals the active relation of man to nature, the direct process of production of his life, and thereby it also lays bare the process of production of the social relations of his life, and of the mental conceptions that flow from those relations.'[76] Even a history of religion, he continued, written in abstraction from this material basis, would be uncritical, and he then went on to contrast two methods in the study of religion:

> It is, in reality, much easier to discover by analysis the earthly kernel of the misty creations of religion than to do the opposite, i.e. to develop from the actual, given relations of life the forms in which these have been apotheosized. The latter method is the only materialist, and therefore the only scientific one.[77]

In here criticising 'the abstract materialism of natural science, a materialism which excludes the historical process',[78] Marx is reiterating his criticism of Feuerbach from the 1840s for descending directly from heaven to earth rather than the other way round.

4.   MARX'S EMPIRICAL COMMENTS

Marx's major statements on religion from his mature writings such as *The German Ideology* and *Capital* are programmatic. In both these works he is very strong, as shown above, on how the various forms of Christianity were 'brought about by wholly empirical causes in no way dependent on any influence of the religious spirit'[79] and how the only 'scientific' method of studying religion is 'to develop from the actual given relations of life the forms in which these have been apotheosised'.[80] Unfortunately, Marx himself gives us only the sketchiest of ideas as to how this might be done. One thing at which, as an ardent polemicist, he *is* very good, is the exposure of the hypocrisy which he thought endemic to religion since the predicates of God were 'nothing but deified names for the ideas of people about their definite empirical relations, ideas which subsequently they hypocritically retain because of practical considerations'.[81] On several occasions in *Capital* Marx hits out, quoting detailed examples, at the hypocrisy surrounding the laws on Sunday working whereby 'Parliament will entertain no complaint of Sabbath-breaking if it occurs in the "process of valorization" of capital'.[82] He cited the example of Quaker industrialists in Yorkshire whose young teenage employees worked for thirty hours continuously over the weekend with only one hour off for sleep. On being taken to court,

> the accused gentlemen affirmed in lieu of taking an oath – as Quakers they were too scrupulously religious to take an oath –

that they had, in their great compassion for the unhappy children, allowed them four hours for sleep, but the obstinate children absolutely would not go to bed.[83]

All this only went to show that 'atheism itself is a *culpa levis* as compared with the criticism of existing property relations.'[84] But Marx's greatest scorn was reserved for the established Church which he saw in conspiracy with 'monopoly capital' and he was much cheered by the massive demonstration in Hyde Park in 1855 against new laws controlling the opening of pubs and shops on Sundays, laws which he saw as the product of an 'alliance of a dissipated, degenerate and pleasure-seeking aristocracy with a church propped up by the filthy profits calculated upon by the big brewers and monopolizing wholesalers'.[85] Marx's attitude is epitomised by his observation in the *Preface* to *Capital* that 'the established Church will more readily pardon an attack on thirty-eight of its thirty-nine articles than on one thirty-ninth of its income.'[86]

Examples of religious hypocrisy arising from direct self-interest are an easy target: in his broader historical analysis of religion Marx is much less convincing. On early religion he has singularly little to say except that the 'ancient worship of nature' reflected the 'low level of the productive process of labour' and hence the 'limited relations between men and nature'.[87] On the religion of ancient society he merely remarked that their real religion was the cult of their nationality and that therefore their religions declined with the disintegration of their societies rather than vice versa.[88] Naturally, Marx had more to say about Christianity whose rise he saw simply as the expression of 'the collapse of the ancient "world conditions"'.[89] The only specific comments, however, that he offers on early Christianity are the mistaken one that most early Christians were slaves[90] and the ludicrous one that they engaged in widespread cannibalism.[91] On the Middle Ages, Marx's comments are more to the point. Feudal religion he saw as reflecting the political form of feudal society:

Hierarchy is the ideal form of feudalism; feudalism in the particular form of the mediaeval relations of production and intercourse. Consequently, the struggle of feudalism against hierarchy can only be explained by elucidating these practical material relations.[92]

More interestingly, in *Capital* Marx alludes to the domination of the Catholic religion in feudal society but denies that this is a counter-example to the materialist conception of history: 'The Middle Ages could not live on Catholicism, nor could the ancient world on politics. On the contrary, it is the manner in which they gained their livelihood which explains why in one case politics, in the other case Catholicism, played the chief part.'[93] And this remark was expanded into a whole new version of historical materialism by such structuralist-inspired Marxists as Althusser and Poulantzas.[94] But, again, Marx offered no explanation of the mechanism by which religion was dominant in feudal society,[95] apart from a dubious generalisation about the inevitable rise of middlemen in all spheres of society – 'in religion God is pushed into the background by the "mediator", and the latter is again shoved back by the priests, who are the inevitable mediators between the good shepherd and his flock' – a view expressed in the context of the rise of capitalist farmers in sixteenth-century England, i.e. just the time when 'priestly' power was declining.[96]

For obvious geographical and historical reasons Marx was most interested in Protestant Christianity. He had considerable admiration for Luther as an economic theorist[97] and thought that Protestantism had played a progressive role in its time.[98] This was largely due to the link between Protestantism and capitalism:

> For a society of commodity producers, whose general social relation of production consists in the fact that they treat their products as commodities, hence as values, and in this material form bring their individual, private labours into relation with each other as homogeneous human labour, Christianity with its religious cult of man in the abstract, more particularly in its bourgeois development, i.e. in Protestantism, Deism, etc., is the most fitting form of religion.[99]

Although he does say that 'Protestantism, by changing almost all the traditional holidays into working days, played an important part in the genesis of capital',[100] Marx is not concerned to establish any causal relationship between capitalism and Protestantism. What struck Marx was the structural correspondence between the two:

> The monetary system is essentially a Catholic institution, the

credit system essentially Protestant. 'The Scotch hate gold.' In the form of paper the monetary existence of commodities is only a social one. It is *Faith* that brings salvation. Faith in money-value as the immanent spirit of commodities, faith in the mode of production and its predestined order, faith in the individual agents of production as mere personifications of self-expanding capital.[101]

Thus although Marx touches on themes later pursued by Weber, he makes no attempt to link Protestantism with the *spirit* of capitalism as elaborated by Weber through his concept of elective affinities.

In his later writings in particular, Marx was mainly interested in the *political* influence of religion. He commended the Commune for trying 'to break the spiritual force of repression, the "parson-power", by the disestablishment and disendowment of all churches as proprietory bodies'[102] and praised measures by which 'the priests were sent back to the recesses of private life, there to feed upon the alms of the faithful, in imitation of their predecessors, the Apostles.'[103] Unlike some of his successors, and many contemporary socialists such as Blanqui and Dühring, Marx had no wish to persecute religion as such. But neither was he in favour of the simple liberty of conscience proclaimed in the Gotha programme of 1875. The workers' party, he declared, should go beyond the demand that 'everyone should be able to attend to his religious as well as his bodily needs without the police sticking their noses in.'[104] This was because 'bourgeois "freedom of conscience" is nothing but the toleration of all possible kinds of religious freedom of conscience, and that it [the workers' party] endeavours rather to liberate the conscience from the witchery of religion.'[105]

The only religion apart from Christianity to which Marx devoted serious attention was Hinduism. His vituperative description of Hindu beliefs reflected both the paucity of his sources and the cultural arrogance of contemporary European prejudice which saw in Hinduism 'a brutalising worship of nature, exhibiting its degradation in the fact that man fell down on his knees in adoration of the sovereign of *Kanuman*, the money, and *Sabbala*, the cow.'[106] More interesting however, was his account of the socio-economic basis of this religion. This basis, he said, was the Asiatic mode of production which consisted in thousands of self-sufficient, unchanging, isolated village communities with primitive production techniques over which towered a despotic state whose centralised administration was needed to produce the essential large-scale irrigation works. Although Marx commented in a letter to Engels that 'the real key even to the oriental heaven' was to be found in 'the absence of private property in land',[107] it was on the primitive village communities that Marx laid most emphasis, thinking that Hinduism was a natural religious counterpart to such a social organisation. In fact these village communities were much less self-sufficient and more dynamic than Marx imagined; nor did he appreciate the political and economic uses of Hinduism, both at village and state level, when manipulated by Brahmin orthodoxy.[108]

5. THE FUTURE OF RELIGION

Marx was confident of the disappearance of religion with the advent of communism:

> The difference between the present upheaval and all earlier ones lies in the very fact that man has found out the secret of this historical upheaval and hence, instead of once again exalting this practical 'external' process to the rapturous form of a new religion, divests himself of all religion.[109]

And indeed in his more sanguine moments he believed that for most people religion had 'now long been dissolved by circumstances'.[110] The hierarchy of alienations led science through from politics and law to art and religion, which, being at the top, was destined for a total extinction which would not overtake, say, art. For whereas there could, from a class-historical point of view, be good or bad art, there could not be good or bad religion. Even the State which was equally destined for abolition, would still have its functions of legislation, administration and adjudication preserved in communist society.[111] But Marx would deny that, in parallel, the institutional/oppressive side of religion might disappear but its functions continue. In his earlier writings, which looked on religion as opium, the reason for this was that communism, being a self-creating society with fully satisfying interpersonal relationships,[112] has no need for religion with its themes of creation, dependency and mediation. Communism, in other words, would be able to satisfy the desires which religion expressed in an alienated form. For religion was merely the expression of deeper alienations –

particularly the alienation of labour – which communism would have overcome. In Marx's later writings, the emphasis was more on the ontological status of religion as an illusion. In *Capital*, he wrote:

> The religious reflections of the real world can, in any case, vanish only when the practical relations of everyday life between man and man, and man and nature, generally present themselves to him in a transparent and rational form. The veil is not removed from the countenance of the social life-process, i.e. the process of material production, until it becomes production by freely associated men, and stands under their conscious and planned control.[113]

The very translucency of society would preclude its representation in an illusory (religious) form. Religion was seen here as an ideology; ideologies dealt with the appearance of society, not with its essence; at the present time, the illusory nature of religion could be exposed by Marxist social science which went beyond appearance to the essence of society; under communism, religion (as also indeed social science)[114] would be redundant.

6. CONCLUSION

One of the difficulties of considering Marx's views on religion is that they are, for the most part, only delivered *en passant*. The most elaborated of his views – that religion is the fantasy of alienated human beings – is representative of his early thought. In later remarks, the element of religion as class ideology and as reflection were dominant. Marx thought religion at once important and unimportant. Important, because the purely spiritual compensation that it afforded human beings frustrated efforts at material betterment. Unimportant, as he considered that his colleagues and particularly Feuerbach had fully exposed the true nature of religion. It was only a secondary phenomenon and, being dependent on socio-economic circumstances, merited no independent criticism.

If the weapons that Marx used – Hegel, Enlightenment rationalism, romanticism – were varied, then so was his target: the word 'religion' embraces a wide range of meanings in Marx from systems of ideas to social and political exploitation of popular belief. The generalisations about 'religion' are apparently based on a narrow range of examples and lack any coherent theoretical interest in religion. A lot of the little empirical evidence Marx cites seems, with hindsight, to be dubious and his statements about the disappearance of religion are highly speculative. Some have therefore doubted whether Marx really was attacking religion as such. Certainly his condemnation of the social functions of Christianity are rather wild generalisations based (if at all) on a particular time and place. Even setting aside the passages where Marx resorts to a crude economic reductionism, his view of religion as a reflection of economic arrangements is inadequate. If many of his views on politics and culture have come to be seen by his disciples as overly reductionist, the same applies *a fortiori* to religion whose significance and importance cannot be exhausted by being characterised simply as a mirror of social defects. Nevertheless, many of Marx's comments on religion are insightful and suggestive; and all his followers – from the Austro-Marxists who saw no problem in combining their Marxism with religious belief to those whose version of materialism ruled out any religious statements as *a priori* false – could find *some* support in Marx himself.

2

Engels

1. PIETIST UPBRINGING

Engels wrote considerably more about religion than did Marx. And – again unlike Marx – he returned at the end of his life to the interest in religion that had so vividly marked his youth. One of his poems, written when he was sixteen, begins:

> Lord Jesus Christ, God's only Son,
> O step down from thy heavenly throne
> And save my soul for me.

It was only after three long years of sometimes anguished soul-searching that Engels finally broke with the beliefs of his childhood and adolescence.

Whereas Marx had been born in the agricultural sector of the Rhineland to a family of decidedly liberal inclination, Engels's family lived in its industrial heartland, the Ruhr, and had strong religious convictions. For Barmen in the valley of the river Wupper was a centre of an extreme version of evangelical Christianity known as Pietism. Originating in the late seventeenth century as a movement to bring new life to the dry official Lutheranism of the time, Pietism continued to exercise a strong influence in the early nineteenth century. Pietist theology was based squarely on the Bible regarded as the directly inspired word of God which was not to be illuminated by reason, but to be simply received through the Spirit in the Church. Pietists were opposed to emphasis on cult or on formal membership: what was vital was the personal relationship of the individual to God. Hence the importance of feeling, of conversion, of moral reform and constant edification. Because salvation involved a break with the world (apart from business endeavours), the consequently necessary asceticism entailed a devotion and self-denial which sometimes degenerated into a series of legalistic negatives – no alcohol, no dancing, no finery.[1]

Engels's father was a convinced follower of the orthodoxies of

Pietism, held office in the local church and inculcated into his family the virtues of hard work and saving. Friedrich Engels, his eldest son, was confirmed in 1837 and his deep religious faith was praised in his school-leaving certificate of the same year. After a year at home helping with the family business he went to the Hanseatic port of Bremen as an apprentice to a very conservative business friend of his father. Engels lodged with one of the local pastors but soon found that the larger perspectives of Bremen led him increasingly to question the tenets of his religious upbringing.

Engels's first interest during the three years he spent in Bremen was literature, and he became an enthusiastic member of the Young German movement which expressed vague feelings of a rejuvenating German nationalism in a trenchant and witty style which formed a pleasant contrast to the narrow Pietism of the Wupper valley. In the middle of 1839 he published a caustic commentary on his birthplace in a series of newspaper articles entitled *Letters from the Wuppertal*. Here he took Pietism to task on two grounds: social and doctrinal. Socially, Engels accused Pietism of hypocrisy since, he claimed, the Pietists were the worst employers of all, while among the lower social strata the kind of mysticism induced by Pietist attitudes was often combined with drunkenness and laziness.[2] The main Pietist doctrine with which Engels took issue was that of predestination which he claimed to be 'in most direct contradiction to reason and the Bible'.[3] The principal exponent of these views, Pastor Krummacher, even believed that the sun moved round the earth – an obscurantist view that Engels was confident would be washed away by 'the surging flood of time'.[4]

His own inner struggle to be clear about his religious convictions is movingly documented in his correspondence during 1839 with the two Graeber brothers, both training to be pastors, whose acquaintance he had made in a Pietist circle in Barmen. In his letters to them, he claims never to have been a Pietist, only a mystic, but now to be 'an honest, and in comparison with others very liberal, super-naturalist' although 'inclining now more, now less to rationalism'.[5] Orthodoxy, in the shape of the doctrine of the literal inspiration of the Bible, was a dead letter whereas reason represented the divine in man and he could not believe that 'a rationalist who seeks with all his heart to do as much good as possible, should be eternally damned'.[6] By June 1839, he writes boldly: 'I have now reached a point where I can only regard as divine a teaching which can stand the test of reason.'[7]

And so many Christian attitudes to science, to education, to the status of the Bible, to eternal damnation, failed to meet this test. He temporarily found refuge in Schleiermacher whose view of religion as a sense and taste for the infinite based on intuition and feeling seemed to Engels to undercut the objections of the rationalist. But his doubts soon reached a point of crisis:

> I had trust and joy when I prayed; I have them now too, I have them even more because I am struggling and need to be strengthened. . . . I pray daily, indeed nearly the whole day, for truth, I have done so ever since I began to have doubts. . . . Tears come into my eyes as I write this. I am moved to the core, but I feel I shall not be lost; I shall come to God for whom my whole heart yearns.[8]

A few months later Engels found the solution to his problems in David Strauss's massive *Life of Jesus*, which had had an immediate and profound impact on the theological scene on its publication in 1835. For Strauss the gospels were imaginations of facts – myths – produced by the collective consciousness of a people who had arrived at a specific stage in their development. This implied that the revelation and incarnation of the divine essence could not be limited to one individual and that its sole adequate field was the whole of humanity. By the end of 1839 Engels could describe himself as 'an enthusiastic Straussian'.[9] Strauss could not be refuted and his new disciple felt himself to be on firm ground at last.

Strauss was also responsible for interesting Engels in Hegel: 'Strauss had lit up lights on Hegel for me which makes the whole thing plausible.'[10] He soon found that Hegel's philosophy of history was written 'as from my own heart' and could report that through Strauss he had entered in 'the straight road to Hegelianism', had adopted the Hegelian idea of God, and joined the ranks of the 'modern pantheists'.[11] This interest in Hegel was fortified by his arrival in Berlin in late 1841 to do this year's military service. He immediately became a prominent member of the Young Hegelian movement. In particular he studied Bruno Bauer's critique of the synoptic gospels, attended seminars on New Testament Studies, and produced notes on the Johannine tradition that were to form the basis of an article published forty years later.[12] When Schelling was recalled to Berlin to combat the new ideas, it was Engels who attacked him in a lengthy pamphlet entitled *Schelling and Revelation*. In contrast to Schelling's view of history as a series of arbitrary events interfered with externally by God, Engels follows Strauss and Feuerbach in identifying the divine with the course of human history. In common with many other Young Hegelians Engels transferred his faith to politics. He was proud to claim later that his anti-Schelling publication was the first Young Hegelian document to admit the charge of atheism.[13]

Having thus definitely abandoned any semblance of religious belief, Engels left Berlin at the end of 1842 to spend two years in his father's Manchester business. At the time of his religious crisis Engels had declared: 'I hope to live to see a radical transformation in the religious consciousness of the world.'[14] His experiences in England soon led him to the conclusion that 'communism was a *necessary* consequence of New Hegelian philosophy'.[15] Engels's continued interest in religion, combined with his adherence to a historical materialist view of the world, gave him the distinction of being the first Marxist to produce a sketch for a Marxist history of religion. This history showed religion, and particularly Christianity, to be in many respects a precursor of socialism.

2. TOWARDS A MARXIST HISTORY OF RELIGION

A. Primitive Religion

Engels's scattered remarks on primitive religion do not easily fit into a coherent perspective. On examination, they seem to be informed more by the rather undeveloped state of cultural anthropology at the time than by any recognisably Marxist orientation.

In his first extended comment on primitive religion, in *Anti-Dühring*, Engels starts from the proposition that 'all religion is nothing but the imaginary reflection in men's minds of those external forces which control their daily life, in which the terrestrial forces assume the form of supernatural forces.'[16] As far as the origins of religion are concerned, 'in the beginnings of history it was the forces of nature which were so reflected, and which in the course of further evolution underwent the most manifold and varied personifications among the various peoples.'[17]

But his essay on Ludwig Feuerbach, written some ten years later, contains a view which seems to contradict the idea of religion as arising from misunderstood natural forces. He writes:

> From the very early times when men, still completely ignorant of the structure of their own bodies, under the stimulus of dream apparitions came to believe that their thinking and sensation were not activities of their bodies, but of a distinct soul which inhabits the body and leaves it at death – from this time men have been driven to reflect about the relation between this soul and the outside world. If upon death it took leave of the body and lived on, there was no occasion to invent yet another distinct death for it. Thus arose the idea of its immortality, which at that stage of development appeared not at all as a consolation but as a fate against which it was no use fighting, and often enough, as among the Greeks, as a positive misfortune. Not religious desire for consolation, but the quandary arising from the common universal ignorance of what to do with this soul, once its existence had been accepted, after the death of the body, led in a general way to the tedious notion of personal immortality.[18]

When Engels continues: 'In an exactly similar manner the first gods arose through the personification of natural forces', he appears to exclude the above discussion from the sphere of religion. But his remarks are taken virtually *verbatim* from Tylor's *Primitive Culture*, where this version of animism is portrayed as the prime origin of religious conceptions.[19] And when Engels writes that 'religion arose in very primitive times from erroneous, primitive conceptions of men about their own nature and external nature surrounding them',[20] he seems to view animism and the misinterpretation of natural forces as twin sources of religious beliefs.

Engels's account has little to do with any distinctively Marxian approach – indeed the animist conception might seem to be directly opposed to it. In a letter to Conrad Schmidt on this subject, Engels explained:

> These various false conceptions of nature, of man's own being, of spirits, magic forces, etc., have for the most part only a negative economic element as their basis; the low economic development of the prehistoric period is supplemented and also partially conditioned and even caused by the false conceptions of nature.

And even though economic necessity was the main driving force of the progressive knowledge of nature, it would surely be pedantic to try and find economic causes for all this primitive nonsense.[21]

Thus Lévi-Strauss can comment that 'Marx and Engels frequently express the idea that primitive, or allegedly primitive, societies are governed by "blood ties" (which, today, we call kinship systems) and not by economic relationships.'[22] Even more striking than this separation of religion and economics, Engels, in contrast to the view previously expressed in *The German Ideology*,[23] portrays religion first as a response to nature and to phenomena such as dreams and only later as a response to socio-economic conditions. This is in line with the curious view expressed in his *Origin of the Family* that the primitive family was a natural and not a social product, and that monogamy was the first form of the family to be based not on natural but on economic conditions: Engels here contrasts natural selection in savage and barbaric societies with new, *social* forces that only emerged later.[24] Moreover, in spite of his characterising primitive religion as being 'spontaneous', Engels's picture of primitive religion is sometimes surprisingly intellectualist. Religion, for him, had its roots 'in the narrow-minded and ignorant notions of savagery'.[25] In the course of further development, the personified gods of nature 'assumed more and more an extra-mundane form, until finally by a process of abstraction, I might almost say of distillation, occurring naturally in the course of men's intellectual development, out of the many more or less limited and mutually limiting gods there arose in the minds of men the idea of the one exclusive God of the monotheistic religions.'[26] The tendency towards monotheism is no more connected to socio-economic factors here than it is in the works of Engels's contemporaries such as Frazer, who also alludes to an instinctive craving for the simplification and unification of ideas.

These 'limited and mutually limiting gods' that succeeded to the personified force of nature were termed by Engels 'national religions'. According to him all primitive religions later developed into 'national religions which arose from and merged with the social and political conditions of the local people'.[27] For with the onset of the division of labour and class society men were subjected to social power which was reflected in extra-terrestrial gods with social attributes. These gods were 'national gods whose domain extended no further than the domain of the territory which they were to protect. . . . They could continue to exist, in imagination, only as long as the nation existed; they fell with its fall.'[28] Although this is difficult to reconcile chronologically with Engels's statement that 'nations only became possible through the downfall of Roman World domination',[29] his general point is clear: that the emergence of monotheism was only effected following the emergence of highly differentiated local religions.

It is also clear that Engels both lacks a coherent approach to the study of primitive religion, and exhibits too great a reliance on authorities whose conclusions, given the state of the art at the time, could at best be only tentative. Engels's major source is Tylor's *Primitive Culture*, whose emphasis on animist roots in religion is questionable – not least because Tylor's sources are sedentary peoples rather than the earlier hunters and gatherers. When Engels does mention specific examples, the evidence he relies on has usually been proved unsound by subsequent research.[30] It is particularly noticeable that, although Engels devotes a lot of space to describing Iroquois society in *The Origin of the Family, State and Private Property*, he was not in a position to give an account of Iroquois religion as an example of his general position. He confines himself to remarking that 'their religion is a cult of elemental forces in process of development to polytheism'.[31] For Engels was prone, in the spirit of late nineteenth-century positivism, to over-simple generalisations. This involved the application of the Darwinian model of evolution to the study of primitive society and the consequent attribution to primitive peoples of both 'childish' ignorance and also a penchant to speculate about the world in the manner of a nineteenth-century rationalist.

B. Early Christianity

The first specific area to which Engels devoted any detailed attention in his study of religion was that of early Christianity. He contrasted Christianity with earlier religions – either primitive or national – in three respects. Firstly, Christianity was an 'artificial religion' as opposed to 'spontaneous' primitive religions: in other words, Christianity at its foundation needed 'deception and falsification of history'.[32] But Engels also realised that 'a religion that brought the Roman Empire into subjection and dominated by far the larger part of civilized humanity for 1,800 years cannot be disposed of merely by declaring it to be nonsense gleaned together by frauds.'[33] The Christian religion could not be 'destroyed through ridicule and invective *alone*, it has to be over-powered scientifically, i.e., historically explained'.[34] This historical explanation involved the other two novel, and closely connected, aspects of Christianity – its abstractness and its universality. In using those concepts, Engels refers back specifically to his Young Hegelian mentors: Feuerbach for the former and Bauer for the latter. The Christian God is 'the product of a tedious process of abstraction, the concentrated quintessence of the numerous earlier national and tribal gods.'[35] 'The one almighty God', he says in another passage, had transferred to him 'all the natural and social attributes of the numerous gods'.[36] Such a description would seem to fit the rich variety of a Hegelian concrete universal rather than any abstraction; and indeed Engels does characterise Christianity as a 'universal' religion – 'the first possible world religion'.[37] Following the last chapters of Hegel's *Philosophy of Religion*, Engels wished to put Christianity in a position of privilege as *the* religion. In harmony with a certain tradition of Christian apologetics and with the Eurocentrism characteristic of his age, Engels sees Christianity as the *Aufhebung* or résumé of all other religions.

Engels attempted, however, to anchor this universality in socio-historical terms. The spread of Roman power around the whole of the Mediterranean basin exerted a levelling influence by dividing the population simply into either Roman citizens or subjects and submitting them to a common system of taxation and law. With the transition from Republic to Empire this process became more acute in that the population was faced by an autocratic ruler supported by a mercenary army. The social and political degeneration caused by 'the levelling iron fist of conquering Rome',[38] produced a general demoralisation and despair. To this sorry condition Christianity was able to offer universal consolation, for

in all classes there was necessarily a number of people who, despairing of material salvation, sought in its stead a spiritual salvation, a consolation in their consciousness to save them from utter despair. . . . Christianity clearly expressed the universal feeling that men themselves are guilty of the general corruption as the consciousness of sin of each one; at the same time it provided, in the death-sacrifice of its judge, a form of universally longed-for internal salvation from the corrupt world, the consolation of consciousness; it thus again proved its capacity to becomes a world religion and, indeed, a religion which suited the world as it then was.[39]

This picture of the Roman Empire (which is, of course, in sharp contrast to the views of such as Gibbon and all who admire the *Pax Romana*) is drawn, as Engels himself tells us,[40] from Bruno Bauer's 1840s studies on early Christianity. From the later Bauer of the 1870s, Engels drew his account of the intellectual preconditions of Christianity's triumph,[41] and in particular the relative contributions of Greek and Jewish elements. Following Bauer, Engels thought that

> Christianity was not imported from outside – from Judaea – into the Romano-Greek world and imposed on it, but, at least in its world-religion form, it is that world's own product. . . . It was only by the intermediary of the monotheistic Jewish religion that the cultured monotheism of later Greek vulgar philosophy could clothe itself in the religious form in which alone it could grip the masses.[42]

In this process, Engels detected three stages. Firstly, there was what he called the 'keystone' – the ideas of incarnation and redemption. Like every great revolutionary movement, Christianity was made by the masses, but, Engels admitted, the manner in which it, and with it the 'keystone' ideas, arose in Palestine is 'utterly unknown to us'. Secondly, there was the stage of a Christianity strongly influenced by Alexandrine Judaism as exhibited in the Book of Revelation which Engels believed to have been written around AD 68.[43] And finally, there were Greco-Roman additions, particularly from Stoic philosophy, mediated through the Jewish theological speculations of Philo. The 'culminating point' of Bauer's researches was, according to Engels, the conclusion that 'the Alexandrine Jew Philo, who was still living about AD 40, but was already very old, was the real father of Christianity, and that the Roman stoic Seneca was, so to speak, its uncle.[44] It is this supposed debt of Christianity to Greco-Roman philosophy that Engels wished particularly to emphasise – to the extent of claiming that 'whole passages in the New Testament seem almost literally copied from Seneca's works'.[45] In a manner more fitting to Bauer the fastidious intellectual aristocrat than to his own Marxism, Engels stresses the vulgar (and by implication degenerate) origins of Christian thought – vulgar Jewish monotheism which had become de-nationalised in the Diaspora and vulgar Greek philosophy which had declined into doctrines of God and immortality.

Engels's comments on the philosophico-cultural origins of Christianity are of dubious value. Many of the sources for determining the answers to his questions were simply not available at the time of writing. Even within these constraints he relies too heavily on the later works of Bruno Bauer. Bauer's whole work on Christianity and Stoicism (in contrast to his earlier writings) is highly speculative and has contributed nothing to Biblical scholarship.[46] In general, recent scholarship on the ideological roots of Christianity has put emphasis on Jewish revolutionary and messianic thought of the intertestamentary period and on Greek Gnostic speculation,[47] neither of which are prominent in Engels's account. More particularly, Engels's chronology is fundamentally vitiated by his belief that the Book of Revelation was 'not only the only book of the New Testament, the date of which is really fixed, but also its oldest book'[48] and therefore worth more than all the rest of the New Testament put together.[49] Engels's speculation about the dating of the book by decoding the 'number of the beast' mentioned in Revelation Chapter 13 and connecting it to the fall of Nero have been shown to be quite unfounded.[50] Engels's ideas are taken straight from notes he made fifty years earlier in Berlin on the lectures of the liberal Hegelian Ferdinand Benary, which Engels claimed to have been 'carrying within me since 1841'.[51] Anyone looking in the Book of Revelation for the original Christian message rather than the obvious sources in Acts and I Corinthians is obviously starting at the wrong end.

It is surprising that Engels devoted so much space to analysing Christian doctrines and their intellectual sources and relatively so little to any recognisably materialist account of their origin and growth. Engels insisted that the Christian World religion fitted 'the economic, political and ideological conditions'[52] of the Roman Empire. And he gives us terse and insightful summations of the social structure of the time in terms of the rich, the propertyless free, and the slaves,[53] and repeatedly describes Christianity as 'the religion of the slaves, the banished, the dispossessed, the persecuted, the oppressed'.[54] Of the slaves, Engels says that they were 'deprived of rights and of their own will and the possibility to free themselves, as the defeat of Spartacus had already proved; most of them, however, were former free citizens or sons of free-born citizens. It must therefore have been among them that hatred of their condition of life was still generally vigorous, though externally powerless.'[55] He points to the three-fold equality of early Christianity as particularly appropriate to slaves:

> Christianity knew only *one* point in which all men were equal: that all were equally born in original sin – which corresponded perfectly to its character as the religion of the slaves and the oppressed. Apart from this it recognized, at most, the equality of the elect, which however was only stressed at the very beginning. The traces of common ownership which are also found in the early stages of the new religion can be ascribed to solidarity among the proscribed rather than to real egalitarian ideas.[56]

But repeatedly Engels fails to subject early Christianity to any serious class analysis. For his view that Christianity recruited 'from the lowest strata of the people, as becomes a revolutionary movement'[57] contrasts with the view of Christianity as having universal appeal in face of the levelling power of Rome. Indeed, he says that 'in all classes there was necessarily a number of people who, despairing of material salvation, sought in its stead a spiritual salvation, a consolation in their consciousness to save them from utter despair.'[58] And when he continues that the majority of those pining for consolation were necessarily slaves, it is not clear whether this is a quantitative necessity – simply because most people were slaves. In any case, recent analysis suggests that the description 'religion of slaves' is highly misleading, as is Engels's opinion that most revolts in antiquity were slave-based. Talking of early Jewish recruitment, a topic neglected by Engels, Gerd Theissen writes that its origin was 'not so much the lowest class of all as a marginal middle class which reacted with peculiar sensitivity to the upward and downward trends within society which were beginning to make themselves felt'.[59] And as far as the social composition of Christianity in the Greco-Roman world goes, Robert Grant marshals a lot of evidence to show that the Christian movement should be regarded 'not as a proletarian mass movement but as a relatively small cluster of more or less intense groups, largely middle class in origin'.[60]

C. Christianity and the Rise of the Bourgeoisie

Engels showed very little interest in the history of Christianity during the thousand years that followed its establishment as a state religion by Constantine. 'In the Middle Ages', he wrote, 'in the same measure as feudalism developed, Christianity grew into the religious counterpart of it with a corresponding feudal hierarchy.'[61] The Young Engels conceded that 'the strong faith of the Middle Ages did indeed give the whole epoch considerable energy',[62] but his more mature view was that the Middle Ages constituted a 'long hibernation' whose main interest for him was that it provided the context for the emergence of capitalism and its religious counterpart, the Reformation. The development of the rising middle class in the towns became incompatible with the maintenance of the feudal system. But for feudalism to be over-thrown in each country, it was essential first to destroy its 'sacred central organization', the Roman Catholic Church, which 'surrounded feudal institutions with a halo of divine con-secration'.[63] This struggle against feudalism was carried out in 'three great decisive battles',[64] each with its concomitant attitude to religion. They were the Reformation in Germany, the Civil War in England, and the French Revolution.

It was to the German Protestant Reformation that Engels devoted most of his attention. He saw its origins as very early:

> from the thirteenth to the seventeenth century all the reformations and struggles carried out under religious slogans that were connected with them were, on the theoretical side, nothing but repeated attempts of the burghers and plebeians in the towns and the peasants who had become rebellious by contact with both the latter to adapt the old theological world outlook to the changed economic conditions and the condition of life of the new class.[65]

Engels specifically refers to the Albigensians as the first exponents of the protestant heresy[66] – though sometimes he attributes their class base to the burghers and sometimes to the peasants and 'plebeians'.[67] The German Reformation was, according to Engels, a bourgeois movement and Luther was the representative of a bourgeois party.[68] The obvious difficulty with this view is to reconcile the description of Lutheranism as the ideology of a rising bourgeoisie with the backward nature of the German economy. According to Engels himself, agricultural and industrial production lagged behind levels achieved in Flanders, the Netherlands, Italy and England, and the English and Dutch were already forcing the Germans off the sea trade routes.[69] It is difficult to see how such a retarded economy could produce a bourgeois revolution – albeit one in a religious guise. It was not until the late 1880s that Engels came across a plausible answer to the problem. Kautsky had just published a series of articles which pointed out that the gold and silver mines in Saxony were the most important mines of their kind in Europe at the time. Writing to Kautsky about his articles, Engels said:

> It is only now that I am quite clear . . . how very much the gold and silver production of Germany (and of Hungary whose precious metals were transferred to the whole of the West through Germany) was the last decisive push which placed Germany from 1470 to 1530 economically at the head of Europe and thus the centre of the first bourgeois revolution in religious disguise – the Reformation.[70]

However, Engels did not have the time to elaborate on this view.[71]

But the main interest of Engels in this period was the Peasants War of 1525, the heroic role of the peasant leader Thomas Münzer and the effect on Luther himself – all dealt with in his *Peasant War in Germany* written during the summer of 1850. In the second edition of his work published in 1874, Engels acknowledged that he had taken 'the entire subject-matter on the peasant risings and on Thomas Münzer'[72] from his Young Hegelian colleague Wilhelm Zimmermann who had published a three-volume history of the Peasants War in 1841–3. But Engels was not only indebted to Zimmermann for his facts: he also shared much of his interpretation. Zimmermann had declared that 'all later manifestations of social movements in Europe are contained in the movements of 1525: it is not only the beginning of the European revolutions, but their microcosm.'[73] In keeping with the Young Hegelian tradition, Zimmermann secularised his interpretation of Münzer whose ideas he viewed as an early step towards the realisation of the Kingdom of God or perfect society on earth.[74] Engels took over from Zimmermann two mistaken emphases of interpretation: firstly, the attempt to minimise the religious

motivation of Münzer and thus portray him as an early Young
Hegelian,[75] and secondly, the attempt to exaggerate the role of
Münzer as leader of the peasant rebellion as a whole; particularly
evident is the mistake of regarding the Anabaptists as being agents
of Münzer.

Engels's account has further difficulties when it wishes to go
beyond Zimmermann and show 'the politico-religious controversies of the times as a reflection of the contemporary class
struggles'.[76] For his approach is governed by his own recent political
experience in the 1848 revolution; 'Luther and Münzer each fully
represented his party by his doctrine, as well as by his character, and
actions. From 1517 to 1525 Luther changed just as much as the
present-day German constitutionalists did between 1846 and 1849,
and as every bourgeois party which, placed for a time at the head of
the movement, is overwhelmed by the plebeian proletarian party
standing behind it.'[77] Later, Engels was even more specific: 'The
German Peasant War pointed prophetically to future class
struggles, by bringing on to the stage not only the peasants in revolt
– that was no longer anything new – but behind them the beginnings
of the modern proletariat with the red flag in their hands and the
demand for common ownership of goods on their lips.'[78] Apart
from the general difficulty of finding a strong bourgeois basis for the
German Reformation, it was also hard to see Luther as a spokesman
for the bourgeoisie in view of his 'reactionary' support for the
Princes in 1525. Luther was an ardent critic of some of the
fundamental practices of capitalism[79] and an advocate of the far
from bourgeois doctrines and practice of early Christianity.[80] The
Lutheran Reformation, says Engels, 'produced a new creed, indeed
a religion adapted to absolute monarchy'[81] which has plausibly
been viewed by some Marxist historians as the final stage of
feudalism rather than a product of the rise of the bourgeoisie.[82] It
was even more difficult to see the peasants as a leading force in a
bourgeois revolution. The reformation continued unabated after the
defeat of the peasants. Indeed many of the demands of the peasants
were reactionary in that they appealed to the type of common land
ownership that antedated feudalism – just as, ironically, many of
the working-class activists in 1848 looked back to pre-capitalist
forms of social organisation for their model.[83] In general, it is
noticeable how little Engels mentions, even in the broadest outline,
the actual religious doctrines of either Luther or Münzer. Any
detailing of these would have cast serious doubt on the concept of a

bourgeois revolution in religious disguise and in particular on the view of Münzer as really a social revolutionary who was forced by the spirit of the age to cloak his ideas in religious phraseology.[84] A measured conclusion is that of Leonard Krieger in his edition of Engels's *Peasant War*:

> Undoubtedly, Engels's early religious experience and his lifelong conviction of a kinship between religion and communism helped him to approach, in the context of the religiosity of the Peasants' War, as close as he would ever get to an integral relationship among the variegated historical activities of man. The connection between the radical sects and the 'peasant-plebeian' classes – the connection that embodied Engels' most penetrating historical perception – remains the one definite relationship that has been accepted by historians on both sides of the Marxist divide. In general, moreover, even if Engels' priority of social interests and his one-to-one correlation of the other religious confessions with social classes have found no such acceptance, the relevance of the social dimension to the religious conflicts of the Reformation era is beyond cavil and the discovery of how this relationship actually worked remains one of the live issues for European historiography.[85]

'But where Luther failed, Calvin won the day.'[86] The second great act of the bourgeois evolution, Engels tells us, took place in England and was supported by the rise of Calvinism in Geneva, Holland and Scotland. In England Calvinism was 'the true religious disguise of the interests of the bourgeoisie of that time'.[87] This was true in two respects: firstly there was a correspondence between the ecclesiastical presbyterian organisation of Calvin's Church and the political views of its members. 'Calvin's church constitution was thoroughly democratic and republican; and where the kingdom of God was republicanised, could the kingdoms of this world remain subject to monarchs, bishops and lords?'[88] More fundamentally, there was a correspondence between Calvin's theology and the economic interests of the bourgeoisie:

> His predestination doctrine was the religious expression of the fact that in the commercial world of competition success or failure does not depend on a man's activity or cleverness, but on circumstances uncontrollable by him. It is not of him that willeth

or of him that runneth, but of the mercy of superior economic
powers; and this was especially true at a period of economic
revolution, when all old commercial routes and centres were
replaced by new ones, when India and America were opened to
the world, and when even the most sacred economic articles of
faith – the value of gold and silver – began to totter and to break
down.[89]

Engels's view contains some difficulties. Although it is quite
possible to see a correlation between the arbitrary predestinations of
God and the irrationality and anonymity of the early capitalist
market, Engels does not mention those links that have most
impressed those who have studied the relationship of Calvinism to
early capitalism, particularly the 'inner-worldly asceticism' involved
in the sober prosecution of a worldly calling and the sustained
rejection of all fleshly pleasures which are said to follow logically
and psychologically from Calvin's theology. Indeed, on Engels's
account, the effort, calculation and self-discipline that characterised
the capitalist entrepreneur would seem to be pointless. There is also
the view, as in Weber's *The Protestant Ethic and the Spirit of Capitalism*,
that gives Calvinism a more influential place in the evolution of
capitalism.[90] And many would even deny any material connexion.[91]
Finally, Engels firmly attributes the origin of this 'second great
bourgeois upheaval' to the Calvinist 'middle-class of the towns'.[92]
The interpretation of the social causes of the English Civil War is a
matter of considerable controversy. Some think that 'the English
puritans included strong anti-capitalist forces and that orthodox
Calvinism, so far from being the ideology of the merchant classes in
the seventeenth century, prevailed largely – in Protestant countries
– among backwoods squires, as in Scotland and Gelderland'[93] and
that the Great Rebellion had its roots in an impoverished gentry
rather than a rising bourgeoisie. And even committed Marxist
historians would want strongly to qualify Engels's views.[94]

As a postscript it should be noted that, in contrast to the
Calvinism of the bourgeoisie, Engels considered materialism in
England, to be an aristocratic doctrine. The English bourgeois 'was
himself religious: his religion had supplied the standard under
which he had fought the king and the lords; he was not long in
discovering the opportunities this same religion offered him for
working upon the minds of his natural inferiors, and making them
submissive to the natural behests of the masters it had pleased God

to place over them.'[95] In contrast, materialism, whose original home, from the seventeenth-century onwards, was England, was anti-bourgeois. Hobbes's materialism was interpreted as a defence of royal prerogative and omnipotence while 'the new deistic form of materialism' of his successors 'remained an aristocratic, esoteric doctrine.[96] What Engels fails to explain is how Hobbes and Locke who (together with Bacon) he considers the founders of English materialism,[97] a doctrine which he explicitly associates with the royalist cause,[98] can at the same time be plausibly viewed as the founders of a specifically bourgeois political theory.[99]

If, for Engels, 'the flag of religion waves for the last time in England in the seventeenth century',[100] it followed that 'the Great Revolution was the third uprising of the bourgeoisie, but the first that had entirely cast off the religious cloak, and was fought out on undisguised political lines.'[101] The materialism which had been born in England as an aristocratic doctrine under a restored monarchy moved over to France where, fusing with the philosophical materialism of the Cartesian School, it became – either as avowed materialism or as deism – 'the creed of the whole cultural youth of France'[102] and the vehicle of a bourgeoisie in revolt against an absolutist monarchy. Engels summarised his views as follows:

In France, the Calvinist minority was suppressed in 1685 and either Catholicized or driven out of the country. But what was the good? Already at that time the free-thinker Pierre Bayle was at the height of his activity and in 1694 Voltaire was born. The forcible measures of Louis XIV only made it easier for the French bourgeoisie to carry through its revolution in the irreligious, exclusively political form which alone was suited to a developed bourgeoisie. Instead of Protestants, free-thinkers took their seats in the national assemblies.[103]

This paradox that 'the doctrine hatched by English Royalists gave a theoretical flag to French Republicans and Terrorists, and furnished the text for the Declaration of the Rights of Man'[104] suggests that Engels would see the relationship of religion to revolution as a highly variable one. His view of unilinear historical progress nevertheless compelled him to assert that a developed bourgeoisie would have no use for religion – at least in its revolutionary phase. (The nineteenth-century religiosity of the English bourgeoisie and the reconversion to Christianity of its

French counterpart were to be explained by their desire to use religion to keep the working class in their place.)[105] So strongly did Engels hold to his view that he could declare: 'The Christian religion in France, as a matter of fact, so completely disappeared in the years 1793–8 that even Napoleon could not reintroduce it without opposition and difficulty; and this without any need for a substitute, in Feuerbach's sense, making itself felt in the interval.'[106] This sweeping assertion ignores several factors: the attempt to establish the cult of a Supreme Being, which Engels simply dismissed as a failure,[107] the widespread existence of revolutionary cults of diverse sorts,[108] the Napoleonic restoration of Christianity which he viewed as artificial, and, most important of all, the fact that most of the French socialist sects of the mid-nineteenth century were heavily imbued with Christianity, albeit of an unorthodox kind. It should finally be noted that Engels's more simplistic statements on the French Revolution come from his essay on Feuerbach. The somewhat (but not much) more subtle account in the Introduction to *Socialism: Utopian and Scientific* comes after the correspondence with Bloch and Schmidt had led Engels to clarify his position on the materialist conception of history by declaring that he and Marx had previously exaggerated the influence of the economic factor and admitting that the 'superstructure' could react back on the 'base'.[109]

3.   RELIGION AND SOCIALISM

A. Contemporary

Engels's historical studies of Christianity led him to see both a continuity and a discontinuity between religion and socialism.

The discontinuity lies in Engels's conviction that after the eighteenth century Christianity no longer had any vitality as a progressive force. Several of his previous analyses had shown that Christianity could be the religion of a rising class. Following the French Revolution however, Christianity 'entered its final stage. It had become incapable for the future of serving any progressive class as the ideological garb of its aspirations. It became more and more the exclusive possession of the ruling classes and these apply it as a mere means of government to keep the lower classes within bounds.'[110]

More interesting is the continuity that Engels perceived between

Christianity and socialist atheism. He was particularly impressed in this connexion by early Christianity, which he viewed as the socialism of its time. In reply to a critic who wondered why socialism had not established itself on the fall of the Roman Empire, Engels replied that 'this "socialism" did in fact, as far as it was possible at the time, exist and even become dominant in Christianity.'[111] He liked to quote Renan's remark that 'when you want to get a distinct idea of what the first Christian communities were, do not compare them to the parish congregations of our day; they were rather like local sections of the International Working Men's Association.'[112] This parallel was expanded in the last substantial piece of writing that Engels produced:

> It is now, almost to the year, sixteen centuries since a dangerous party of overthrow was likewise active in the Roman empire. It undermined religion and all the foundations of the state; it flatly denied that Caesar's will was the supreme law; it was without a fatherland, was international; it spread over all countries of the empire, from Gaul to Asia, and beyond the frontiers of the empire. It had long carried on seditious activities in secret, underground; for a considerable time, however, it had felt itself strong enough to come out into the open. This party of overthrow, which was known by the name of Christians, was also strongly represented in the army; whole legions were Christian. When they were ordered to attend the sacrificial ceremonies of the pagan established church, in order to do the honours there, the subversive soldiers had the audacity to stick peculiar emblems – crosses – on their helmets in protest. Even the wonted barrack bullying of their superior officers was fruitless. The Emperor Diocletian could no longer look on while order, obedience and discipline were undermined. He interfered energetically, while there was still time. He promulgated an anti-Socialist – beg pardon, I meant to say anti-Christian – law.[113]

But Engels wanted to go further than structural parallels between Christianity and socialism. Not only did they share a common constituency in oppressed people, a common promise of salvation, a common opposition to the prevailing society which led to persecution, and a common assurance of ultimate victory:[114] there was also something in the actual content of the Christian message that led to a socialism which sometimes in Engels appears as little more than a secularised Christianity. His investigation into the history of religions had led him to see an evolution from natural/ primitive religions, through national religions, to the three universal religions of Buddhism, Christianity and Islam. Of these three, only Christianity seemed to Engels to qualify both practically and intellectually as truly universal insofar as it paved the way for the universality of socialism. For 'after Christianity, after absolute, i.e., abstract religion, after "religion as such", no other form of religion can arise . . . not even pantheism.'[115] Already in 1842 Engels had come to the conclusion that 'Christianity contains premises which, if developed, could lead to atheism',[116] and even pointed out the following year in his discussion of Carlyle that, on Carlyle's pantheistic view, 'it is not we but our Christian opponents who would be the true atheists.'[117] In a sense, therefore, socialism was the Christianity of Engels's time.

It was particularly socio-political considerations that led Engels to equate Christianity with reaction. He had been disappointed to find in the 1840s that 'the French Communists, being a part of a nation celebrated for their infidelity, are themselves Christians.'[118] In England, however, the role of religion came closer to his expectations. He was indeed puzzled by his impression that 'the English are the most religious nation on earth and at the same time the most irreligious' in that 'they worry more about the next world than any other nation and at the same time they live as though this world were all that mattered to them.'[119] But he soon became convinced that this religiousness was an attribute of the bourgeois. Recalling his own first impressions, he wrote some thirty years later:

About the middle of this century, what struck every cultivated foreigner who set up his residence in England, was what he was then bound to consider the religious bigotry and stupidity of the English repectable middle class. We, at that time, were all materialists, or, at least, very advanced free-thinkers, and to us it appeared inconceivable that almost all educated people in England should believe in all sorts of impossible miracles, and that even geologists like Buckland and Mantell should contort the facts of their science so as not to clash too much with the myths of the book of Genesis; while, in order to find people who dared to use their own intellectual faculties with regard to religious matters, you had to go amongst the uneducated, the 'great unwashed', as they were then called, the working people, especially the Owenite Socialists.[120]

On the Continent, too, following the upheavals of 1848, the bourgeois began to look gratefully to religion as a support:

Nothing remained to the French and German bourgeoisie as a last resort but to silently drop their free thought, as a youngster, when sea-sickness creeps upon him, quietly drops the burning cigar he brought swaggeringly on board; one by one, the scoffers turned pious in outward behaviour, spoke with respect of the Church, its dogmas and rites, and even conformed with the latter as far as could not be helped. French bourgeois dined maigre on Fridays, and German ones sat out long Protestant sermons in their pews on Sundays. They had come to grief with materialism. *Die Religion muss dem Volk erhalten werden*, – religion must be kept alive among the people as the last means to save society from utter ruin. Unfortunately for themselves, they did not find this out until they had done their level best to break up religion for ever. And now it was the turn of the British bourgeois to sneer and to say: 'Why, you fools, I could have told you that two hundred years ago!'[121]

Since Engels was clear that 'neither the religious stolidity of the British, nor the *post festum* conversion of the continental bourgeois will stem the rising proletarian tide',[122] he was naturally inclined to expect the working class to be antipathetic to religion, particularly in the most advanced industrial country, England. He found that 'the English Socialists are far more principled and practical than the French' in that 'they are engaged in a practical struggle against the various churches and do not want to have anything to do with religion.'[123] The workers, at least in Manchester, were busy reading Paine and Voltaire. Two years later, in his *Condition of the Working Class in England*, Engels came to the conclusion that, with the exception of the Irish, 'the workers are not religious and do not attend church. . . . Among the masses there prevails almost universally a total indifference to religion.'[124] It is difficult to see how this view could have been anything but the product of wishful thinking, particularly as the period during which Engels was writing marked the high point of religious practice in Victorian England, particularly where the Free Churches were concerned.[125]

And Engels does indeed backtrack somewhat when he observes later in the book that 'English Socialism affords the most pronounced expression of the prevailing absence of religion among the working men, an expression so pronounced indeed that the mass of the working men, being unconsciously and merely practically irreligious, often draws back before it.'[126] Engels entertained similar illusions about the working class in Germany and France. 'The working people of our country', he implausibly claimed in 1845, 'read and digest the writings of the greatest German philosophers such as Feuerbach, etc., and embrace the results of their enquiries, as radical as this result may appear. The people of Germany have no religion.'[127] Thirty years later Engels said of the German Social Democratic workers that they had 'purely and simply finished with God, they live and think in the world of reality and are therefore materialists. This seems to be the case in France too.'[128] When confronted with a specific example of popular interest in religion, Engels could only account for it as artificially produced by government propaganda.[129] Engels was little interested in providing empirical foundations for his view. Religion was for him irretrievably a part of bourgeois ideology which merely served to render the workers subservient. His faith in the inevitable growth of proletarian self-consciousness and in the consequent triumph of socialist principles, and his eagerness to chart the development of this process[130] entailed both a belief in the eventual disappearance of religion and an unfounded anticipation of this event.

B. The End of Religion

Why did Engels believe that religion would disappear with the advent of socialism? Religion, for him, was imaginary – 'the fantastic reflection of human things in the human mind.'[131] It was not only that religion 'stands furthest away from material life and seems to be most alien to it':[132] unlike law and morality, religion did not simply reflect material conditions. As something 'fantastic', it involved a mistake. Socialist law, therefore, and socialist morality were conceivable, but socialist religion was not. This view suggests a very intellectualist attitude to religion and the reasons advanced for the disappearance of religion, particularly in the *Dialectics of Nature*, reflect this view which is a corollary of Engels's intellectualist account of the origins of primitive religion.[133] On this account, since religion is an incorrect reflection of nature, 'only real knowledge of the forces of nature ejects the gods or God from one position after another.'[134] In keeping with Victorian positivism in general, Engels took the view that 'what can be brought under laws, hence what one *knows*, is interesting; what cannot be brought under laws, and therefore what one does not know, is a matter of indifference and can be ignored.'[135] God was just another name for ignorance which the progress of materialist science would render completely redundant. More particularly, Engels considered the essence of Christianity to be the opposition of the spiritual and the material. With the advance of natural science, however, and the opportunities this afforded to control the production process, it would become increasingly impossible to maintain 'this senseless and unnatural idea of a contrast between mind and matter, man and nature, soul and body, such as arose after the decline of classical antiquity and attained its highest elaboration in Christianity.'[136]

This view, of course, has nothing particularly Marxist about it. In *Anti-Dühring*, by contrast, Engels sketches a position in which it is not natural science but social science that will lead to the disappearance of religion. Here Engels begins with the familiar view that 'all religion is nothing but the fantastic reflection in men's minds of those external forces which control their daily life, a reflection in which the terrestrial forces assume the form of supernatural forces.'[137] In primitive times it was natural forces that assumed a religious form. But soon social forces, too, entered the process. Alongside the forces of nature 'social forces begin to be active – forces which confront man as equally alien and at first equally inexplicable, dominating him with the same apparent natural necessity as the forces of nature themselves. The fantastic figures, which at first only reflected the mysterious forces of nature, at this point acquire social attributes, become representatives of the forces of history.'[138] As long as men continue to be under the domination of natural and social forces, religion will continue to exist. Under prevailing bourgeois conditions, he continued, men were subject to the means of production that they themselves had produced. Mere knowledge was insufficient to bring these social forces under the domination of society. What was above all necessary was a social *act*. For,

> when society, by taking possession of all means of production and using them on a planned basis, has freed itself and all its members from the bondage in which they are now held by these means of

production which they themselves have produced but which confront them as an irresistable alien force; when therefore man no longer merely proposes, but also disposes – only then will the last alien force which is still reflected in religion vanish; and with it will also vanish the religious reflection itself, for the simple reason that then there will be nothing left to reflect.[139]

Engels's views on the disappearance of religion depend on two questionable assumptions. The first is a teleological account of religious development from primitive 'natural' religion through to Christianity and atheistic socialism. But many would see natural religion – in the sense of the celebration of rites of passage – as extremely resistant and far from *dépassé*.[140] If this is the case even with natural religion it casts grave doubt on the discrete evolutionary stages that Engels posits. Secondly, it is by no means clear, even with the restricted definition of religion that Engels uses, that the incompatibilities are as he suggests. Authors as far apart as Zaehner and Althusser have argued for the compatibility of Engels's dialectical materialism (in the case of the former) and his historical materialism (in the case of the latter) with the continuing existence of religion.[141]

CONCLUSION

Although Engels wrote considerably more on religion than Marx, his views are not thereby more interesting. Brought up in a strongly pietist household, it is natural that Engels should be interested in religion in his early years; his return to the investigation of religion in his later years is due partly to a survival of interest in those questions – as specifically in his article on the Book of Revelation. More immediately, the growing size of the Marxist movement put Engels under considerable pressure during the last two decades of his life to systematise and, to some extent, to popularise a Marxist world view; and this, of course, had to deal with the question of religion.

The superficiality of Engels's approach to religion is dictated, in large parts, by the kind of Marxism he came to espouse. The account of historical materialism outlined in his letters to Bloch and Schmidt reiterated the unfortunate metaphor of base and superstructure, referred to economic, political and ideological 'factors' and maintained that the economic factor determined in the last instance. Religion, as the part of the ideological factor furthest removed from the base, naturally assumed a very pale role in the historical process. Furthermore, Engels's adoption of a materialist metaphysic, in the shape of what later became known as dialectical materialism, left little room for an account of religion other than pure illusion.

In elaborating these broad models of history and philosophy, Engels was strongly influenced by the side of scientistic positivism that flowed so strongly in the last decade of the nineteenth century. It was this spirit that informed Engels's teleogical and evolutionary view in which religion would eventually be replaced by the progress of science. There is a tension in Engels's thought between the view that religion has some genuine content on which socialism is called upon to realise – and the view that religion is an illusion due largely to ignorance. The growing prestige of positivism caused that latter view to prevail in Engels's later work.

His conceptual tools and intellectual milieu go a long way to explaining why Engels, who could be so good a historian, is so weak when it came to dealing with religion. In the three periods to which he devotes serious attention – primitive religion, early Christianity, and the Reformation Engels relies uncritically in a single authority. For primitive religion, he relies on Tylor, for early Christianity on Bauer, and for the Reformation on Zimmermann. Tylor was a positivist and a rationalist, Bauer a conservative idealist, and Zimmermann a radical Young Hegelian. And Engels makes only the most meagre efforts to combine their views with any sort of Marxism. For the kind of Marxism he elaborated simply did not have the conceptual wherewithal to come to terms with his authorities.

3

German Social Democracy

1. INTRODUCTION

The legacy of Engels to German Social Democracy in matters of religion was an attitude of indifference if not outright hostility. Some of his earlier writings – or indeed even his later articles – may have indicated fruitful connexions between socialism and Christianity, but the major work for which Engels became known was his *Anti-Dühring*. It was through *Anti-Dühring* that most leading Social Democrat intellectuals, from Kautsky and Bernstein downwards, found their way to Marxism. This 'more or less connected exposition of the dialectical method and of the communist world outlook',[1] as Engels himself called it, became an encyclopedia or handbook of Marxism for the next generation. Its jejune treatment of religion foreshadows that adopted, with few significant exceptions, by German Social Democracy.[2] The period between the Erfurt Programme of 1891 and the outbreak of the First World War was the least propitous for any interaction between socialism and Christianity. The adoption of the Erfurt Programme marked the eclipse of Lassalle whose socialism, heavily influenced by German Idealism, did not appear to conflict with religious values. With its adoption of Marxism, however, Social Democracy began explicitly to be propagated as an alternative to Christianity.

With the significant exception of the Austro-Marxists discussed below, the Marxism of German Social Democracy was imbued with the spirit of scientific positivism. The popularisation of scientific materialism in the 1850s and 1960s by such writers as Vogt, Moleschott and Büchner was continued by Ernst Haeckel. His *Riddle of the Universe*, which sold 100 000 copies within a year of its publication in 1899, marked the high point of this movement. Haeckel had set out to convert Germany to a form of Darwinism whose metaphysical – and specifically anti-religious – claims went far beyond any intention of its founder. And these views rapidly became a philosophical adjunct for the growing Marxist party. As early as 1871 Darwin's work in biology had been seen as the guarantor of Marx's social science. The penetration of Darwinism *à la* Haeckel into the socialist consciousness was facilitated by three interconnected factors. Firstly, the vague feeling that religion, at least in specific and institutionalised form, was against the interests of the working class favoured the propagation of a materialist outlook. This outlook was all the more attractive when the crude materialism of Haeckel, who could assert as a matter of 'knowledge' that the soul was a sum of plasma movements in the ganglion cells, was supplemented by the ethical dimension of a self-confident socialist movement. Secondly, the average party member needed a fairly accessible and easily propagated view of the world with which to buttress his or her socialism. Given the prestige of natural science at this time, it was inevitable that Marxism would be assimilated to philosophical materialism as a (natural) science of society. The fact that Haeckel himself had a profound dislike of socialism was irrelevant. Thirdly, the influence of Hegel, from which Protestant theology had learnt so much and to which was due much of the pregnancy of Marx's (and Engels's) remarks on religion, was almost totally eclipsed. As one of the Social Democratic leaders declared at the 1899 Party Congress: 'In our campaigns, let us substitute for "dialectic" the much more precise and rich concept of "development". It is also much more intelligible to the workers. Bebel has mentioned the spirit of the great Darwin. We stand nearer to him than to Hegel.'[3] With this shift Marxism ceased to share even the roots of a common language with Christianity.

Among Marxists in general, with significant exceptions such as Labriola, the positivist side of their ideas triumphed over the critical. By the turn of the century this positivism, although under severe attack in other countries, was still well entrenched in Germany in which the ideas of Darwin, now elaborated into a total explanation of the universe, had more continued influence than in any other country. Religion in Germany was thus widely on the defensive intellectually. Socially and politically, too, there was a ready equation of Christianity with attitudes that were hostile to the working class. Exhausted by the grim political struggle of the *Kulturkampf*, the Catholic Church made virtually no contribution to the country's intellectual life. There was no German equivalent to a Claudel or a Blondel. The *Kulturkampf* had also enhanced the power of Rome over the German Church. On his succession in 1903 Pius X rapidly stifled the relatively open-minded attitude to intellectual and political innovation of his predecessor Leo XIII. Nor was

German Protestantism in a much better state. Bismarck's attitude to the Catholics had forced the Protestants, too, to concentrate their minds too much on Church–State relations. Confronted with the ideas of Haeckel, they managed only to produce the thin idealism of Harnack. The widespread reverence for authority meant that there was no feeding-in of ideas from the experience of the rank and file as in the Anglo-Saxon world. The dominant tone of German philosophy had favoured the spread of an agnostic attitude among the middle classes. And the Church leaders could produce no convincing response to the extraordinary vitality of German theology in such areas as the New Testament criticism following in the wake of Strauss, the revision of Old Testament scholarship necessitated by Wellhausen's *History of Israel*, and the spread of comparative religious studies. Even the revival of interest in religious – or at least spiritual – values exemplified by Nietzsche or Bergson had little influence on organised Christianity.

Thus the theoreticians of the SPD, insofar as they touched on religion, tended either to consider its historical influence and how to fit religion into their evolutionary scheme of history or to concentrate on immediate questions of disestablishment, interest in which was stimulated by the Church–State conflict in France in the 1900s. The sixth point of the Party's Erfurt programme of 1891 had reaffirmed the stance of the Gotha programme of 1875 by declaring religion to be 'a private matter', a view accepted even by Wilhelm Liebknecht and August Bebel who nevertheless proclaimed atheism to be a logical and historical consequence of socialism. Kautsky, Cunow and their colleagues were not interested in any 'dialogue' with Christianity as the contemporary Churches did not offer much material for conversation. Few prominent churchmen had any sympathy for socialism. There were a few strong advocates of social reform such as Adolf Stöcker who founded a Christian Social Workers' Party in 1878, Friedrich Naumann who was very active in advocating a Christian socialism in the 1880s and 1890s, and Christopher Blumhardt who actually joined the SPD in 1899. All three were Lutheran pastors, but Stöcker's views were developed inside a distinctly conservative political and social framework, Naumann rejected Marxism for preaching class hatred, and Blumhardt, who did have a genuine sympathy for the Marxist point of view, was forced by the Church authorities to resign his orders.[4] Nevertheless, although they might not have much sympathy for organised socialism, there *was* growing interest and activity in the

Churches concerning 'the social question' as evidenced on the Catholic side by the Encyclical *Rerum Novarum* of 1891. Also, many SPD members, however antipathetic they felt towards institutional Christianity, continued to harbour instinctive religious feelings of the sort popularised in the 1840s by Weitling and Kriege to which Marx had been so hostile.[5] The willingness to enlarge a rather jejune Marxism with an ethical socialism of Christian inspiration was common in the revisionist circles of German Social Democracy. But this was a trend naturally resisted by SPD Marxists who, in addition to dealing with immediate political questions such as the disestablishment of the Church (effected in France in 1903), attempted to give a historical materialist account of religion in general and Christianity in particular which would clearly subordinate religion to the principles of scientific socialism.

2. DIETZGEN, BEBEL AND LAFARGUE

The growing influence of 'scientific' Marxism in the SPD, and the consequently changing attitude to religion, can be appreciated by comparing the writings of Joseph Dietzgen with those of later Marxist publicists such as Bebel and Lafargue. Dietzgen, a self-taught and relatively prosperous tanner, produced his main work, entitled *The Nature of Human Brainwork*, in 1869. The book was a thorough-going attempt to construct a materialist epistemology. In the early 1870s Dietzgen wrote a series of articles for the SPD newspaper *Vorwärts* under the surprising title *The Religion of Social Democracy*. The tone was set by the opening sentences: 'The teachings of Socialism contain the material for a new religion which, unlike any other religion, appeals not merely to the heart and emotions, but at the same time to the brain, the organ of knowledge. From all other earthly knowledge socialism is distinguished by its religious form, by its fervid appeal to the heart and soul of man.'[6] The old Gospel depended on faith, the new one on science, and Work was the name of the new Redeemer. Much of Dietzgen's work echoed the early German socialist followers of Weitling with their simple view that Christianity equalled communism and that Jesus Christ was the first communist. Indeed, Dietzgen appealed explicitly to Feuerbach whom he considered to have 'brought the conclusive and irrefutable proof that all religion is simply a substitute for human ignorance'.[7] And Dietzgen's message was a typical Feuerbachian reversal: 'In order to emancipate humanity from religion not only vaguely but distinctly and really, it is necessary to overcome religion by analyzing and fully comprehending it.'[8] Dietzgen wished to distinguish clearly the parts of Christianity which could be readily accepted by socialists – they included 'mortifying the flesh as a means against non-married lust or brotherhood of man against national jealousies'[9] – from those which were incompatible with socialism – the preaching of a love which excluded class hatred and the rejection of the scientific method as the only criterion of truth. But in spite of his advocacy of 'anti-religious social democracy',[10] Dietzgen was evidently ambiguous about the status of 'religion'. It is not surprising that his later editor suggests that the reader could safely change the title from *The Religion of Social Democracy* to *Social Democracy and Religion*.[11]

Dietzgen's ambivalence was echoed by Wilhelm Liebknecht, founder of the Marxist party in Germany, who told the Reichstag deputies that the attitude of the Social Democrats 'is *a religion*, not the religion of the Popes but the *religion of humanity*'.[12] But no such ambivalence afflicted August Bebel who uncompromisingly rejected all religion. 'The Bible', he declared, 'has brought more people into the madhouse than any other book. . . . Christianity and Socialism stand opposed to each other like fire and water. The so-called good kernel in Christianity is not Christian but universal and human, and what is peculiar to Christianity – the doctrine and the dogma – is inimical to humanity.'[13] Bebel continued the theme of the incompatibility of Christianity with contemporary intellectual and material progress in his *Woman under Socialism*, published in 1879, which was, together with *Anti-Dühring*, the most widely-read book in German Social Democracy. In the final section of the book Bebel discussed the future of religion which was merely 'the transcendental reflection of prevailing social conditions'.[14] Bebel quoted the early Marx to the effect that religion was a striving after illusory happiness which stemmed from the social condition that necessitated such an illusion and would disappear as soon as the masses understood the nature of genuine happiness and how to obtain it. Fetishism, polytheism, monotheism and pantheism had been successive stages of religious belief which was not being completely dissolved: 'The natural sciences have reduced the dogma of the creation of the earth in six days to a myth; astronomy and mathematics have made heaven into a mere structure of air, and the stars in the firmament, on which the angels are enthroned, into planets and fixed stars, the nature of which excludes all angelic life.'[15] Naturally the ruling class clung to religion to bolster their authority, considering that 'religion must be preserved for the people'. Morality could exist without religion, for morality involved the relations of human beings with each other, while religion involved their relations with supernatural beings. Bebel added the usual social democratic rider that 'if someone should still have religious requirements, let him satisfy them in the company of like-minded people. Society does not concern itself with the matter.' But he was convinced that religion would die an early death in the new socialist society for 'constant human progress and unadulterated science are its motto'.[16]

These themes were pursued by Marx's son-in-law Paul Lafargue who published in 1905–6 a series of articles in the leading German Social Democrat periodical *Die Neue Zeit* entitled 'The Causes of Belief in God'. The problem he set out to solve was why the bourgeoisie, in spite of their general level of education and the propaganda of free thinkers, were still largely Christian whereas the 'ignorant' proletariat were remarkable for an unreflecting but obstinate indifference to all things religious. (For the proletariat, Lafargue quoted Charles Booth's reports on the East End of London, but provided no evidence for the religiosity of the bourgeoisie.) Lafargue began his answer with a brief section on primitive religion which was rather out of place. Dreams, he said, had given rise to belief in the Soul and Immortality, to the offering of prayers and gifts to supposedly powerful dead souls and to monotheism where God was considered to be the most powerful of all the souls. Christianity merely assembled and organised myths that had been around for centuries. More to the point, Lafargue, who adopted elsewhere in his writings the thorough-going reductive materialism of the later Feuerbach, claimed that bourgeois social scientists 'could not and cannot entertain the conviction that social phenomena just as much as natural phenomena are dependant on the law of necessity, and precisely because they could not attain to this conviction, belief in God is a necessity for even the most cultivated bourgeois mind.'[17] Investigation into natural science was free and unprejudiced, for the success of bourgeois production depended on it. But not so in social science, where investigation uncluttered with idealist prejudice would undermine bourgeois rule. Elsewhere, Lafargue admitted that bourgeois writers of the Englightenment (Locke, Condillac) had adopted a materialist epistemology, but this had been abandoned once the bourgeoisie had attained power in favour of the Platonic idealist view that abstract ideas could be directly intuited by the mind independently of physical sensation. This implied that human beings were more than mere physical entities and thus opened the way for the idea of supra-sensible cognition and religious mystification.[18]

This mystification had, according to Lafargue, a real basis in bourgeois economics. Just as primitive religion arose from ignorance of the natural world, so the bourgeois belief in God arose from ignorance of the social world. For bourgeois society was ruled by chance. Dealings in stocks and shares, the expansion and retraction of credit made all business enterprises into a gamble and bourgeois society as a whole into a giant game of roulette. No wonder, then, that a mystical power was believed to lie behind this game of chance. Belief in God as a mysterious being without material substance has its parallel in the bank note which incorporated a social power that was quite incommensurate with its material substance. More specifically, the capitalist believed in the after-life, since for him there was no activity without profit, and an after-life was the only way in which he could get compensation for his losses on earth. More interestingly, Lafargue asserted that the impersonal role of property in capitalism as exemplified by the joint stock company gave rise to the idea of a universal faceless God. Just as share certificates were nameless and characterless, so the typical expression of bourgeois religiosity was the characterless God of the Deists. And such beliefs would persist as long as capitalist society existed: once the means of production were socially controlled, society would no longer be opaque and the idea of God would disappear. The sharp superficiality of these remarks – and the crudeness of Bebel's hostility – are highlighted by the contrast with the careful treatment of such questions by Karl Kautsky, the great systematiser of Marxist thought in the two decades before 1914.

3. KAUTSKY

A. Origin and Function of Religion

In his earliest writings, Kautsky followed the views of Engels's *Anti-Dühring* on primitive religion by writing that 'the intellectual roots of religion, the causes of religious thought and feeling, lie in the existence of superhuman and incomprehensible forces, in the face of which man is helpless, whose operations he can neither control nor foresee, and which exert such a decisive influence upon his weal and woe that he feels the need of propitiating them.'[19] Kautsky did, however, go on to say that these forces could be either natural or social: under primitive communism social forces 'played no part', and since men still felt themselves to be 'a part of nature' it followed that 'of religion there is as yet little mention'.[20] Indeed, the social root of religion only began to play a part with the rise of commodity production, was quiescent in Antiquity and the Middle Ages, and only really came to the fore in the Renaissance. Although these latter remarks are difficult to make much sense of, Kautsky did continue to maintain the general position that primitive religion was largely due to ignorance of nature.[21]

The publication in 1913 of Cunow's book on primitive religion[22] caused Kautsky to change many of his previously asserted views on religion – as he himself admitted.[23] For Cunow's work, and Tylor's animism on which it was based, argues forcefully that the view of Marx and Engels, that primitive religion was the product of the fear of nature, was mistaken. For Engels had attributed too great a power of objective reflection about nature to primitives, neglected the fact, emphasised by Cunow, that religion had a social basis from the very beginning, and failed to realise that the origin of religion lay in the phenomenon of dreaming. (Kautsky seems to have forgotten Engels's passage on this very subject in *Feuerbach*.)

More generally, Kautsky emphasised the integrative function of religion in the face of threatening forces. Religion drew its strength from social morality in that the 'most essential characteristic of religion' was 'the social obligation to believe in God and serve him'.[24] Indeed Kautsky's comments in his later work *The Materialist Conception of History* (1927), on religion as social morality objectified in the form of 'collective representation' bear striking similarities to the work of Lévy-Bruhl and Durkheim.[25] Attention paid to the gods was, on this view, a function of social need and thus primitive human beings were less religious than, e.g., Renaissance man since they only needed the gods from time to time, whereas more modern people lived in almost constant poverty. In keeping with this approach, Kautsky shared little inclination to connect early religion with the division of labour, exploitation, the forces of production, and so on.

B. Primitive Christianity

Kautsky's views on primitive religion were derivative and rather confused; by contrast, his substantial work *Foundations of Christianity* remains one of the major Marxist contributions to the history of religion. He had already dealt with early Christian communism in the first part of his *Precursors of Modern Socialism* (1895). When preparing a second edition of *Precursors* and considering the criticisms of reviewers, Kautsky became more deeply interested in the history of early Christianity about which there had recently been a flood of publications.[26] Moreover, he claimed that his activities in the proletarian movement of his own times gave him a privileged insight into his topic: for 'a man who has learnt to live in the feelings and aspirations of the proletariat, fighting by their side, may lay claim to an ability to understand many things about the beginnings of Christianity more easily than scholars who have always viewed the proletariat only from afar.'[27] Moreover, in contrast to bourgeois historians who believed in eternal ethical principles, the historical materialist was well equipped to avoid reading the present into the past. He insisted that 'whatever the great accomplishments, the petty defects, and defeats of the ancient proletarians, they could mean nothing in forming an estimate of the nature and the prospects of the modern proletariat, either from a favourable or an unfavourable standpoint',[28] and therefore Kautsky could make the implausible claim that 'he who accepts the standpoint of the economic conception of history can adopt a completely unprejudiced view of the past, even though he be actively involved in the practical struggles of the present.'[29] Kautsky nevertheless wished to see his work as some sort of contribution to the self-understanding of the modern proletariat – a point to which we shall return in considering the conclusion to his work.

Undoubtedly the weakest section of Kautsky's book is the short first part on sources for studying the personality of Jesus. For in pursuit of his two firm views that Jesus himself was a putschist and that *organisation* was at the origin of Christianity, he had a strong tendency to dismiss anything he did not like in the sources as either completely unreliable or else as forgery. The evangelists were 'extremely ignorant men'[30] – though the two examples he gives of this ignorance (Augustus's census and Jesus's trial procedure) are in fact highly complex issues in which it would be far too simple to say that the Gospel account was erroneous. In general, Kautsky considered the historical value of the Gospels to be no greater than of Homer or the *Nieberlungenlied* since they afforded 'not the slightest information'[31] about Jesus's teaching or influence, that it was not certain that any of Paul's epistles were genuine, and that the passages in Josephus and Pliny that mention Jesus and his followers were forgeries. Such views (partially contradicted by the detailed discussion that Kautsky himself devoted to the doctrines and influence of Jesus) simply reflect the underdeveloped level of biblical scholarship at the time.

When, however, Kautsky turns, in Part Two, to the socio-economic conditions of the Roman Empire that acted as a ground for Christianity, he is at his most impressive. Building on Engels's scattered remarks, Kautsky drew a picture of an Empire declining economically as the system of slave labour on latifundia grew less capable of expansion. The decline of the free peasantry had meant less good soldiers, a stabilisation of the frontiers, fewer slaves and therefore a halt to economic development both in agriculture and in the increasingly populous cities. The loosening of social ties that resulted gave rise to an individualist, sceptical ethos and, equally, a growing credulity caused by idealist philosophies and the spread of urbanism. The growth of large cities and economic decline also led to an estrangement from nature and an emphasis on individual spirituality which were preconditions for the emergence of monotheism, belief in 'a single spirit whose emanation and counterfeit constitutes the inscrutable and uniform spirit in all individuals'.[32] All these factors, together of course with the internationalism of Rome, prepared the way for Christianity which, drawing on its Jewish roots for its monotheism, its belief in a redeemer, and its strong sense of solidarity, acted as a universal antidote to the general ghastliness of the Empire.

In his treatment, in Part Three, of Jewish religion as a precursor of Christianity, Kautsky saw the Babylonian exile as decisive. He considered early Jewish religion to be polytheistic fetishism, with the Ark of the Covenant as the supreme example. The development of the plastic and graphic arts in, for example, Egypt and Greece reinforced polytheism by giving it a material foundation in that 'the invisible men now became visible and therefore capable of being present in the same manner in the minds of all; now the various gods were permanently differentiated from each other, all confusion between them having disappeared.'[33] In Israel, by contrast, the very backwardness of industry and art 'made it easier for the Israelites to accomplish the step that freed them from polytheism when they become acquainted with the philosophical and ethical monotheism that arose in various large cities, at the culmination of ancient civilization.'[34] Kautsky pointed out that the monotheistic national religions were derived from nations that were still at the nomadic stage of thought and had not developed by important industry and art – Jews, Persians and Islamic Arabs who accepted monotheism as soon as they came in contact with a higher urban culture. This might seem paradoxical but Kautsky drew attention to the ability of the backward peasant village to make the leap straight from the oil lamp to the electric light invented in the city, thus bypassing the stage of gas illumination. In dealing with the Babylonian exile, Kautsky saw it as reinforcing Jewish chauvinism in religion but also exposing the Jews to an urban lifestyle which, with its merchants, trade, leisure and wealth, led to the development of mathematics and abstract philosophy which facilitated the emergence of monotheism. It was this 'uneven development' that enabled Kautsky to explain what he saw as the contradictions in Jewish religion – between the God who only wanted the pure in heart but who was located in a temple and served by a privileged priestly caste, or between the God who was the God of all men but especially of the Jews. Kautsky's account of Jewish religion is rather sweeping and speculative, but it does raise four specific problems. Firstly, it depends crucially on the view that pre-Babylonian religion was polytheistic which is a highly controverted question.[35] Secondly, Kautsky's chronology is extremely vague, for his discussion of monotheism – to which he explicitly refers when discussing its adoption by the Jews[36] – locates its rise at the time of Rome's decline. Thirdly, it is clear that Kautsky knew next-to-nothing about Babylonian religion which was very far from monotheistic. And fourthly, his view of the prophets as revolutionary leaders of the oppressed peasantry drastically misunderstands their role.[37]

In the first half of his book, Kautsky claimed to have shown how the Jews

were enabled to offer the most acceptable pabulum to the minds of the declining ancient world, which doubted their own traditional gods, but did not have sufficient energy to create a view of life without a god or with one god only, the more so since the Jews combined with their belief in a single primitive ethical force also a belief in the coming of a Redeemer for whom the entire world was then longing.[38]

In order then, in Part Four, to show why Christianity should be the form in which Israel conquered Rome, Kautsky began, in good Marxist fashion, by analysing the class formation of Israel in the time of Jesus. He saw the opposition of the Pharisees to the Saducees in the dominant group to be fundamentally not a religious but a class opposition similar to that between the nobility and Third Estate before 1789.[39] The Saducees were representatives of the priestly nobility who controlled the Jewish state. The Pharisees were a more popularly based patriotic party who appealed to traditional Jewish law and practice to justify their opposition to what they saw as the compromising attitude of the Saducees. At the bottom of the social scale Kautsky discerned three parties described as 'proletarian'. These were the Zealots who united the Jerusalem proletariat with the rural bandits of Galilee; the Essenes who were not willing to wait for the Messiah to appear but wished to build their new communist communities immediately; and the Christians who found unsatisfactory the purely nationalistic character of the Zealots yet did not wish to live in the country like the Essenes. Kautsky claimed that 'it is generally recognized that the Christian congregation originally embraced proletarian elements almost exclusively, and was a proletarian organization. And this was true for a long time after its proletarian beginnings.'[40] But Kautsky's extremely loose usage of 'proletarian' means that this is not as precise a statement as it sounds.

In order to demonstrate the proletarian character of early Christianity, Kautsky searched the Gospels for evidence of class hatred and communism. Class hatred he found in the many condemnations of riches in the Gospel of St Luke which he considered – eccentrically and on no evidence – to be the earliest gospel. Such doctrines were watered down in the 'later' Matthew and Mark as non-proletarian elements joined the congregation. Being 'proletarians' it was natural that the early Christians should aim at communism and Kautsky was at pains to demonstrate this from the early chapters of *Acts*. This communism was parallel to that of the Essenes and was one of distribution and consumption, not of production. Such a communism necessarily found family ties a burden and Kautsky attempted to demonstrate that early Christians were hostile to the family and even promoted sexual licence. This involved a highly selective reading of the Gospels and particular reliance on later Gnostic literature.

The main thrust of Kautsky's interpretation of early Christianity lay in his view of Jesus as a proletarian Messiah. According to Kautsky, Jesus's proclamation of the imminence of the Kingdom of God was in keeping with the general Jewish expectation of the arrival of the Messiah within a generation. And, in contrast to Engels, he believed that the original Christian message involved the establshment of a material Kingdom. Kautsky therefore portrayed Jesus as a rebel: Christianity had its origin in the Jerusalem proletariat and the roving bands of Galilee and 'we must therefore assume at the outset that Christianity was characterised by violence in its beginnings.'[41] Of course, there is little evidence in the New Testament of this, but Kautsky made the most of the sparse references to swords. The accounts of the arrest of Jesus do seem to deny Kautsky's interpretation of the events as a failed *coup d'état* and he could only take refuge in his view that Christianity was the most contradictory of religions.

When united, the twin factors of communist organisation and faith in the Messiah became irresistible. The era of growing peace in the Roman Empire meant

> a gradual elimination of all rebellious elements from the image of the Jesus God, thus transforming the aggressively rebellious Jesus gradually into a passive figure, who had been murdered not because of an insurrection but simply because of his infinite goodness and sanctity, and the viciousness and malice of treacherous enemies.[42]

In a somewhat contradictory vein, Kautsky also maintained that Christianity would become a universal religion as it was inspired by class hatred – which was a universal phenomenon: 'only the social Messiah, not the national Messiah, could transcend the bonds of Judaism.'[43] The doctrine of the Resurrection (not characteristic of Messianic thinking in general) was functional to the growth of the organisation: 'it was not the faith in the resurrection of the Crucified which created the Christian congregation and gave it its strength, but, on the contrary, it was the vigour and strength of the congregation that created the beliefs in the continued life of the Messiah.'[44] Gradually, Christianity lost its proletarian and communist elements: communism could not develop as Christianity was primarily urban, and the domestic workers, shop keepers, *Lumpenproletariat*, etc., were not the sort of classes who could progress from common consumption to common production. The proletarian elements were also eager to attract the rich into the Church and help charitable enterprises – a process which eventually led to the abandonment of class hatred. Parallel with this development was the emergence of a hierarchy which culminated in the consolidation of the Papacy which Kautsky saw as enhanced by the struggle of bishops against monasteries, just as the European absolute monarchies grew from the antagonistic equilibrium of a declining feudalism and rising capitalism.

In the final section of his book Kautsky considered the relationship of Christianity to socialism. What guarantee was there that socialism would not turn out to be just as exploitative as Christianity? Kautsky admitted that socialism, like Christianity, would have to create a bureaucracy. He also insisted, as against Engels, that Christianity had originally been a proletarian movement and not, therefore, a religion of slaves. But there were nevertheless profound differences between early Christianity and modern socialism. Firstly, socialist bureaucracy would not be in a position to exploit the workers since the modern proletariat, as the productive class, constituted the basis of society – in contrast to ancient Rome where the proletariat tried to live off society and was therefore forced to compromise with the rich in the early Church: different modes of production would give rise to different superstructures. Secondly, the general decay of Rome eventually bred a lack of resistance to the emergence of dominant powers, whereas the modern proletariat was growing in numbers and self-confidence. Thirdly, in the Roman Empire concentration of wealth involved a decrease in productivity, whereas the reverse was true in modern times which meant that a communism of production (as opposed to mere consumption) was now possible. Fourthly, socialism could not develop the divisions that characterised Christianity as the proletariat was in a position to abolish all classes and thus remove the basis for such divisions.

Troeltsch was exaggerating when he described Kautsky's book as 'the dreary dogmatism of the familiar socialist reconstruction of history' in which 'the theory of the one-sided dependence of religion on economically determined class conditions appears as a dogmatic presupposition'.[45] But it remains true that Kautsky has little feel for religion. He is willing to recognise positive elements in early Christianity – its humanitarianism, its attitude to slavery, its generally progressive impact – but this involves him in contradictory views that he can only try to reconcile by describing Christianity itself as 'rich in contradictions'.[46] In addition to the one-sided emphasis on economics, his work relies on the researches of bourgeois scholars and merely tries to fit their results into a Marxist perspective, with curious results, as, for example, in his discussion of the Christian and Jewish proletariat: Kautsky is visibly embarassed at having to describe 'the proletariat' as being credulous and superstitious and makes up for it by constantly emphasising their bravery. More generally, the emphasis on the primary of socio-economic forces is too simplistic, as was recognised by even such a sympathetic commentator as Max Adler.[47] The most impressive sections of Kautsky's book are where he develops Engels's sketch of Roman society and its intellectual decay. But he is much less convincing when he reduces the content of Christianity to social interests and portrays Jesus as a political dissident, a proletarian leader aiming at social revolution. Here Kautsky's own work is yet another example corroborating his statement that 'the descriptions of Jesus in the Twentieth Century . . . do not depict what Jesus actually taught, but what the producers of these images wish he had taught'.[48] Moreover, the picture of Jesus as a political revolutionary just does not accord with available evidence;[49] and recent sociological research has shown that the constituency Jesus appealed to could in no way be described as proletarian, even on Kautsky's loose definition, being rather 'essentially a petty-bourgeois movement'.[50] Moreover, Kautsky seems to have been curiously oblivious to the eschatological dimension of New Testament thinking.[51] Had Kautsky taken this eschatology seriously, he would not have berated the early Christians for not taking a more positive attitude to social questions and not supposed that Jesus could have created a detailed organisation for the movement.

C. The Reformation

In his book on early Christianity, Kautsky had described the strength of religion from the Roman Empire to the Reformation as 'one of the forces which accelerated the social evolution, as long as social goals were accessible to the masses only when clothed in religious garb.'[52] Earlier he had been more emphatic. In his *Thomas More* of 1890 Kautsky showed considerable enthusiasm for the 'old, feudal, popular Catholicism'.[53] In what amounted almost to a panegyric of the mediaeval Church, he wrote:

> The Church taught the Teutons improved methods of agriculture – the monasteries were model agricultural institutions until the late Middle Ages. It was also priests who taught the Teutons arts and handicrafts. Not only did the peasant thrive under the protection of the Church, but the Church also protected the majority of the towns until the latter were strong enough to protect themselves, and she encouraged trade. . . .
>
> When the Teutons invaded the Roman world empire, they were confronted with the Church as the inheritor of the Caesars, as the organisation which held the State together. . . .
>
> That all the knowledge of the Middle Ages was to be found in the Church, that she supplied builders, engineers, doctors, historians, and diplomats, is well known. The whole material life of mankind, as well as its mental life, was an outflow from the Church.[54]

By contrast, the morbid religious introspection caused by the economic upheavals of the Reformation formed a sharp contrast with the carefree, life-loving Catholicism of the Middle Ages. This view of the Reformation as, in many respects, a retrogression was, of course, also in sharp contrast to the attitude of Marx. Kautsky's relatively positive attitude to mediaeval Catholicism was no doubt enhanced by his antipathy to its destroyer, capitalism, by his evident admiration for Thomas More and also, possibly, to the structural parallels between the mediaeval Church and his own aspirations for the SPD.

In his main work on the Reformation,[55] however, Kautsky took a less negative view of certain of its aspects. Generalising rather wildly about Europe from the thirteenth to the sixteenth centuries, Kautsky saw the 'proletariat' of the Middle Ages as transitional between the proletariat of the Roman Empire and the modern proletariat: early Christianity had its roots in the idle *Lumpenproletariat*, which was unpolitical and passive, whereas mediaeval and Reformation communists were diligent, respectable and sober, politically aware, rebellious, and aiming at the dictatorship of the proletariat. Since Roman law favoured the bourgeoisie, communism found its natural ideological basis in earlier Christian concepts. And since the production of knowledge was in the hands of the lords, the ignorance of the masses produced mysticism; a hopelessly downtrodden class would always oppose knowledge – Kautsky referred to the example of the Taborites. The resultant radical tendencies could obtain a force out of all proportion to its class basis in Germany as it was favoured by the ruling class in its opposition to the papacy. This explained why there was no Protestantism in Italy or France both of which had been protected, for some time at least, by the Pope; England had already been too frightened by the peasants' revolt. After the Great Schism, Germany was the only country with no national Church to defend it against Roman spoliation.

Although largely following Engels's account, Kautsky made it more specific by trying to show connections between urban commerce and industry and the rise of Calvinism,[56] and in particular by drawing attention to the mining industry as an immediate cause of the German Reformation. In the fourteenth century the rise of the Taborites had been due to the Bohemian silver mines producing inflation, with the peasants wishing to sell their surplus rather than hand it over to the lords, ex-serfs taking refuge in the towns and an increasing struggle over private property in land.

In the following century the Saxon mines produced an increase of wealth for the nobles and the towns but not for the peasants or the growing rural *Lumpenproletariat* who found their spokesman in Münzer. In 1892, Kautsky had portrayed Münzer as introducing revolutionary new doctrines, following Engels and Zimmermann. By the time he wrote *Precursors*, Kautsky considered that Münzer had no ideas that were to be found in the early communist sects – he simply excelled in revolutionary energy and statesmanlike discernment.[57]

Kautsky's assessment of this period was certainly superior to Bernstein's mechanical reading of positions from class interests;[58] and some of his remarks on the early communist sects such as the Waldenses retain their interest. But he does not give a sufficiently detailed account of the ideas of either Luther or Münzer to be able to illuminate them. There is no description of the relationship between Luther's thought and the emerging bourgeois relationships in Saxony. Nor does Kautsky explain why it was a peasants' war rather than a miners' war. Finally, his account of the derivative status of

Calvinism is difficult to reconcile with its power and influence in pre-Industrial Scotland.[59]

D. The Future of Religion

Kautsky was curiously ambivalent about the future of religion. He was quite clear that the progressive features of early and mediaeval Christianity 'constituted only a means of retarding progress when the religious mode of thought was superseded by the methods of modern science, with the result that it is cherished only by backward classes and strata of the population, or backward regions, and may not in any manner continue to serve as an envelope for new social goals.'[60] In the section on Christianity and Socialism at the end of his *Foundations of Christianity* Kautsky did not pursue Engels's idea that Christianity might have some content that socialism would realise. Their similarity in Kautsky's eyes was limited to the fact that they were both movements of the poorer classes. Kautsky was more struck by their opposition:

> the period of the rise of Christianity is a period of the saddest intellectual decline, of the flourishing of an absurd ignorance, of the most stupid superstition; the period of the rise in socialism is a period of the most striking progress in the natural sciences and a speedy acquisition of knowledge by the classes under the influence of the Social-Democracy.[61]

And in his 1893 articles he stressed the familiar theme that the progress of natural science and technology left an ever decreasing space for the gods. By contrast, Kautsky nevertheless detected signs of a turn to religion in contemporary society which he explained in terms of social conditions: the exploiting classes turned to religion as a prop for the social order and the exploited found in religion support for anti-establishment values, while in general the uncertainty and fluidity of capitalist society impelled towards religion as affording some orientation in an otherwise unpredictable world. Nevertheless, the class struggle was destined eventually to annihilate religion completely.

Kautsky considered himself to be continuing the work of Marx and Engels by considering religion under the dual aspects of compensation and class manipulation while at the same time making it more 'scientific' by keeping abreast of the latest

developments in ethnography and historical research. At the same
time, he was less hostile to religion than Marx and Engels – and not
only in his assessment of mediaeval Catholicism: his interest in
animism as the origin of religion led him to see it as less easily
reducible to social and economic circumstances. Nevertheless, he
always regarded religion as essentially an opiate and was strongly
influenced by the intellectual and political climate of the
contemporary socialist movement:[62] his neo-Darwinan view of the
role of consciousness led him to view religion as (at best) an
increasingly intellectually irrelevant form of ethical idealism; and
the political position of the SPD inclined him to wish to banish
religion from politics and confine it (at best) to the politically
irrelevant status of a 'private matter'.

4.   CUNOW AND PRIMITIVE RELIGION

Given the immense impact of Darwin and consequent popular
interest in evolution and origins, it was to be expected that Marxists,
too, would interest themselves in the beginnings of religion. The
most serious attempt to give a Marxist interpretation of the growing
body of research on primitive religion was provided by Heinrich
Cunow, whose widely read book, *The Origin of Religion and of Belief in
God*, was published in 1913. Cunow's general thesis was that recent
research stressing animist rather than nature worship as the origin
of religious belief confirmed the Marxist approach to the study of
religion. The Preface proclaimed his ambitious intention 'to
demonstrate that not only does the belief of peoples in God and
immortality stem everywhere from the same simple basic
conceptions, but also that all religious development follows the
same paths and in a strict and law-like manner.'[63]

The materialist philosophers of the eighteenth century, such as
Hume, had destroyed the notion of the revelation of God in the
Judaeo-Christian tradition. For Hegel, Cunow had nothing but
contempt: his attempt at compromise had consisted in 'empty
ideological constructions' which had, in any case, been exploded by
Feuerbach. But it was not until the mid-nineteenth century that any
serious attention was paid to the origins of religion. Then the
popular view, reinforced by Sanskritologists such as Max Müller in
his studies of the origins of Indo-European mythologies, was that
religion began with the divinisation of natural forces and that gods

were no more than personified natural phenomena. Cunow claimed that this view was 'utterly incorrect'.[64] He admitted that Marx and Engels had been strongly influenced by this school. But *Anti-Dühring* was wrong when it portrayed the cult of nature as the original religion which was only later influenced by social relationships. On the contrary, wrote Cunow,

> it was not in fact external natural events as thunder, lightning, earthquake, storm, cloudburst, etc., which first awakened in mankind the feelings of fear and dependency and provided obscure riddles to their simple minds. It was rather his own nature, his own origin, growth and passing away, above all death. Moreover, even at his most elementary level of development, man lived not only in nature but also in community with his fellows, and this communal life and its consequent social conditions of existence obtained early on a quickly increasing and constantly expanding influence on his conceptual world.[65]

The empirical material now available afforded the opportunity for 'a strictly scientific inductive investigation of the origins of religion'.[66]

As the first major work to have challenged the Sanskritologists, Cunow expressed his admiration for Tylor's *Primitive Culture*. Nevertheless, Tylor portrayed animism as too unitary and self-contained a stage, neglecting both the stages within animism and the complex development from animism to higher stages. More importantly, Tylor was, according to Cunow, still the prisoner of contemporary comparative mythology in his attempt to explain myth causally from natural phenomena and Tylor could not free himself from the old belief in the primacy of the worship of natural forces. Subsequent research, however, had shown that primitive religion was not determined by natural phenomena 'but, in a degree which continually increases with cultural development, by the social conception of life which in turn is itself dependent on the ways and means of gaining a livelihood'.[67] Society predominated over nature in that conceptions of nature were themselves conditioned by the techniques men employed to obtain their means of subsistence; and also nature merely provided the raw material or local colouring for the construction of religion.

Basing himself on recent reports of the Australian Aborigines and the Polynesians, Cunow claimed that animist ideas originated among primitive peoples as a result of misunderstanding phenomena such as dreams or fainting. Thence grew the idea of placating dead souls, making offerings for success in war and the establishment of a group of people – magicians – who knew how to manipulate these ghosts. Thus arose the cult of ancestors of which totemism was one version. Cunow's main point was that these developments were socially determined: the Australian aboriginal hordes could be shown to have adopted totemic names in order to keep a track on their provenance once exogamy became the rule. And as the hordes became totem groups, so all their social arrangements became commands of their totem god. When the Australian tribes moved into larger units known as phratries they looked for gods that were 'overgods' of many tribes; whereas in Africa, where there was no large settled tribal organisation, there were no tribal or national gods – only the persistence of the cult of dead relations. The nature of beliefs about the after-life can be shown to reflect social arrangements and 'the ethical outlook that primitive man allots to his spirits and gods demonstrates how dependant is the form of the gods on the social conduct of their worshippers. All the rules and customs that stem from life in society, once they have achieved general validity, are portrayed and conceived of as originating in the spirits, i.e. as having been ordained by them in former times.'[68] Subsequently, however, with the transition to farming and the differentiation of society, specialised gods began to emerge. For a cult of nature arose when men began to be dependant on natural phenomena such as rain for the success of their labours. According to Cunow, it could be shown that what remained of nature worship in American, Chinese, Babylonian and early Egyptian religion grew gradually from an earlier cult of souls and ancestors. The worship of animals in Egypt and Babylonia, for example, has descended from the worship of totemic animals. Even in the idealised nature cult of ancient Greece, traces of ancestor worship could still be found. To the followers of Max Müller who might admit this for the rest of the world, but deny it for India, Cunow quoted the Rigveda at great length to the effect that there, too, belief in spirits and an ancestor cult lay at the basis of their nature worship.

Cunow's conclusion was that his demonstration that even the Vedic religion (a *par excellence* example of nature worship according to some) had its origins in spirit and ancestor cults, served to confirm his general thesis that 'all religions development follows the same law-like paths – not a free play of the imagination but an expression in thought of a particular organization of life.'[69] Kautsky admired Cunow as the first Marxist to give a materialist account of the origins of religion.[70] But, as will be seen from this conclusion and the vagueness of other formulations quoted above, Cunow's approach had very little that was specifically Marxist about it. Given the nature of the material, it could scarcely be otherwise. The most that he had shown was that the results of post-Tylor ethnography were more in keeping with a Marxist approach than were earlier views of primitive religion.

5.   AUSTRO-MARXISM

A. Introduction

The only Marxist thinkers to have an occasionally positive attitude to religion in the period preceding and immediately after the First World War were the Austro-Marxists. Based in Vienna, the Austro-Marxists were a group of socialist intellectuals who, from 1905 onwards, developed a Marxism which was rigorously scientific in intention while retaining a strong revolutionary perspective. After the War they held a mid-way position between the reformist German Social Democrats and the Russian Bolsheviks. Their attitude to religion was largely determined by their efforts to incorporate the Kantian method into their Marxism.

There had been a revival of academic interest in Kant in German-speaking circles from the 1860s onwards. The influence of Hegel had faded in the 1840s after his disciples split into radical and conservative wings. There was a growing feeling among liberal intellectuals at the end of the nineteenth century that the progress of natural science could not in itself produce a convincing world-view and consequently needed philosophical supplementation. The 'critical' method of Kant with its radical distinction between phenomena and noumena, between fact and value, seemed to be able to join together both a rigorous insistence on scientific method and a liberal or even socialist political outlook. In his *Critique of Pure Reason* Kant had attempted to reconstruct the necessary conditions of knowledge: things could never be known 'in themselves' – all the mind could know were phenomena which were structured by the categories through which the mind perceived them. As far as morality and religion were concerned, Kant believed that he had succeeded, in the *Critique of Practical Reason*, in demonstrating the impossibility of knowledge about such matters in order to make way for belief. Knowledge being limited to the sense world, God could not be the object of knowledge and thus all traditional metaphysical discussion of God was invalid. Nevertheless, it was possible to argue from the categorical imperative of duty to the reality of freedom, immortality and God, all three being entailed by the existence of moral duties.

Although most socialists were not interested in Kant's philosophy of religion, his ethics were popular among revisionist Marxists, including Bernstein, from the turn of the century onwards. Thinkers such as Kautsky tended to consider a thorough-going materialism as necessary for radical Marxism – a view strongly, if crudely, supported by Lenin in *Materialism and Empiriocriticism*. But there was no inevitable link in practice between Kant and revisionism. The Austro-Marxists, in particular, wished to accept the orthodox view of the objective, scientific side of Marxism.

But they insisted that materialism, whether in the monist interpretation of Plekhanov or the neo-Darwinian version of Kautsky, could give no foundation for moral imperatives and thus could not ultimately 'justify' socialism. To the Austro-Marxists the materialism of much of orthodox Marxism represented a return to the pre-critical ideas that had preceded Kant and Hegel. And just as the dialectical world-view of Hegel had allowed some place for religion, so too did the neo-Kantian Marxist view that both science and morality had a common basis in 'the central concept of Marxist sociology, not society but socialised man'.[71] This 'religious space' was explored most fully by Otto Bauer and Max Adler.

B. Otto Bauer

Bauer's main work on religion was *Sozialdemokratie, Religion und Kirche* published in 1927, though he had developed its main ideas at least twenty years earlier. Its practical purpose was to demonstrate that socialism and religion were not intrinsically incompatible and thus to allow for inclusion in the struggle for socialism in Austria of religiously-minded people and in particular the many strongly Catholic workers who had recently come into the cities off the land. Bauer began by drawing a sharp distinction between the Church with its powerful hierarchies and diplomatic manoeuvrings, and the naive religious beliefs of simple people. Examining religion on the basis of Marx's statement in the *Communist Manifesto* that 'man's ideas, views and conceptions, in one word, man's consciousness, change with every change in the conditions of his material existence, in his social relation, and in his social life',[72] Bauer found that religion was an instrument of bourgeois social control. At the time of the Enlightenment, leading bourgeois thinkers had been opposed to religion: now that they were the dominant class, they had adopted the slogan that 'the religion of the masses must be preserved'. They had even revived Kant's epistemology to this end, limiting science to observable phenomena and thus leaving room for religion. Although the advance of science had rendered the bourgeoisie irreligious, among the proletariat capitalism had reinforced the traditional function of religion:

> whereas previously the root of religion was the helpless fear of mankind in the face of the terrifying powers of nature, capitalism has subjected the mass of working people to social powers which are just as unintelligible, just as incapable of being mastered by the mass of the people, and dispense the fate of individual and mass just as grimly as the powers of nature themselves.[73]

In the words of Marx, therefore, religion was 'the opium of the people'.

But religion was not necessarily on the side of reaction. 'Every historical epoch,' wrote Bauer, quoting Marx, 'every class, fashions its own Christianity.'[74] Sects such as the Waldensians, Taborites and Anabaptists were the forerunners of modern socialism. Awakening proletarian consciousness had constantly linked the promises of socialism with those of the gospel. 'Religion is the opium of the people as long as the people bear the domination of capitalism without fighting back; but religion also provides the first and earliest rebellions of the proletariat with their ideology.'[75] In England, in particular, the plethora of non-establishment churches had engendered a sort of competition and necessary adjustment to the interests of the workers with the result that the English proletariat found no difficulty in accepting Christian ethics into its outlook. With the development of capitalism on the continent, however, large sections of the proletariat had become alienated from religion since enforced social mobility drew many away from their traditional cultural roots and the Church adopted a reactionary political stance. Although this was the case in Austria for the hard core of the urban proletariat, the peasantry and those who had recently moved into the cities were significantly religious, and socialists should not exclude them on that count. Indeed, according to Bauer, 'true' religion was found almost exclusively among the proletariat, the bourgeoisie being only religious on social grounds. As 'the sigh of the oppressed', religion was acceptable when practised by the working classes: but it was definitely *not* acceptable when practised by parasitic prelates.

What, then, should be the contemporary attitude of socialists to religion? In answer, Bauer quoted extensively from Marx and from *Anti-Dühring* on the functions of religion in a class society. But he took issue with the view of Marx and Engels that religion would necessarily disappear in a socialist society. He was clear that the outlook of socialist human beings would be

> free from those popular religious conceptions whose root is the daily worry for work and bread, whose essence is the projection into heaven of unmastered social powers, whose dogmas about the nature of the world are contradicted by the findings of science, and whose ethic is a morality of the subordinate, the exploited and the submissive.'[76]

But socialist society would be highly differentiated and highly individualistic and Bauer thought it still legitimate to ask whether

> when the citizens of the future society strip away from historical religions everything in them that is simply a reflection of the conditions of life in a class society, will not then be revealed for the first time, what in religion is not conditioned temporarily and socially but is a need of the human soul independant of the conditions of social life? When the religions taught by priests, pastors and rabbis disappear, will not consciousness be at last free for religion in the sense of the philosophers?[77]

Bauer certainly did not himself answer these questions in the affirmative, but simply pointed out that Adler had managed to do so.

Turning to current party policy, Bauer claimed that contemporary clericalism turned, as Marx had said, 'secular questions into theological ones'. It made religion a matter of party politics by portraying the class struggle of proletariat and bourgeoisie as a struggle between the Christians and the godless. Social Democracy should change theological questions into secular ones and strive to make religion a non-party, private matter. For, despite its free thinking origins, social democracy could not use power without forming a bloc to include some, at least, of the religiously-minded members of the proletariat, the petty bourgeoisie and the peasantry. This made sense for two main reasons: on historical materialist grounds it was clear that religion, as a reflexion of socio-economic circumstances, would be around for a long time to come; and it was the duty of the party to rally the whole of the working class. This political stance was also justified philosophically, for a reductionist natural scientific materialism was not a necessary part of Marxism. Just as doctors or biologists, though agreed on the principles of their profession, should disagree about the meaning of the world, so could 'theoreticians, who agree on the development of human society, have very different views on the origin, essence, and meaning of the world'.[78] Lenin and Plekhanov did indeed make a reductionist natural scientific materialism part of their world view. But Friedrich Adler, although a genuine historical materialist, took another option based on the work of Mach and denied that Marxism was inherently atheistic, as did Max Adler who based himself on the work of Kant. Bauer's conclusion was that it was not his purpose

to decide which world-view is right – whether the materialist (Plekhanov, Lenin), the positive (Friedrich Adler), or the Kantian (Max Adler). My point is much rather to show from these examples that among the theoreticians of scientific socialism we find adherents of very different world-views: adherents both of anti-religious materialism, and of religiously indifferent positivism and of religious critical idealism.[79]

As far as immediate party policy was concerned, Bauer insisted that, although a free-thinking organisation within the party was necessary, it should not try to impose its views on the whole party. The idea that anti-religious propaganda could possibly be a primary political object was an old liberal illusion which had unfortunately been revivified by the Bolsheviks who refused to treat religion as a private matter and admitted into their ranks only the irreligious. This was possible because their party was a 'vanguard' one, not a party of the whole working class. Such a vanguard party was not, in any case, appropriate in the more developed countries of the West, and consequently the Bolshevik attitude to religion was unsuited to Austria where the party should insist that it was not against religion as such but against the role that the Churches played in politics. The separation of Church and State was absolutely essential – a demand which was itself of religious origin, having first been advanced by the Anabaptists. Bauer's views on religion were worked out in the context of the rise of aggressive free-thinking in the party, particularly after 1918.[80] Although a free-thinker himself and profoundly anti-clerical, Bauer questioned the wisdom of those who wished to revise the traditional position of the Party on religion as a private matter. And to those free-thinkers who quoted Marx's opium phrase, he replied that the Party was against alcoholism but still admitted drinkers.

C. Max Adler

Adler was distinguished by being the only prominent Marxist leader of the time who freed himself from the anti-religious attitude of Marx and Engels and took a positive view of religion. His attitude to religion derived from the enthusiasm that, as a philosopher, he felt for Kant. Neo-Kantianism had entered SPD circles with Viktor Adler's funeral oration at Engels's death in 1895, and it was not uncommon for revisionists such as Bernstein to proclaim a 'return to Kant' as a moral foundation for their rather eclectic social science.[81] But Max Adler was different: he insisted that his attempt to relate Marxism to Kant had nothing to do with the fashionable idea of 'supplementing' Marx by Kant. His adherence to Kant and thus to religion was intrinsic to a Marxism which, in his eyes at least, was comparable to that of any of his German-speaking colleagues in its scientificity and radicalism.

For Adler, classical German philosophy in the shape of Kant was the philosophy of socialism, and Marx stood in the same relationship to Kant in the social sciences as did Newton in the natural sciences.

Classical German philosophy [he wrote] always aspired to be a philosophy of action. But it could only achieve this in idea; Marxism gave it the scientific knowledge that allowed it to realise this action historically. If the idealism of Kant and his followers was the philosophy of the conceptual possibility of socialism, the scientific socialism of Marx becomes the theory of the actual reality of idealism.[82]

This was possible because in Marxism the materialist conception of history and the theory of social progress derive their meaning and their certainty from the concept of socialised man, or, as we now understand, of socialized consciousness'.[83] The aims of philosophy were the ideal norms of human nature activated by reason, and the concept of human nature was only to be derived from a scientific sociology. This scientific sociology had been achieved by Marx, whose *Capital* was, as its subtitle indicated, a 'critique' similar to that of Kant: penetrating below the surface phenomena of capitalist society, Marx had discovered, in the value form, for example, the necessary conditions of their appearance.[84]

What room did such a view afford for religion? Adler admitted that some forms of historical materialism, particularly that of Engels in *Anti-Dühring*, did sound as though they excluded religious belief. But an examination of Marx and Engels's *Holy Family* would show that they were only concerned to continue the work of Bacon and Locke in grounding all knowledge in experience and thus disposing of mataphysics. The anti-religious implications of such a materialism belonged 'not to the philosophical essence of materialism but only to its historical effectivity. For you could draw atheistic or positivistic consequences either from a system of pantheism (Spinoza) or spiritualism (Fichte).'[85] The move from materialism to atheism was due to the lack of epistemological sophistication[86] with the result that the dogmatic materialism of some of the disciples of Marx and Engels was no better than dogmatic religion: 'materialism and Marxism have found their sacred texts and Sunday preachers, even their priests, who are in no way less intolerant and in no way less dogmatic than their colleagues in tonsure and soutane.'[87] Thus Adler accepted the empirical side of books such as Kautsky's *Foundations of Christianity* but claimed that the positivism inherent in Kautsky's approach could not deal with the question of the meaning of religion. Since 'from science there is neither a road to God nor away from him since in its own field it makes no connexion at all with God.'[88] Adler's own efforts were directed at elucidating this meaning by discussing questions which the positivist framework could not even pose.

On Adler's interpretation of Kant, religion was the union of the two spheres of nature and morality, it was 'belief in the coherence of the two and in the necessity of their coherence'.[89] Thus God was an axiom which guaranteed the rationality and meaningfulness of a world which would otherwise be empty and senseless. The idea of God was posited by the autonomy of practical reason in that, without the reconciliation of desert and reward through God and immortality, human life would be unbearable. God was not, therefore, as the old metaphysics had it, external to the world, but rather 'a particular attribute of our consciousness',[90] the subjective *a priori* that united the theoretical and moral worlds in a whole that had sense and meaning. The concepts of God and immortality had no independent existence as such: they gained their force from the fact that we, as rational beings, were obliged to will them. In other words, God was a superior power who made possible the tasks of mankind viewed as a kingdom of ends. Kant's injunctions in the *Groundwork* were necessarily social and contained the concept of humanity. For Kant's realm of reason could, according to Adler, be equated with the social world.[91] Moreover, Kant's definition of God as 'the end (*Zweck*) which needs no other as the condition of its possibility'[92] implied the notion of development and progress. The idea of progress led to religion, as the certainty of progress was not to be obtained from theory or from morality but only from a religious consciousness since God was that order of the world which made it possible to think of nature and morality as a unity and thus entertain a positive conception of development of which the empirical manifestation was scientific socialism.

In a long excursus, Adler argued that this idea of development could not be equated with evolution as presented by Spencer and Darwin since evolution in the sense of progress was unthinkable in any purely natural terms. Marxism itself was often conceived in terms of a natural evolution. But Marx and Engels clearly marked off their own views from natural scientific materialism. Their materialism was always of a *social* nature which 'exhibits the same confirmation to the laws of causality as the rest of nature, but in a different form, the social form, i.e. inside the forms in which humanity has been socialised.[93] And Adler quoted the *Theses on Feuerbach* to demonstrate the centrality of *praxis* to social relationships. Deciding, evaluating, willing, hoping and believing were all necessary for social causality. Scientific sociology might discover contradictions in a mode of production, but 'progress in historical development only comes about insofar as there exists a will for improvement and a belief in the achievement of this end, i.e. become causal factors of revolutionary praxis.'[94] Thus there was no necessity to reject religious ideas, provided only that Kant's critique of religious consciousnes was born in mind, namely,

> that its essential characteristic does not lie in any particular creed and therefore not in belief in God either but that this belief in God, when it has a *religious* aspect, is itself nothing but a particular direction and energy of the consciousness, namely one that involves belief in a meaning to existence and the intention to live and work for this meaning.[95]

This explained the force of chiliastic, and indeed all mass revolutionary movements which invariably relied on this 'religious' component. And equally, concluded Adler, as soon as a party lost this component, it would fail in a crisis – however revolutionary its phraseology might be. An awful reminder of this truth was the attitude of the SPD in August 1914. Thus the investigation of the origins and possible realisations of various ideals did not rob them of their rationality. On the contrary, this was the very reason why

> Marxism can speak of the causal necessity of a development to socialism although the belief in socialism is such an important part of this development that without it the victory of the proletariat as a revolutionary principle would never be achieved. Marxist socialism does not deny the basic sentiment of all real revolutions: My kingdom is not of this world.[96]

Marxism was indeed a scientific theory of social development. But this did not mean that 'the subjective factor, which Marxism recognises, thereby ceases to function. Knowledge of the necessary advent of socialism does not replace belief in socialism because that necessary advent will only come about through this belief.'[97]

In the final section of his book, Adler argued that socialism needed religion. A string of causes could only be viewed as a progressive development through an interpretation which itself had a religious quality: the fact that all change in the universe, even in the inorganic realm, only acquired meaning and value by reference to organic and rational development was 'the basic reason why not only religion and mysticism but also such consciously anti-religious

systems of thought as Marxism are informed by a religious spirit as
soon as they talk of the unity of the world and its all-over coherence
which as it were incorporates God into the laws of the world.'[98]
Adler went on to elaborate on the way in which Kant's notion of the
categorical imperative was an essentially social concept which also
implied the concept of God. It was therefore not surprising that
religion was often the greatest help to progress. Even Saint-Simon,
for all his opposition to Christian 'superstition', wanted a 'new
Christianity' – and so did Comte. It was necessary to forget old
conceptions of religion, regard religion not as a doctrine but as an
attitude of consciousness and then 'the conception that the idea of
social progress is anchored in religious ground will no longer appear
strange but seem self-evident.'[99] For all religious concepts were best
treated as 'symbols which express the inevitable human striving for
salvation, mankind's hope in the future and its conviction in
unfettered moral development.'[100]

There are three main points to be made about Adler's treatment of
Marxism and religion. Firstly, his conception of religion is rather
thin. Kant himself sometimes sounded as though religion was little
more than the obligation to view duties as divine commands and
Adler often reduces religion to morality or, at most, conceives
religion, like Schleiermacher, to consist in a vague feeling of
dependence on something greater. He therefore has little sympathy
with historical religion and its myths which he views as precursors
of his 'rational' religion. If God was 'no longer a being separate from
humankind, a power outside and alien to the world, something
outside the human personality, but rather nothing but a particular
direction of our consciousness into which we find ourselves
necessarily led as soon as we attempt to adopt a unitary conception
of the world',[101] it was difficult to see the difference between
religion and philosophy – which, indeed, Adler declared to be 'only
two different inner paths to the same goal'[102] and his own version of
religion to be 'philosophical belief'.[103] Secondly, Adler is not
concerned to show any *connexion* between Marxism and religion: the
most that he demonstrates is that their spheres of operation are so
separate that they are necessarily compatible. Thirdly, in his
interpretation of Marx and Engels, Adler is perhaps too ready to
view both Marx's *Theses on Feuerbach* and Engels's *Anti-Dühring* as
being one sort of (sociological) Marxism as opposed to the
(metaphysical) materialism of Plekhanov.[104] Many would think that
the division – if such there is – would be more plausibly drawn

between Marx and Engels. This difficulty springs from Adler's desire to reduce Marxism to an empirical science of society. His conception of Marxism, like that of religion, is rather thin.

4

Soviet Marxism

1. ORTHODOXY AND UNDERDEVELOPMENT

It is more true of the Bolsheviks than of any other Marxist tradition that their attitude to religion was informed by the kind of religion that confronted them. Marx's critique was aimed mainly at fundamental Lutheranism, and Engels and Kautsky were engaging, at least sometimes, with the more variegated Christianity of their own times; when Russian Marxists talked of religion, they had principally in mind the Orthodox Church and their wholesale opposition to religion was a consequence of the political subservience and doctrinaire other-worldliness that they perceived Orthodoxy to represent.

Since its inception, the Eastern branch of Christianity had lived in a symbiotic relationship with political authority, the Emperor in Constantinople being also head of the Church. The various Orthodox Churches were national Churches and they invariably tended to map themselves into the political organisation of their respective states. This tendency was increased in the Russian Orthodox Church by the reforms of Peter the Great in the early eighteenth century which secularised the Church and integrated it into the state apparatus. The Patriarchate was abolished and replaced by a Holy Synod which had full responsibility for administering the Church and whose head was sometimes not even a cleric. The will of the monarch came to be identified with the will of God and the Church was simply a department of State. In spite of a strong reform movement following the 1905 revolution, the Church thus became increasingly identified with the reactionary policies of the regime.[1]

This identification of the Church with the autocracy meant that it continuously alienated the educated classes. The Church was anti-intellectual and, for much of the time, not even interested in exploring its own doctrines let alone engaging others in dialogue. This political and intellectual conservatism explains the strong antagonism that existed throughout the nineteenth century between the Russian intelligentsia and the Orthodox Church. For the intelligentsia, the Church was the main bastion of a feudal autocracy and the chief enemy of enlightenment, progress and political liberty. Most of Lenin's utterances on religion are clearly in this tradition and echo the strident anticlericalism of such writers as Belinsky, Lavrov and Bakunin and the abstract, highly principled dogmatism that characterised the Russian intelligentsia in general.

Subservience to the State and innate conservatism corresponded to the actual doctrines of Orthodoxy. The emphasis on changelessness and tradition often led to resignation, withdrawal and a strong anti-world stance. The apophatic approach to God characteristic of Orthodoxy stressed the transcendence of God and the unapproachability of his essence. This view was implicit in the original doctrinal schism between West and East which centred on the Eastern rejection of the *filioque* – the doctrine that the Spirit proceeded from the Son as well as the Father. Whereas in the West the Spirit tended to be subordinate to the Son, whose human side was fully emphasised, the East tended towards an extreme spiritualism which, in its interpretation of Christ, stressed his Transfiguration and Resurrection rather than the more earthly aspects of incarnation and crucifixion. This lack of concern with worldly affairs necessarily meant a dearth of any development thinking on political, social or economic matters. It is significant that the only serious schism experienced by the Russian Church – that of the Old Believers in the seventeenth century – was not, as in the Reformation, of progressives but of conservatives implacably opposed to any change. In Western Europe, where Engels and Kautsky were writing, many Churchmen were wondering how to accommodate their religious beliefs to scientific and social developments; in Russia, the change was, if anything, in the opposite direction, towards increased mysticism and other-worldliness.

It is also true that the Bolsheviks' attitude to religion was informed by the paucity of their own philosophical concepts. This, in its turn, was due in large measure to the peculiar development – or lack of development – of Russian society. Even after the emancipation of the serfs in 1861, Russia continued to be an underdeveloped agrarian society with an autocratic, centralised state lacking serious industrial development and its concomitant bourgeois class that could mediate and diffuse political power. The extreme political and intellectual position of the religion that buttressed this autocracy

called forth equally extreme and unmediated opposition in the form
of a vulgar materialism. Under roughly similar economic
circumstances in France in the eighteenth century and in Germany
in the nineteenth century a thorough-going metaphysical
materialism had become influential. This materialism of the French
Encyclopaedists and of thinkers such as Büchner, Vogt and
Moleschott in Germany had been a weapon in the hands of a rising
middle class in its fight against royal and aristocratic privilege. In
Russia, at least in the Leninist view of things, this same struggle
against a mediaeval autocracy devolved, in the absence of a strong
middle class, upon the proletariat. Owing to Russia's retarded
development, the proletariat faced, in many respects, the same
intellectual scene as that confronted by the bourgeoisie in France
and Germany in previous centuries and were led to wield the same
weapon – the bludgeon of an unyielding and simplistic materialism.
The subtlety of the dialectical approach that characterised the best
analyses of society and politics by Russian Marxists deserted them
when it came to religion, a deficiency which was partly caused by
the fact that many members of the Russian intelligentsia had, in any
case, first learnt their philosophy in the Germany of the 1860s
where, as indicated, a vulgar materialism was rife. Hence the
naïvety, as compared with Marx or Engels, of many of the Bolshevik
pronouncements on religion was due not so much to lack of
intellectual sophistication (though there was that, too) as to the
socio-economic, political and intellectual configuration of Russian
society out of which grew the polar opposites of Bolshevik
materialism and Orthodox spiritualism.

2.   PLEKHANOV

This attraction for eighteenth-century materialism was evident in
the writings of Plekhanov,[2] the 'father' of Russian Marxism, who
established the orthodox line in political and philosophical matters
that was to guide the Russian Marxists in the decade and a half
preceding the Revolution of 1905. Plekhanov was the most
philosophical of the early Russian Marxists, and saw a simple
opposition between his own philosophical materialism and religion.
Philosophy, he felt, had grown within, and at the expense of,
theology. The relationship between knowledge and faith was an
instance of the general law that 'every new solid or philosophical

principle is born in the womb of – and consequently on the nutritive juice of – the old, which is its *opposite*.'[3] Like Engels, who had a strong influence on him, Plekhanov started from an immediate dichotomy between materialism and idealism.[4] Like Engels again, he was inclined to draw on Tylor and claim to find the origins of idealism in the animism of primitive religions.[5]

The undialectical quality of Plekhanov's materialism is best indicated by his almost unqualified enthusiasm for Feuerbach.[6] The basic thesis of Feuerbach that 'thought is conditioned by being, not being by thought' was, according to Plekhanov, 'a view of the relations between being and thought which was adopted by Marx and Engels and was made by them the foundation of their materialist conception of history.'[7] Further, Plekhanov wished to claim the monist philosophy of Spinoza as a foundation for Marxism: 'Spinozism, freed from its theological lumber by Feuerbach, was the philosophy which Marx and Engels adopted when they broke away from idealism.'[8] Plekhanov differed from Feuerbach in denying that there was any natural need for religion. Following Comte and later positivists, Plekhanov considered religion (here equated with myth) to be an inferior stage in humanity's intellectual development, destined to pass away with the growth of science. Any emotional needs that religion might have catered for in the past could be adequately met by music and art – and he suggested turning churches into theatres. For the present, it was sufficient to criticise religion through an exposition of materialist principles and a certain irony – an intellectualist view for which he was later criticised in Bolshevik circles.

The basis of Plekhanov's approach was that 'a consistent socialist outlook is an absolute disagreement with religion.'[9] He therefore contested the German Social Democratic view that religion was a private matter:

> Modern scientific socialism rejects religion as a product of an erroneous view of nature and society and condemns it as an obstacle to the all-round development of the proletariat. We have not the right to close the doors of our organisation to a man who is infected with religious beliefs; but we are obliged to do all that depends on us to destroy that faith in him or at least to prevent – with spiritual weapons of course – our religious-minded comrade from spreading his prejudices among the workers.[10]

Plekhanov nevertheless considered that there was no necessary connexion between the materialist conception of history and a rejection of religion. In dealing with the thesis of Edwin Seligman that one could accept the materialist explanation of history and not draw the atheist conclusions of most of its adherents,[11] Plekhanov admitted that 'Seligman is right in his way: with a certain inconsistency the logical operation which he suggests is obviously possible.' Plekhanov's own inconsistency here is due to his imagining that historical materialism needs supplementing by something very different – the philosophy of dialectical materialism, and not being clear as to how to reconcile the two. Indeed, one of his main contributions to Marxist theory was to stress the influence of geographical factors and claim that 'the peculiarities of the geographical environment determine the evolution of the forces of production, and this, in its turn, determines the development of the economic forces and, therefore, the development of all the other social relations.'[12] When dealing with the problem of how 'the very same fund of ideas' could produce the militant atheism of the French materialists, the religious indifference of Hume, and the 'practical' religion of Kant, his rather unsatisfactory answer was that 'similar in their nature but dissimilar in their degree of development, the elements of society combined differently in the different European countries, with the result that in each of them there was a very particular state of minds and manners which expressed itself in the national literature, art, etc.'[13] But exactly how this was so is not investigated. And his answer to the problem of explaining why the French utopian socialists, though successors to the eighteenth-century materialists, were so religious, was simply that

> they entered into 'contradictions' to the Encyclopaedists on some questions – particularly, that is, on the organization of society – and there appeared in them the striving 'to do the opposite' to the Encyclopaedists. Their attitude to religion was simply the opposite of the attitude to it taken up by the 'philosophers'.[14]

Plekhanov was more at home in philosophy than history and was not really interested in the question of how atheism followed from a materialist interpretation of history. For him, the question of the relationship between religion and socialism was primarily a philosophical one and he sought the answer to it in a dialectical materialism taken over from Engels. In Western Europe there were obvious historical connexions between socialism and various forms of Christianity; in Russia this was not the case and Plekhanov was not inclined to follow Engels and his German Social Democrat successors into such matters.

3. LENIN

A. Early Formulations

In his attitude to religion, as in many other fields, Lenin was strongly influenced by Plekhanov, who taught him his unremitting hostility to religion as an outlook which had nothing to contribute to social progress and was incompatible with Marxist materialism. At least in his earlier writings, Lenin's approach is even more simplistic than that of Plekhanov: living in the West in a cosmopolitan atmosphere, Plekhanov was interested in the cosmological aspect of religion; Lenin was more firmly rooted in Russia and viewed religion mainly from a political angle. Initially Lenin was not interested in philosophy nor in the comparative history of religion. He mentioned the 'democratic revolutionary spirit'[15] of early Christianity and referred to an unspecific time when 'the struggle of democracy and of the proletariat went on in the form of a struggle of one religious idea against another.'[16] But he was completely uninterested in exploring the implications in the manner of Engels and his claim that 'the idea of God *always* put to sleep and blunted "social feelings"'[17] only has the remotest plausibility in an exclusively Russian context. For in Russia atheism among radicals traditionally had social sources; it was the attitude of the Orthodox Church rather than the supposed conflict between science and religion that led Lenin to equate atheism with freedom and progress.

Both Lenin's parents were religiously minded and he was brought up in the Orthodox tradition. He seems to have broken with religion at the age of sixteen, though mentions of religion in his earlier writings are brief and always in the context of some particular political question. Lenin's basic theme was that

in a society so organised that an insignificant minority enjoys wealth and power, while the masses constantly suffer 'privations' and bear 'severe obligations', it is quite natural for the exploiters to sympathise with a religion that teaches people to bear 'uncomplainingly' the hell on earth for the sake of an alleged celestial paradise.[18]

In general, Lenin's views were more vitriolic than those of Marx and Engels, and anticlerical rather than atheist. He also accorded more importance than did Marx and Engels to an active struggle against religion as an integral part of any successful revolutionary politics.

Lenin only ever published one article specifically on religion, written in 1905 when there was an increasing interest in Russian society in religious questions. In this article, entitled *Socialism and Religion*, Lenin summarised his main thesis as follows:

> Religion is one of the forms of spiritual oppression which everywhere weighs down heavily upon the masses of the people, over-burdened by their perpetual work for others, by want and isolation. Impotence of the exploited classes in their struggle against the exploiters just as inevitably gives rise to the beliefs in a better life after death as impotence of the savage in his battle with nature gives rise to belief in gods, devils, miracles, and the like. Those who toil and live in want all their lives are taught by religion to be submissive and patient while here on earth, and to take comfort in the hope of a heavenly reward. But those who live by the labour of others are taught by religion to practise charity while on earth, thus offering them a very cheap way of justifying their entire existence as exploiters and selling them at a moderate price tickets to well-being in heaven. Religion is opium for the people. Religion is a sort of spiritual booze, in which the slaves of capital drown their human image, their demand for a life more or less worthy of man.[19]

Nevertheless, continued Lenin, the modern proletariat, under the influence of large-scale factory work and urban life, would progressively free itself from religious prejudices:

> The proletariat of today takes the side of socialism, which enlists science in the battle against the fog of religion, and frees the workers from their belief in life after death by welding them together to fight in the present for a better life on earth.[20]

Lenin saw religion chiefly as a *distraction* from political struggle.

In terms of immediate demands, this meant pressing for recognition by the State that religion was a private affair. Thus, the Russian Social Democratic Labour Party should demand the complete separation of Church and State – as a corollary to their demands for political freedom. This demand would be supported by those among the clergy who were dismayed by the Church's conservative stance and 'we socialists must lend this movement our support, carrying the demands of honest and sincere members of the clergy to their conclusion, making them stick to their words about freedom, demanding that they should resolutely break all ties between religion and the police.'[21]

This support for dissident religious movements was part of Lenin's overall political strategy for drawing minorities of all kinds into the political struggle. His attitude to religious sectarians parallels his treatment of national minorities.[22] In an address of 1903 to the peasantry, Lenin proclaimed that 'the Social Democrats . . . demand that everybody shall have full and unrestricted right to profess any religion he pleases' and continued: 'No official should have the right even to ask anyone about his religion: this is a matter for each person's conscience and no one has any right to interfere. All religions and all churches should have equal status in law.'[23] The tactical aim here was to drive a wedge between the Tsarist autocracy and its religious supporters and thus win ground for Social Democracy among the religious minorities. Pointing to 'the growth of religious sects and rationalism among the peasantry', he declared that 'political protests in religious guise are common to all nations at a certain stage of their development, and not to Russia alone.'[24] But Lenin never pursued this view of religion as a precursor of socialism, though the Bolshevik party did publish in 1904 a periodical designed to appeal to the more progressive sects. In the same context, Lenin's attitude to the brief prominence in the revolutionary movement achieved by the dubious figure of Father Gapon at the beginning of 1905 was to welcome the appearance of 'Christian Socialists and Christian Democrats, the resentment of the heterodox, sectarians etc.' as 'this serves the purpose of the revolution and creates exceedingly favourable conditions for agitation for the complete separation of the Church from the State.'[25]

But however much Lenin supported, for tactical reasons, the proposal that religion should be a private matter as far as the state was concerned, it could not be so for the Party which could not be 'indifferent to lack of class-consciousness, ignorance or obscurantism in the shape of religious belief'.[26] For the demand for the disestablishment of the Church was 'so as to be able to combat the religious fog with purely ideological and solely ideological weapons . . .'.[27] To the question why, in that case, atheism was not part of the Party's programme, Lenin replied that since the programme was based entirely on 'the scientific, and moreover the materialist, world-outlook', an explanation of the programme 'necessarily includes an explanation of the true historical and economic roots of the religious fog. Our propaganda necessarily includes the propaganda of atheism.'[28] On the other hand, 'under no circumstances ought we to fall into the error of posing the religious question in an abstract, idealist fashion, as an "intellectual" question unconnected with the class struggle.' For

it would be bourgeois narrow-mindedness to forget that the yoke of religion that weighs upon mankind is merely a product and reflection of the economic yoke within society. . . . unity in this really revolutionary struggle of the oppressed class for creation of a paradise on earth is more important to us than unity of proletarian opinion on paradise in heaven.[29]

This subordination of the religious question to tactical political ends is characteristic of all Lenin's earlier writings.

B. Materialism and the God-builders

The aftermath of the revolution of 1905 forced Lenin, at least apparently, to consider religion from the point of view of theory as well as of practice. The ferment of 1905 in Russian society included a marked shift of interest towards religion and even idealism among the intelligentsia. In St Petersburg an influential Religious and Philosophical Society had held meetings from 1901 to 1903 to bring about a *rapprochement* between intellectuals – known as 'god-seekers' – and the Church. More particularly, a number of prominent intellectuals, who had been interested in Marxism, now developed an interest in the Orthodox Church. Notable among them was Sergei Bulgakov, who took up Dostoyevsky's idea that Orthodoxy was 'our Russian Socialism' and, while attacking contemporary Socialists, wished to rejuvenate the Church with socialist principles. Although conservative in his cultural values,

Bulgakov was a radical collectivist in his social and political attitudes and even founded an unsuccessful socialist party. Nicolai Berdayev, on the other hand, was an extreme libertarian whose eclecticism went even further than Bulgakov and combined the most disparate elements in a revolutionary Christian anarchism.[30]

Nor was the Bolshevik party immune from the *Zeitgeist*. In his early writings Lenin had thought that Marxism did not need a philosophy and even after 1905 he still believed that there should be no 'party line' in philosophy and was content to leave discussion of these questions to the brilliant group of professional philosophers and intellectuals, such as Bogdanov, Lunacharsky and Gorki, who had joined the Bolsheviks in 1905. However, by 1908 and 1909, years of low ebb for the Bolsheviks, Lenin was forced to intervene in philosophical discussions. These discussions had begun to have political implications because Bogdanov was threatening his leadership by advocating the boycott of the Third Duma and thus outflanking him on the left. This gave their Menshevik critics the opportunity of attacking the Bolsheviks by drawing a parallel between their alleged deviation in politics and their deviation in philosophy. For Bogdanov and his colleagues had developed an enthusiasm for bringing Marxism up to date with contemporary developments in the philosophy of matter and in particular for the potentially idealist philosophy of Ernst Mach. Around the turn of the century there had developed among scientists a critical attitude to the rather crude materialism of their immediate predecessors. This was epitomised by the shift from Dalton's long-standing view of the solid atom as the basic building block of the world to viewing the atom as a cloud of negatively charged electrons. To put it crudely, 'matter' seemed to have disappeared. Anticipating the line of scientific advance, Mach attempted to construct a view of the world which consisted entirely in sensations: what we call objects (including the self) were merely groupings of sensations classified in the most economical and coherent manner.[31]

Lenin violently opposed the Russian Machists in his book *Materialism and Empiriocriticism*, which reasserted the traditional materialist basis of Marxist philosophy as against those such as Bogdanov whose monism seemed to Lenin to abolish the distinction between thought and matter.[32] Rejecting his previous idea that, at least from a tactical point of view, certain religious beliefs were progressive, Lenin no longer looked to the function of religious beliefs, but tried to use materialist propositions to disprove them.

He started from a basic dichotomy, the two fundamental 'lines' in philosophy, the antithesis between materialism and idealism: 'Are we to proceed from things to sensation and thought? Or are we to proceed from thought and sensation to things? The first line, the materialist line, is adopted by Engels. The second line, i.e., the idealist line, is adopted by Mach.'[33] Lenin equated idealism with fideism and constantly asserted throughout the book that those who abandoned his sort of materialism would have no defence against fideism – a term which Lenin defined as putting faith above reason and which had obvious religious overtones. Indeed much of the polemic of *Materialism and Empiriocriticism* can be read as indirectly aimed at religion. 'Once you deny', Lenin wrote, 'objective reality, given us in sensation, you have already lost every weapon against fideism, for you have slipped into agnosticism or subjectivism – and that is all fideism requires.'[34] And Lenin agreed with Dietzgen that 'the materialist theory of knowledge is a universal weapon against religious belief.'[35] It is noteworthy in this context that one of the few authors to get praise from Lenin was Ernst Haeckel. In spite of Haeckel's neo-Darwinian opposition to socialism, Lenin welcomed his *Riddle of the Universe* on the grounds that Haeckel gives 'a slap in the face' to all theological rejections of natural-scientific materialism.[36] Lenin, as a philosopher, was still fighting the battles of the eighteenth century. Since religion in Russia occupied a position roughly analogous to that found in Western Europe in the eighteenth century, it is not surprising that Lenin in his attack should resort to the same kind of materialism as the Encyclopaedists. Hence the lack of reference to Hegel and the otherwise surprising fact that Lenin chooses to begin his book with a discussion of Berkeley. The emphasis that Lenin placed on materialism (and his narrow definition of it) can be gauged from the difference between him and Engels on agnosticism. Whereas for Engels agnosticism was 'shamefaced materialism', for Lenin agnostics were all too often shamefaced idealists.[37]

Further light on Lenin's attitude at this time is to be found in the extensive notes he made on Feuerbach in 1909.[38] The work of Feuerbach that Lenin is excerpting is the *Lectures on the essence of Religion* of 1849 and thus less Hegelian than the Feuerbach who so influenced Marx's formulations on religion. Nevertheless it is noticeable how Lenin concentrates on those passages where Feuerbach equates religion with ignorance and superstition and omits any references to Feuerbach's less negative views.

Lenin had another opportunity to comment on the relation between religion and socialism with the growth inside the Bolshevik party of the so-called 'God-builders'. Unlike the God-seekers, who wished to revivify religion by means of socialist ideas, the God-builders, who were Party members, aimed to raise socialism to the status of a religion. Finding scientific Marxism too jejune a philosophy of life, they wished to supplement Marxism with a kind of mysticism that saw human history as the process whereby God was created. Prominent among the God-builders were Lunacharsky, Gorki and Bazarov. Drawing on Comte's religion of humanity, Feuerbach's critique of Christianity, as well as the works of Dietzgen and Nietzsche, they wished to give their atheism a religious aspect by equating their vision of socialist progress with the 'building' of God. Referring to the achievements of humanity, Lunacharsky wrote: 'In contemplating the handiwork of genius, do we not say to ourselves: what manner of man is this that even the winds and the waves obey him? . . . Do we not sense the nascent power of the new-born . . . God?'[39] For the God-builders, Marxist socialism was the fifth great religion to have sprung from Judaism: the first was primitive cosmism; the second and third were Platonism and Judaism which combined to give rise to Christianity out of which emerged the fifth religion of labour. The schema was elaborated in Lunacharsky's two-volume work, *Socialism and Religion* (1908). Following Kautsky, he saw socialist elements in the Christian tradition which had continually been suppressed by its authoritarian organisational structures. Marx himself was an heir to this tradition:

I dare to say that this philosophy [of Marx] is a *religious philosophy*, that is has its source in the religious quest of the past, engendered by the economic growth of mankind, and that it gives the brightest, most real, most active solution to the 'cursed questions' of human self-consciousness, which were resolved in an illusory way by the old religious systems.[40]

Moreover, Bogdanov was the only contemporary thinker continuing this splendid tradition making a return to a 'genuine unvulgarised, unplekhanovised Marx' which provided 'splendid soil for the growth of the socialist religious consciousness'.[41] What Lunacharsky advocated was a religion whose function was to reconcile the hopes of human-kind with the hard facts of nature and give an added psychological attraction to the otherwise rather jejune Marxist outlook. This new religion, he wrote, 'the religion of humanity, the religion of toil, has no guarantees, but I suppose that even without God and without guarantees, which are but masks of the same God, it remains a *religion*.'[42]

As well as disliking Lunacharsky's emotionalism, which could declare that 'religion is an enthusiasm and without enthusiasm people can create nothing great',[43] Lenin linked the God-builders with the ultra-left tendency that wished to boycott elections to the Third Duma.[44] As a consequence, he was responsible in June 1909 for a resolution for his faction which condemned God-building as 'a perversion of scientific socialism' which 'breaks with the foundation of Marxism and brings . . . harm to the revolutionary social-democratic work of enlightening the working masses'.[45] Lenin viewed the efforts of the God-builders as in the same category as the ideas of Tolstoy which, for all their merciless criticism of capitalism, indulged in 'the preaching of one of the most odious things on earth, namely, religion, the striving to replace officially appointed priests by priests who will serve from moral conviction, i.e. to cultivate the most refined and, therefore, particularly disgusting clericalism'.[46] For Lenin considered the ideas of Lunacharsky and his friends to be reactionary. 'For some', Lenin wrote, 'the statement "Socialism is a religion" is a form of transition from religion to socialism; for others it is a form of transition *from* socialism to religion'[47] – and the God-builders definitely came into this latter category.

In contrast, Lenin stressed the social roots of religion in modern capitalist society:

The deepest root of religion today is the socially down-trodden condition of the working masses and their apparently complete helplessness in the face of the blind forces of capitalism, which every day and every hour inflicts upon the ordinary working people the most horrible suffering and the most savage torment, a thousand times more severe than those inflicted by extraordinary events, such as wars, earthquakes, etc. 'Fear made the gods'. Fear of the blind force of capital – blind because it cannot be foreseen by the masses of the people – a force which at every step in the life of the proletarian and small proprietor threatens to inflict, and does inflict 'sudden', 'unexpected', 'accidental' ruin, destruction, pauperism, prostitution, death from starvation – such is the root of modern religion.[48]

In the face of such an indictment, the confused rhetoric of the God-builders served merely to conceal the real issues. Lenin returned to the subject in a long letter written to Gorki in 1913. Here he dismisses as another version of God-building Gorki's definition of God as 'the complex of those ideas, worked out by the tribe, the nation, mankind, which awaken and organise social feelings, having as their object to link the individual with society and to bridle zoological individualism.'[49] This, to Lenin, sounded very like the theories of Bogdanov and Lunacharsky. And lumping them altogether with the rather different God-seekers, Lenin dismissed them:

> God-seeking differs from God-building and god-creating or god-making etc., no more than a yellow devil differs from a blue devil. To talk about god-seeking, not in order to declare against *all* devils and gods, against every ideological necrophily (all worship of a divinity is necrophily, be it the cleanest, most ideal, not sought-out but built up divinity, it's all the same), but to prefer a blue devil to a yellow one, is a hundred times worse than not saying anything about it at all.[50]

Gorki's ideas were also – like Christian socialism which was the 'worst distortion' of socialism – clearly reactionary. For however innocent the intention might be, the beautifying of the idea of God could only serve to beautify the illusions of ignorant workers. Gorki's idea of God as the complex of ideas which awaken and organise social feelings was also simply untrue in that it was an idealist view which neglected the material origins of such ideas in the brutal subjection of man, by nature and class exploitation. Although Lenin admitted that 'there was a time in history when, in spite of such an origin and such a real meaning of the idea of God, the struggle of democracy and of the proletariat went on in the form of a struggle of one religious idea against another', nevertheless 'nowadays both in Europe and in Russia *any*, even the most refined and best-intentioned defence or justification of the idea of God, is a justification of reaction.'[51] Lenin's forthright and unqualified conclusions was: 'The idea of God *always* put to sleep and blunted the "social feelings", replacing the living by the dead, being *always* the idea of slavery (the worst, hopeless slavery). Never has the idea of God "linked the individual with society": it has always *tied* the oppressed classes *hand and foot* with faith in the divinity of the oppressors.'[52]

Towards the very end of his life, Lenin seems somewhat to have modified his ideas on religion, at least to the extent of taking up Plekhanov's idea that theatre and secular rites should be encouraged to fill the gap left by religion.[53] Nevertheless his fundamental intellectual opposition to religion is in evidence in his philosophical notebooks on Hegel. In spite of his enthusiasm for Hegel – so different from the almost entire neglect of *Materialism and Empiriocriticism* – Lenin equates religion with idealism, becomes consistently intolerant of Hegel when he talks of religion, and maintains that God should be consigned 'to the rubbish heap'.[54] For Lenin expected that the proletarian revolution, with the concomitant advance of science and extension of education, would cause religion to disappear altogether. But this view did not preclude his talking of initiatives to hasten religion's decline. Lenin strongly disapproved of the German SPD's doctrine that religion was a private matter: he attacked Plekhanov for saying that religion would disappear automatically through a change in world view rather than as a result of class struggle. In spite of guarantees in the Constitution of 1918 of freedom of conscience and the right to conduct religious propaganda, Lenin included the following statement of intent in the party programme for the following year:

> With regard to religion, it is the policy of the Russian Communist Party (Bolsheviks) not to content itself with the already decreed separation of the Church from the State and of the School from the Church. . . . The party strives for the complete dissolution of the ties between the exploiting classes and the organisation of religious propaganda, as well as for the real emancipation of the toiling masses from religious prejudices; to this end, the party organises the widest possible scientific, educational and anti-religious propaganda.[55]

Given the increasing coalescence of party and state structures, the distinction previously drawn by Lenin between the attitude of the Party to religion and that of the State became obsolete and the active persecution of religion was inevitable.[56]

In his last pronouncement on this subject, Lenin alluded to fashionable 'philosophical trends . . . which are now seeking to clutch at the skirts of Einstein',[57] and warned against the way in which they were connected with bourgeois support for religion. To counteract this, Lenin, following Engels and Plekhanov, recommended the translation of 'the militant atheist literature of the late eighteenth century for mass distribution among the people'.[58] Concerning the philosophical problems raised by recent developments in natural science, he stated:

> For our attitude towards this phenomenon to be a politically conscious one, it must be realised that no natural science and no materialism can hold its own in the struggle against the onslaught of bourgeois ideas and the restoration of the bourgeois world outlook unless it stands on solid philosophical ground.[59]

To this end, he advocated the foundation of a 'society of Materialist friends of Hegelian Dialectics'.[60]

The philosophical eclecticism evident in the last two proposals – combining the materialism of the Encyclopaedists with the dialectics of Hegel – demonstrates both how little intellectual consideration Lenin accorded to the religious question and how the social formation of Russia inclined him to return to the simple oppositions of the eighteenth century. Unlike his predecessors, there is little of intrinsic interest in Lenin's view of religion. He was far less knowledgeable than Engels or his SPD followers about the history and complex manifestations of religion. Apart from a grudging remark on the 'democratic revolutionary spirit' of early Christianity, he paid no attention to the revolutionary contribution of schismatic movements. The bluntness of his analysis is epitomised by his substitution of the phrase 'opium *for* the people' in place of Marx's 'opium *of* the people', his constant linking of the religious question with the pre-Hegelian opposition of materialism to idealism, his penchant for Enlightenment materialism, and his consequent conviction that religion was purely and simply false. As well as inducing a rather too schematic philosophical approach, and quite illegitimate generalisations, the Russian social formation led Lenin entirely to subordinate his views on religion to the class struggle. He could not share the optimism of his German Marxist colleagues on the 'withering away' of religion. This might well be so in Western Europe, but in Russia the close linking of Church power and Tsarist autocracy demanded a revolutionary class struggle, inspired by the active and unremitting hostility which characterised the whole of Lenin's approach.

4.   TROTSKY, BOGDANOV AND BUKHARIN

The views of Lenin were typical of the Bolshevik Party as a whole, though some of the leaders expressed themselves more subtly. Trotsky found himself in a kind of sympathy with well-organised and forceful religious groups. In *Their Morals and Ours* he came to the defence of the Jesuits over the question of the ends justifying the means. The Jesuits, according to Trotsky, were superior to other parts of the Church in that they were 'more consistent, bold and perspicacious' and 'represented a militant organization, strictly centralized, aggressive and dangerous not only to enemies but also to allies'.[61] The Puritans – albeit at the other end of the Christian spectrum – attracted Trotsky's admiration no less. In a well-known passage, he drew a striking parallel between Marxism and Calvinism:

> Calvinism, with its iron predestination, was a mystic form of approach to the systematisation of an historical process. The rising bourgeoisie felt that the laws of history were on its side, and this consciousness it clothed in the form of the doctrine of predestination. The Calvinistic denial of free will in no wise paralysed the revolutionary energy of the Independents; on the contrary, it provided a mighty rallying point for it. The Independents felt that they were called to fulfil a great historic act. One may with a certain justice draw an analogy between the doctrine of predestination in the Puritan revolution and the role of Marxism in the revolution of the proletariat. But in the one and in the other a tremendous activity is based not on a subjective arbitrariness, but on an iron systematisation – in the one case mystically and in the other scientifically known.[62]

Trotsky, who during 1921–2 headed the 'Society of the Godless' which was devoted to spreading anti-religious propaganda, writing in the early 1920s was nevertheless quite clear about the incompatibility of religion and Marxism: 'We consider atheism, which is an inseparable element of the materialist view of life, to be a prerequisite for the theoretical education of the revolutionist. Those who believe in another world are not capable of concentrating all their passion on the transformation of this one.'[63] The only exception was the 'raw revolutionary recruits from the East' where the immediate renunciation of Islam as a condition of party membership would be impracticable[64] – though he did encourage, in 1922, the Living Church Movement since it opposed the Orthodox establishment and adopted what he saw as a more progressive, rational stance towards religion.

Nevertheless, Trotsky's rejection of religion was absolute, along with all substitutes for it. Religion reflected man's weakness in the face of nature and his helplessness within society. In Russia, religion was the highest expression of the serf-owning ideology which had in the past been accepted in more or less good faith by all members of society; but 'as the bourgeois order develops and religious mythology comes into even greater contradiction with it, religion becomes a source of greater and greater trickery and deliberate deception'.[65] Contemporary religious movements, even apparently reformist ones, were thoroughly bourgeois:

> In the first four years, the Church fenced herself off from the proletarian Revolution by a sombre defensive conservatism. Now she is going over to the NEP [New Economic Policy]. If the Soviet NEP is a mating of socialist economy with capitalism, then the Church NEP is a bourgeois grafting on to the feudal stem.[66]

The theoretical basis for Trotsky's view, in as far as there was one, was that 'taken in a broadly materialist and dialectical sense, Marxism is the application of Darwinism to human society'[67] and Darwinism was irreconcilable with belief in God – whatever Darwin himself may have thought. And Trotsky was enthusiastic in supporting the virtual equation, in party documents, of anti-religious propaganda and propaganda for the natural sciences. According to Trotsky, the problem of religion had 'colossal significance'. Religion was a kind of fictitious knowledge of the universe:

> Fearing nature or ignoring it, being unable to analyse social relations or ignoring them, man in society endeavoured to meet his needs by creating fantastic images, endowing them with imaginary reality, and kneeling before his own creations. The basis of this creation lies in the practical need of man to orient himself, which in turn springs from the conditions of the struggle for existence.[68]

As a support for versions of absolute morality, Trotsky saw religion as Marxism's main ideological competitor in that 'heaven is the only fortified position for military operations against dialectical materialism'.[69] The struggle against religion could only be successful if religion failed to respond to class needs in a new social environment as was the case, so Trotsky believed, with the 'advanced' sections of the working class. But

> the complete abolition of religion will be achieved only when there is a fully developed socialist system, that is, a technology that frees man from any degrading dependence upon nature. It can be attained only under social relationships that are free from mystery, that are thoroughly lucid and do not oppress people. Religion translates the chaos of nature and the chaos of social relations into the language of fantastic images. Only the abolition of earthly chaos can end forever its religious reflection. A conscious, reasonable, planned guidance of social life, in all its aspects, will abolish for all time any mysticism and devilry.[70]

As for immediate measures, Trotsky believed that Orthodox religion had never succeeded in deeply penetrating the consciousness of the masses, as it relied on ceremonial and had a merely mechanical and habitual relationship to its members. As a substitute, therefore, the cinema was the most promising instrument for forming a new, socialist, a-religious culture.[71]

Intellectually the most gifted of the Bolshevik leaders, Bukharin, displayed more serious interest in religion than did either Lenin or Trotsky. His *Historical Materialism: A System of Sociology*, published in 1921, soon became one of the most widely read Marxist textbooks on the subject. Bukharin centred his study on the concept of 'equilibrium' between society and nature inside society, an equilibrium which was being constantly disturbed and constantly re-established. In early times,

> a need was felt for something to hold together all these 'knowledges' and 'errors', that would realise an equilibrium between them. Religion and general science had to provide this uniting principle; it is that which had to furnish the answer to the most abstract and general questions.[72]

The origin of religion was to be explained on animist principles, but very different from those of Engels following Tylor. According to

Bukharin, the notion of spirit was a reflection of the particular economic form of society when, through differentiation in clan structure, the division of labour led to the segregation of administrative work. The mode of production then became a pattern for the interpretation of all phases of existence, particularly man himself:

> the 'spirit' guides the 'body' and is as much superior to the body as the organizer and administrator is superior to the simple executant. . . . All the rest of the world began to be considered according to the same scheme of things: behind each thing, man saw the 'spirit' of this thing; all nature became animated with a 'spirit', a scientific conception which is known as 'animism'. . . . This conception, once established, necessarily led to the origin of religion, beginning with the worship of ancestors, of the elders of the clan, of supervisors and organizers in general.[73]

In Bukharin's opinion, this view had been confirmed by the material present in Cunow's *Ursprung der Religion*, although he criticised Cunow for giving natural rather than social explanations. Bukharin quotes considerable material in support of what he calls the 'Marxian' view – including a lot from Weber on Eastern religions, though he says nothing of Weber's own interpretation of this material. Bukharin's general view is that religion is a 'super-structure' and that 'the Church, in addition to serving as a pacific of the masses, restraining them from violations of the established order of things, itself was and is a portion of the exploiting machinery, constructed according to the same general plan as the larger exploiting society.'[74] Using Weber, Bukharin claimed that there was a good 'fit' between religious structures and other social structures, but then went on simply to assume that this showed that 'the religious superstructure is determined by the internal conditions of human existence; its nucleus is the reflection of the socio-political order of society.'[75] To the evident objection that it is difficult to see why monotheism, claimed to be a product of a social order, should persist in capitalism where political power is diffused, Bukharin answered that the 'economy is characterized, on the one hand by a relation of domination and submission, and on the other hand by unorganized exchange relations; the preservation of religion at all is due to the former circumstance, while the latter explains the meagre and fleshless character of God today.'[76]

Bukharin claimed to have got his theory of religion from Lenin's old rival Bogdanov, who was one of the few Marxist intellectuals to attempt a genuinely Marxist theory of religion.[77] Bogdanov traced successive world-views to the successive modes of production and exchange. To the three stages – primitive, authoritarian, and exchange – corresponded the pre-religious, the religious, and the secular world-views. In the primitive stage, labour was simple and based on the satisfaction of immediate needs. As society developed, however, the organisation of this labour became more sophisticated and produced hierarchical organisations. The social divisions between the organisers of work and its implementors inaugurated the authoritarian period of society which, in turn, gave rise to an authoritarian metaphysics and causality in which the whole universe was divided into active agents and passive objects. The authoritarian relations of production also accounted for the dichotomy between spirit and matter and the growth of a belief in spiritual forces to explain events which had no visible cause. The active organisers of society also needed the strength of tradition to support their position. These two tendencies – the authoritarian form of causality and the growing reverence for ancestors – led to the emergence of religion proper: 'deified ancestors were looked on as the organisers of all human practice, as the source of all knowledge.'[78] This religious world-view – based on the legacy of the ancestor-organisers and valid enough in its own time – began to decline with the growth of an exchange economy in which the authority figures were removed from direct participation in production. Once the economy was organised by exchange, the old organisers were robbed of any function and had to rely solely on tradition for their continuity. The religious world-view became increasingly detached from everyday life, which was governed now by the secular considerations of science and philosophy in which vertical authoritarian causality was replaced by a kind of horizontal, infinite chain of cause and effect governed by natural necessity, a world-view that, in its turn, would be replaced by socialist relations of production and the empiriomonism that he advocated.

Bogdanov did not pursue these ideas on religion systematically. After the 1917 revolution he became the founder and organiser of the short-lived Proletkult and the Proletarian University in the context of which he concentrated on elaborating his new science of tectology in which he saw (in a striking anticipation of modern cybernetics) the formation of society not in the ownership of the means of production but in the possession of organising experience. Contrary to many one-sided versions of Proletkult, Bogdanov did not completely reject the heritage of religion. In his opinion, the proletariat should imitate the free-thinkers who, while opposing religion when it obscured thought or weakened the will, were at the same time 'capable of turning all religions into a precious cultural legacy for themselves and others'.[79] The knowledge of this legacy was also important for instrumental reasons. Religion had served to sustain an authoritarian way of life. 'The authoritarian world is superannuated, but it is not dead; its traces surround us on all sides, both secretly and, increasingly, often in all possible defensive disguises – even the least expected. To conquer such an enemy, you must know him, know him profoundly and seriously.'[80] And this warning, Bogdanov added presciently, extended to 'the problem of the role of Party leaders, of the authorities, and that of the meaning of the collective control exercised over them, etc.'[81] But the proletariat had another heritage, too, from religion, namely 'all the artistic richness of popular experience crystallized in all sorts of legends and sacred writings, pictures of a different and original life, harmonious in its own way, widening the horizon of humankind, playing a full part in the world movement of humanity, bringing forth a creation that was new, autonomous and freed from traditional environments and ingrained habits of thought.'[82] And Bogdanov drew a parallel here with the story of Hamlet. Of course, Shakespeare was imbued (according to Bogdanov) with the authoritarian outlook characteristic of feudal times. Nevertheless, 'can and should the working class elaborate and construct its own type of organization otherwise than by confronting and comparing it with other types of organization, other than by criticizing and reworking them, other than by using their elements?'[83] The message of Hamlet concerning the organisational problem 'retains its power both for the contemporary scene and for the proletariat as a class wherever there is a clash between the thirst for harmony and the dry imperatives of struggle'.[84] Although Bogdanov is far from explicit about it, the implication is that religion, too, has some sort of universal content which is not entirely vitiated by the authoritarian forms with which it has hitherto been connected.

Bogdanov, a doctor by training, died in 1928 as a result of an experiment in blood transfusion which he performed upon himself. With the triumph of Stalin in the late 1920s, even the meagre discussion of religion that had previously existed among the

Bolsheviks ceased completely. Increasingly, severe measures were taken against any public manifestation of religion. This campaign was reinforced by Stalin's emphasis, in his interpretation of historical materialism, on the '*tremendous role* of new social ideas' which 'organize and mobilize the masses'.[85] Dialectical materialism as interpreted by Stalin ruled supreme for a quarter of a century. And to religion Stalin, the former theology student, made absolutely no reference.[86]

5

Gramsci and the Frankfurt School

1. INTRODUCTION

For all its apparent diversity, pre-1914 Marxism in Western Europe enjoyed a unity of common political and philosophical presuppositions that was soon fractured by the impact of the First World War. The followers of Lenin and Kautsky went their separate ways as the split between Social Democracy and the newly Bolshevised Communist Parties increasingly divided the European Left. The failure of revolutionary Marxism in Western Europe led to an emphasis on theory rather than practice, a turning away from the more straightforwardly materialist elements in Marxism and a seeking for explanations which involved the superstructure of society just as much as the base. This was accompanied by a resurgence of interest in the Hegelian roots of Marxism – roots which had been drastically neglected by the Marxists of the Second International. Hegel had been a great influence on the development of German theology: with the emergence of interest in him, the possibility of a more positive attitude to Christianity also reappeared. This turn is most evident in Georg Lukács's *History and Class Consciousness*, a work of immense influence in spite of later repudiation by its author. Lukács gave an overfull place to Hegel in his interpretation of Marx and influenced the subsequent discussion of religion by reintroducing the concept of reification into Marxist discourse – which permitted a different approach from that of the idea of religion as a reflection of class interests which had dominated the previous more positivist generation. This renewal of interest in ideology was most marked in the work of the Frankfurt School. But the outstanding Marxist theoretician in this area was Antonio Gramsci who combined an interest in superstructural questions with a strong commitment to the classical Marxist tradition and whose subtle historical perspective resulted in some of the most interesting Marxist discussions of religion.

113

2.   GRAMSCI

Gramsci has been called the Marxist theoretician of the superstructure; and nothing illustrates this more clearly than the centrality which the problem of the role of the intellectuals occupies in his thought. Through a series of historical studies, Gramsci elaborated a distinction between traditional intellectuals – who mistakenly considered themselves to be autonomous of social classes and bearers of an unchanging message – and organic intellectuals who genuinely articulated the specific collective consciousness of their class. One of the functions of intellectuals, in addition to ensuring the economic organisation and political power of their class, was to preserve the hegemony of that class over society as a whole by means of a justifying ideology of which they were the agents. Gramsci broadened the concept of hegemony and, through it, laid great stress on the role of ideology in the historical process: to understand the roots of ideology and to win the ideological/cultural battle was a precondition of Marxist success in the West in a way that it had never been in Tsarist Russia where the state institutions had not been protected by a strongly entrenched bourgeois culture.

Given his concern with intellectuals and with cultural hegemony, it will come as no surprise that the problem of religion was one of Gramsci's chief interests. Unlike all his Marxist predecessors, Gramsci had a serious and abiding interest in religion which made many of his comments nearer to the spirit of Weber than to that of Engels. What Gramsci sought to study above all was the historical role of the Catholic Church. In the *Prison Notebooks* he was concerned to analyse in detail the changing relationship between the Church and its members as providing the traditional model for the relationship of intellectuals to the masses. Thus the history of the Church provided him with examples of both traditional and organic intellectuals, the mediaeval Catholic world was a supreme example of the exercise of hegemony, and the Reformation was a model for the intellectual and moral reform movement that Gramsci wished to see spearheaded in his own time by the Communist Party. The Party as the Modern Prince, the collective intellectual of the working class, should learn the lesson of intellectual hegemony from the Church it was due to replace. A critical assessment of the role of the Church was made all the more acute by the fact that the peasantry, who Gramsci saw as a necessary ally of the working class, were still strongly influenced by Catholicism.

Gramsci's early political journalism contained passing remarks on religion which were extremely negative, as, for example, when he claimed that Marxism had 'guillotined the idea of God'. The *Prison Notebooks* show a much calmer and more reflective approach. The reflective and exploratory nature of his approach means that Gramsci's central concepts are notoriously difficult to define – and religion is no exception. Gramsci sometimes used the word religion in the narrow sense of belief in a transcendent divinity, but typically in the *Prison Notebooks* the sense given to religion is much broader. Gramsci himself posed the question as follows: 'Note the problem of religion taken not in the confessional sense but in the secular sense of a unity of faith between a conception of the world and a corresponding norm of conduct. But why call this unity of faith "religion" and not "ideology", or even frankly "politics"?'[1]

This broad definition comes from Croce for whom religion was 'a conception of the world which has become a norm of life'.[2] Yet Gramsci also wished to distinguish religion from ideology. There were three basic elements to any ideology: its philosophy, produced by the intellectuals of the ruling class, directed towards the members of that class, and the cornerstone of any ideological constellation; common sense, which was 'the philosophy of non-philosophers' and whose fundamental characteristic was that 'it is a conception which, even in the brain of one individual, is fragmentary, incoherent and inconsequential, in conformity with the social and cultural position of the masses whose philosophy it is';[3] and folklore, which was the collective name for the popular beliefs, opinions and superstitions that gain their authority from tradition. Although religion had a role to play in all three elements of ideology, it was by nature closer to common sense and folklore, which provided its ideological sediment, than to philosophy. 'Every religion', wrote Gramsci, '. . . is really a multiplicity of different and often contradictory religions: there is a Catholicism for the peasants, a Catholicism for the petty bourgeoisie and urban workers, a Catholicism for women, and a Catholicism for intellectuals which is itself obscure and incoherent.'[4]

It was its incoherence that marked religion off from philosophy and made it a conception of the world suitable for subordinate classes. Moreover, insofar as religion attempts to embrace the whole of society, it is bound to be incoherent. Gramsci conceded that 'the strength of religions, and of the Catholic Church in particular, has lain, and still lies, in the fact that they feel very strongly the need for the doctrinal unity of the whole mass of the faithful and strive to ensure that the higher intellectual stratum does not get separated from the lower.'[5] Nevertheless, this success was short-lived. One of Gramsci's major concerns in the *Prison Notebooks* is to suggest a conception of the world that avoids both the speculative idealism of Croce and the positivistic materialism of Bukharin. In his view, religion combines both these errors in that it contains both the conceptual speculations of the theologians and the materialism of popular religion. Moreover, the Catholic doctrine of creation and notions of the independent reality of the external world could only serve to reinforce the kind of materialism proposed by Bukharin. Religion reinforced the metaphysical nature of both idealism and materialism and thus made the relationship between individuals and of individuals to the natural world into mechanical relationships. Gramsci, on the contrary, wished to stress the dialectical and organic nature of these relationships by proposing a view of human nature and society akin to that of the early Marx.

This contradiction between the practical materialism of religion and its theoretical idealism explains the close relationship between religion and utopia. In a striking passage Gramsci wrote:

. . . religion is the most gigantic utopia, that is the most gigantic 'metaphysics', that history has ever known, since it is the most grandiose attempt to reconcile, in mythological form, the real contradictions of historical life. It affirms, in fact, that mankind has the same 'nature', that man in general exists, in so far as created by God, son of God, therefore brother of other men, equal to other men, and free amongst and as other men; and that he can conceive of himself as such, mirrored in God, who is the 'self-consciousness' of humanity; but it also affirms that all this is not of this world, but of another (the utopia). Thus do ideas of equality, fraternity and liberty ferment among men, among those strata of mankind who do not see themselves as equals nor as brothers of other men, nor as free in relation to them. Thus it has come about that in every radical stirring of the multitude, in one way or another, with particular forms and particular ideologies, these demands have always been raised.[6]

Thus Gramsci's attitude to Christianity is not entirely negative:

> For a period and in determinate historical conditions, the
> Christian religion has been, and continues to be, a 'necessity', a
> necessary form taken by the wishes of the popular masses, a
> determinate form of the rationality of the world and of life. . . .
> But, in this case, it must be a simple form of Christianity, not the
> jesuitical form which has become a pure narcotic for the mass of
> the people.[7]

Gramsci was more interested in the form of activity encouraged by
Christianity at different times and in different places rather than in
an examination of its formal content. The role of Christianity had to
be in its historical context, and Gramsci picked out four contexts
for discussion: early Christianity, traditional Catholicism, the
Reformation and his own epoch, with most importance attaching to
the last two.

Early Christianity

Gramsci's interest in primitive Christianity was as an example of a
thorough-going, total revolution. Christianity represented 'a
revolution in the fullness of its development, that is, a revolution
which has gone to its extreme consequences, to the creation of a new
and original system of moral, juridical, philosophical and artistic
relationships.'[8] It is interesting to compare Gramsci's approach with
that of Engels. Engels was interested in early Christianity as an
ideology and in the social bases of this ideology; Gramsci was
interested in early Christianity as an example of successful
revolutionary practice. This success depended on the production of
appropriate intellectuals who could transform the religious
impulses of primitive Christianity into practical and effective
activity. It is in this context that Gramsci draws a parallel between
the relationship of Lenin to Marx and that of Paul to Jesus. It was
Paul who organized the expansion of Christianity, its revolutionary
strategy, and therefore 'historically Christianity could be called
Christo-Paulinism and this expression would be more exact (only
belief in the divinity of Christ prevented this happening but this
belief is itself an historical element, not a theoretical one).'[9] For
Gramsci, early Christianity was not so much a class phenomenon as
the general form of spiritual resistance that the people of Hellenistic

civilisation offered to Roman domination. The attitude of the early Christians was essentially passive. It was not overtly political, still less military. Moreover, its ideology was strongly determinist, an attitude which 'becomes a formidable force of moral resistance, of cohesion, of patient and obstinate perseverance'.[10] The force of Christianity came from a sense of material impotence combined with that of cultural superiority: 'I am conquered now but the force of circumstances is working for me in the long term, etc.'[11] The victory of Christianity thus provided Gramsci with one of his key concepts – that of 'passive revolution', which designated a perod of profound social, political and economic change in which the ruling elite nevertheless managed to secure its own continuity by incorporating popular movements. This is what happened with the Edict of Milan: the Christian world-view, because it did not seek to replace the current social and political system, became incorporated by it: 'Christianity has confirmed what happens in periods of restoration as opposed to periods of revolution: the attenuated and camouflaged acceptance of the principles against which the struggle had been conducted.'[12]

The eventual result of this incorporation was that the clergy became, in mediaeval times, the prototype of another of Gramsci's central categories – that of organic intellectual. The mediaeval Church overlapped in many instances with the feudal ruling class and enjoyed an intellectual monopoly. The Church was both part of the ruling class and also an intellectual caste. Gramsci found the historical explanation for the domination of ideology in feudal times in the fact that the Church was at the origin of feudal society: during the rise of feudalism, it was the intellectual strata who gave birth to the dominant class and thus became its organic intellectuals.

As the Middle Ages progressed, the Church was faced with a dual problem. Firstly, there was a tension between the social basis of the Church in the feudal ruling class and the religious principle it inculcated which had originally emanated from the lower classes. Secondly, political authority tended to liberate itself from ecclesiastical control and lay intellectuals wished to challenge the ideological monopoly of the Church. It is in this context that Gramsci considered the mediaeval heresies and saw them very differently from Engels, who viewed them simply as proto-bourgeois movements and forerunners of the Reformation. For Gramsci, interested in the political and cultural aspects of religion, the mediaeval heresies were a symptom of the growing rupture between the Church and the masses produced, in Italy for example, by the communal movement. These heresies took the form of non-violent protest movements which the Church had sufficient vitality to re-absorb. For,

> the heretical movements of the Middle Ages were a simultaneous reaction against the politicking of the Church and against the scholastic philosophy which expressed this. They were based on social conflicts determined by the birth of the Communes, and represented a split between masses and intellectuals within the Church. This split was 'stitched over' by the birth of popular religious movements subsequently re-absorbed by the Church through the formation of the mendicant orders and a new religious unity.[13]

But what was possible in the thirteenth century was no longer possible in the sixteenth. Gramsci did not deny the bourgeois aspect of the Reformation that Engels was at such pains to emphasise: but he was more interested in the changing relationships of intellectuals to masses. Among the intellectuals charged with diffusing an ideology, there was always a tendency to develop a solidarity with the masses. And this solidarity could turn into open revolt in times of crisis. Thus it was that the very religious orders founded to contain religious opposition in the high Middle Ages provided heretical leaders in the sixteenth century – for example, Savonarola from the Dominicans, Luther from the Augustinians. Gramsci further distinguished between two types of heresy: that issuing from the lower classes which desired, still within the framework of traditional religion, a return to the sources, a purification; and a heresy which stemmed from the intellectuals themselves and moved beyond the bounds of traditional religion by putting at the centre of their view national-popular aspirations as a protest against the theocratic universalism of Rome.

This schema was only very vaguely sketched out by Gramsci, but was made a little more specific in the case of Italy where his major interest lay. The question Gramsci tried to answer was: why was there no Reformation in Italy? Italy had a comparatively developed economy in the two centuries preceding the Reformation and a very high degree of cultural attainment. But, unlike Germany and England, the popular movements pressing for a return to the pristine purity of Christianity did not develop a nationalist dimension. In Italy the bourgeoisie did not become a national class producing its own intellectuals. There were two reasons for this. Firstly, there was the economic decline of Italy: 'A change to principalities and fiefdoms, a loss of bourgeois initiative and the transformation of the bourgeoisie into landowners. Humanism was a reactionary phenomenon because the whole of Italian society had become reactionary.' Secondly, the Catholic Church became increasingly Italianised and thus managed to incorporate Italy's leading intellectuals: 'as far as Italy is concerned the central fact is precisely the international or cosmopolitan function of its intellectuals, which is both cause and effect of the state of disintegration in which the peninsular remained from the fall of the Roman Empire up to 1870.'[14] Thus the Italian Renaissance was fundamentally parasitic because 'politically domination was in the hands of an aristocracy composed largely of self-made men, gathered in the courts of the nobility, and protected by bands of mercenaries: it produced the culture of the sixteenth century and helped the arts, but was politically limited and ended up under foreign domination.'[15] Since the Renaissance was 'not a national and political phenomenon' but essentially, if not exclusively, 'the phenomenon of an aristocracy cut off from the people-nation',[16] a political role was open for the Church:

> . . . in the political conception of the Renaissance, religion was consent and the Church was civil society, the hegemonic apparatus of the ruling group. For the latter did not have its own apparatus, i.e. did not have its own cultural and intellectual organisation, but regarded the universal ecclesiastical organisation as being that. The only way in which this differed from the Middle Ages was the fact that religion was openly conceived of and analysed as an *instrumentum regni*.[17]

Hence the importance for Gramsci of Machiavelli who was the only intellectual to see that Italy could only progress by the overthrow of Papal political authority and the creation of a genuinely popular national culture. But Machiavelli was isolated and remained 'the theoretician of what happened outside Italy, not of Italian events'.[18]

Gramsci's view of the German Reformation is, again, different from that of Engels. For Engels, the German Reformation was a proto-bourgeois movement with Luther and Calvin as representative intellectuals, combined with a peasant revolt which was abandoned by the Lutherans in a compromise with the aristocracy. For Gramsci, however, the Reformation was above all a popular movement which only gradually produced intellectuals of its own. The Reformation was sterile in the area of high culture, since:

> a great movement of intellectual and moral regeneration insofar as it is embodied in large popular masses, as was the case with Lutheranism, assumes initially vulgar and even superstitious forms; this was inevitable simply because it was not a small aristocracy of great intellectuals but the German people who were the protagonists and standard-bearers of the Reformation.

Gramsci's remarks on Calvinism are very similar to those of Weber. Gramsci saw Protestant versions of predestination, like other forms of deterministic Christianity, as 'a form of worldly rationality which provided a general framework for real practical activity'.[19] Calvinism was a prime example of the motive power of ideologies in that it constituted a classical example of 'transition from a conception of the world to a norm of practical conduct' and was 'one of the greatest impulses to practical action in the history of the world'.[20] By contrast, 'the Counter-Reformation has rendered sterile this upsurge of popular forces. The Society of Jesus is the last of the great religious orders. Its origins were reactionary and authoritarian, and its character repressive and "diplomatic".'[21] The link between intellectuals and masses was well and truly severed and the Church took a more and more authoritarian and disciplinary role. It is significant that Jansenism, the only religious movement produced by the Counter-Reformation, was not a mass movement and did not even issue in the establishment of a new religious order.

However interested Gramsci was in history and however acute his observations in the past, they were always made with an eye to the political present. Like Marx and Engels before him, Gramsci saw Marxism as, in some sense, the inheritor of Christianity.

> The philosophy of praxis presupposes all this cultural past: Renaissance and Reformation, German philosophy and the French Revolution, Calvinism and English classical economics, secular liberalism and this historicism which is at the root of the whole modern conception of life. The philosophy of praxis is the crowning point of this entire movement of intellectual and moral

reformation, made dialectical in the contrast between popular culture and high culture. It corresponds to the nexus Protestant Reformation plus French Revolution: it is a philosophy which is also politics, and a politics which is also philosophy.[22]

In thus linking Luther to Hegel, Calvin to Ricardo, and – more imaginatively – Machiavelli to the Jacobins, Gramsci is following Engels's famous tripartite division of the origins of Marxism, though with more emphasis on the importance of ideas. Marxism was destined to embody the cultural as well as the social and political revolution that Christianity had tried to implement, but failed.

From his Italian standpoint, Gramsci saw Christianity as a much more differentiated phenomenon than did many of his Marxist predecessors. In particular, he did not see Protestantism as more progressive than Catholicism. True, it was the lack of a Protestant Reformation that meant that the Italian people as a whole had not been introduced to the culture and political life of a nation. Nevertheless, Protestantism, by basing itself exclusively on the sacred text of the Bible, had tended to become an intellectual religion divorced from the masses. By contrast,

> the strength of the Catholic Church has consisted and still consists in the fact that it feels strongly the necessity for the doctrinal unity of all the mass of 'religious' people and strives to prevent the intellectually superior levels from splitting away from the inferior levels. The Roman Church has always been the most tenacious in the struggle to prevent the 'official' formation of the two religions, that of the intellectuals and that of the ordinary believer.[23]

Catholicism had at least attempted to solve the problem since 'the official religion of the intellectuals attempts to impede the formation of two distinct religions, two separate strata, so as not to become officially, as well as in reality, an ideology of restricted groups.'[24] Nevertheless, the Roman Church

> tends to maintain a purely mechanical contact, an external unity based in particular on the liturgy and on a cult visually imposing to the crowd. . . . Although it has organised a marvellous mechanism of 'democratic' selection of its intellectuals, they have

been selected as single individuals and not as the representative expression of popular groups.[25]

Therefore Gramsci's projected work on the Modern Prince, i.e. the Party as collective intellectual, 'will have to be devoted to the question of intellectual and moral reform, that is, to the question of religion or world-view'.[26] For the Modern Prince, 'as it develops, revolutionises the whole system of intellectual and moral relations. . . . In men's consciences, the Prince takes the place of the divine or categorical imperative, and becomes the basis for a modern laicism and for a complete laicisation of all aspects of life and of all customary relationships.'[27]

Thus Gramsci wished to qualify Marx's description of religion as the opium of the people. As far as Catholicism went, this was only true after the Reformation and particularly after the French Revolution when Catholicism became little more than the ideology of a fading aristocracy incapable of expressing the needs of the people. Indeed, Gramsci drew some striking parallels between the evolution of Catholicism and of Marxism. For, like Catholicism, Marxism had tended to split into two trends. The few important intellectuals 'were not linked to the people, did not come from the people, but were the expression of traditional intermediate classes to which they returned during the great "turning points" of history: others remained, but to submit the new conception to a systematic revision, not to favour its autonomous development.'[28] This left the path open for the development of a vulgar Marxism relying on simple notions of materialism and determinism. This, like religious determinism, might be stimulating at times, but ultimately robbed the masses of all initiative. Gramsci's problem, therefore, was to prevent Marxism from becoming another popular religion by the creation of genuinely organic intellectuals. However much this challenge proved impossible to meet in the event, Gramsci's meditations on the lessons to be learned from a comparison between Marxism and Christianity remain, at least in a socio-political perspective, the foremost Marxist contribution to the study of religion. His discussions are, of necessity, frequently fragmentary and allusive: but for their sympathy, insight, and suggestiveness they are rarely equalled.

3. THE FRANKFURT SCHOOL

Gramsci, for all his emphasis on superstructural elements, stands in
the classical Marxist tradition in his analysis of religion. The same
cannot be said for what has come to be known as 'Western
Marxism', the main representative of which was the Frankfurt
School, which constituted the chief innovating force during the long
night of Stalinism. Although the School laid considerable emphasis
on superstructural factors, they did not offer much sustained
analysis of religion. However, the leading member of the Frankfurt
School, Max Horkheimer, did have an abiding, if peripheral,
interest in religion. In one of his earliest papers, Horkheimer
pointed to the iconoclastic potential of Christianity, in that the idea
of a radically transcendent divinity implied a relativization and even
criticism of all political and social arrangements.

> The concept of God [wrote Horkheimer] was for a long time the
> place where the idea was kept alive that there are other norms
> besides those to which nature and society give expression in their
> operation. Dissatisfaction with earthly destiny is the strongest
> motive for acceptance of a transcendental being. If justice
> registers with God, then it is not to be found in the same measure
> in the world. Religion is the record of the wishes, desires and
> accusations of countless generations.[29]

Thus Horkheimer went beyond Marx, whose attitude to religion he
considered to be limited by historical circumstances. For Marx had
neglected 'the progressive elements of religion' which were
contained in the 'longing for something quite other' which
Horkheimer considered to be the essence of religion.[30] He had much
praise for primitive Christianity as a revolutionary force and a
qualified respect for the mediaeval Church whose scholasticism at
least provided, in common with Marxism, a unity of theory and
practice and a meaning for the life of all members of society. But he
had only scorn for modern Protestantism whose secularizing and
demythologizing tendencies afforded no bulwark against the main
enemies – positivism, pragmatism and the solely instrumental view
of reason.[31] But religion was not destined to disappear completely:

> Mankind loses religion as it moves through history, but the loss
> leaves its mark behind. Part of the drives and desires which

religious belief preserved and kept alive are detached from the inhibiting religious form and become productive forces in social practice. In the process even the immoderation characteristic of shattered illusions acquires a positive form and is truly transformed. In a really free mind the concept of infinity is preserved in an awareness of the finality of human life and of the unalterable aloneness of men, and it keeps society from indulging in a thoughtless optimism, an inflation of its own knowledge into a new religion.[32]

The legacy of religion was the idea of perfect justice which, while it might be impossible of realisation in this world, yet served as a constant basis of opposition to the powers that were.

There was also a limited sympathy with theological motifs in the writings of Adorno, whose first major work was a discussion of Kierkegaard. But Adorno's treatment of theology remained at a purely secular level and it was to art that he finally looked as the preserve of those values denied in the contemporary world.[33] In Adorno's younger friend, Walter Benjamin, however, these theological motifs were more marked. Benjamin derived his theological – or, rather, mystical – attitudes from his aesthetics and developed a 'negative' theological position in which mysticism and materialism converged. The allusive nature of Benjamin's approach is exemplified in the passage which opened one of his last essays:

A puppet in Turkish attire and with a hookah in its mouth sat before a chessboard placed on a large table. . . . Actually, a little hunchback who was an expert chess player sat inside and guided the puppet's hand by means of strings. One can imagine a philosophical counterpart to this device. The puppet called 'historical materialism' is to win all the time. It can easily be a match for anyone if it enlists the services of theology, which today, as we know, is wizened and has to keep out of sight.[34]

Although Benjamin called himself a historical materialist, his images and language was heavily imbued with theological themes such as redemption and messianism and, much to Adorno's annoyance, he was loath to mediate the theological with the secular. Benjamin's expressions were deliberately, as he put it, 'Janus-faced', simultaneously strongly religious and strongly revolutionary materialist.[35] As Michel Lowry has well put it:

The elective affinity is not here mere analogy, but active interpenetration and combination of both elements. There exists an intimate link, a *correspondance* in the Baudelairian sense, between each term of the profane revolutionary utopia and of the sacred Messianic sphere, between the history of redemption and the history of class struggle: to the Lost Paradise corresponds the pre-historic classless communist society, egalitarian and non-authoritarian, living in edenic harmony with nature; to the expulsion from the Garden of Eden, or to the Tempest blowing men away from Paradise, towards Hell, correspond 'progress', industrial civilization, capitalist-commodity society, the modern catastrophe and its pile of wreckage; to the Coming of the Messiah, the proletarian-revolutionary interruption of history; and to the Messianic Age, the re-establishment of Paradise with its edenic adamite language, corresponds the new libertarian-communist classless society and its universal language. *Ursprung ist das Ziel* and *restitutio in integrum* are the spiritual quintessence of this peculiar 'theology of revolution'.[36]

In his aesthetic criticism, Benjamin tended to juxtapose empirical, rationalist elements with theological or supernatural images in order to illuminate them. In this he was moved by a mystical reverence towards objects or literary texts, being much inspired by the method of Kabbalistic exegesis in which objects of writings were viewed as hieroglyphs containing meanings far removed from the intentions of their authors, and their everyday significance. The model here was the Talmudic teaching of the forty-nine levels of meaning inherent in every passage in the Torah.

More historically specific analyses were offered by two peripheral members of the School – Franz Borkenau and Erich Fromm. Borkenau, in his massive work on *The Transition from Feudal to Bourgeois World-View*, took issue with Weber's discussion of the relationship of Calvinism to capitalism. While admitting that the protestant work ethic did indeed precede its application in the capitalist production process, Borkenau claimed that Calvinism, along with such other things as discoveries in the natural sciences or shifts in trade routes 'assumed importance only in connexion with the disintegration process of feudalism and were determined by it'.[37] For religions were not mere reflections of class conditions: new religions 'make possible different processes of adaptation, that is to say, they direct energies towards a form of life which is not yet in existence.'[38] And Borkenau proceeded to analyse with considerable subtlety the ways in which Calvinism, while originating in many different social strata, was gradually transformed into a systematic capitalist ethic. What interested him was the way in which religious beliefs developed out of the efforts of groups to adapt themselves to fundamental change in the total social structure. Although it is difficult to see how Borkenau's views really differ from Weber's concept of 'elective affinity', Borkenau's scholarship and imagination marked a definite advance over the classical Marxist treatments.

Erich Fromm's essay *The Dogma of Christ*, first published in 1931, was described by Borkenau as 'the first attempt to demonstrate by means of a concrete example the connexion between Marxism and Freudian psychoanalysis'. A brief survey of the historical evidence led Fromm to conclude that Christianity was initially a messianic-revolutionary movement springing from the poor, uneducated and revolutionary masses. He emphasised strongly their eschatological expectations and their hatred of the upper classes: 'the first Christians were a brotherhood of socially and economically oppressed enthusiasts held together by hope and hatred.'[39] While agreeing with Kautsky's emphasis on the class hatred of the early Christians and on their proletarian origins, he took issue with Kautsky on several points. In particular he questioned the emphasis that Kautsky placed on the practical activities of the early Christians at the expense of their ideas and dreams. Fromm claimed that Kautsky 'overlooks the fact that a movement may have a class origin without the existence of social and economic motives in the consciousness of its instigators' and thus consequently 'his contempt for the historical significance of religious ideas demonstrates only his complete lack of understanding of the meaning of fantasy satisfaction within the social process.'[40] Drawing on his Freudian background, Fromm claimed to find in the early Christian idea of a man's being elevated to a god oedipal undertones representing concealed hostility to God the Father, to the emperor and to authority. By the middle of the third century Christianity had lost its eschatological impulse and turned from a religion of the oppressed to a religion of the rulers and of the masses manipulated by them. The masses 'no longer identified with the crucified man in order to dethrone the father in fantasy, but, rather, in order to enjoy his love and grace. The idea that a man became a god was a symbol of aggressive, active, hostile-to-father tendencies.

The idea that God became a man was transformed into a symbol of the tender, passive tie to the father.'[41] This psychic change was conditioned by the transformation of the Roman Empire into a 'feudal class state' in which 'the social system was stabilized and was regulated from the top, and it was imperative to make it easier for the individual who stood at the bottom to be content with his situation.'[42] Fromm's essay was a pioneering work. However, it rested on a selective reading of the early Christian tradition and, as Fromm himself later admitted, one-sided in its stress on the social function of religion as a substitute for real satisfaction and a means of social control. But the main difficulty with his approach is the vagueness of the connexions drawn between psychological and socio-economic forces.

4. GOLDMANN

Probably the most impressive specific analysis of religion produced by Western Marxism was the discussion of Jansenism by Lucien Goldmann, a pupil of Lukács. For Goldmann, any great philosophical or literary work was the expression of a 'world vision' which was a sort of collective consciousness linking together members of a social group in opposition to other social groups. Pascal's genius lay in his expression of a tragic world vision which Goldmann defined as

> the paradoxical nature of the world, tragic man's conversion to essential existence, his demand for absolute truth, his awareness of the limitations of man and of the world, his refusal of any ambiguity or compromise, his loneliness and knowledge of the infinite abyss which separates him both from God and from the world, his wager that this God whose existence cannot be proved nevertheless does exist, and his decision to live wholly and exclusively for this God who is always absent and always present.[43]

The coherence and self-awareness of Pascal's exposition led Goldman to classify him as an eminently dialectical thinker and a worthy predecessor of Hegel and Marx. Western thought had long been dominated by rationalism – first Thomist and then Cartesian.

By renewing the Augustinian tradition, Pascal inaugurated a dialectic approach which emphasised the synthesis between theory and practice. Thus, structurally at least, the *Pensées* of Pascal were in the same mould as Marx's *Theses on Feuerbach* and Lukács's *History and Class Consciousness*. More specifically, Goldmann considered Pascal's thought to represent the 'great turning-point in Western thought' away from the atomistic view of the world embodied in the rationalism and empiricism associated with the rise of the bourgeoisie. It was in the ability to be both inside bourgeois society and outside the bourgeois *Weltanschauung* that linked Pascal to socialist theory: 'It is precisely because Pascal both rejected the world and lived in it, because he combined living in it, refusing it and analysing it, that his work attained the highest philosophical and scientific level that a thinker of his time could achieve.'[44] Descartes's God, as Pascal remarked, was only there to 'give a little tap to start the world off'[45] and this view amounted to practical atheism. Pascal's God, by being ever present and ever absent, afforded a wider and more critical perspective.

This tragic vision of Pascal was to be explained by reference to the social group of whose collective consciousness it was the pre-eminent example. Goldmann traced the genesis of Pascal's ideas to the development of royal power in seventeenth-century France. At the beginning of the previous century the King had exercised his power indirectly through the feudal system with support from the growing influence of the towns and the Third Estate. This support enabled the monarchy to acquire definitive authority over the other nobles and eventually to establish an independence not only from the nobles but also from the Third Estate itself. This authoritarian government realised by Richelieu relied on an administrative corps directly appointed by the crown, which maintained thereby a balance of power between the different classes. And Jansenism first appeared during this transition from limited to absolute monarchy. Pascal belonged to a social group whose traditional legal and administrative functions made them dependent on a monarchy which was bent on acquiring independence from them. Thus, according to Goldmann, 'this put them in an eminently paradoxical situation – and one which in my view provides the infrastructure for the tragic paradox . . . of the *Pensées* – where they were strongly opposed to a form of government which they could not try to destroy or even to alter in any radical manner.'[46] Jansenism, with its

insistence on the essential vanity of the world and consequent
advocacy of withdrawal from it provided the ideological counterpart
to this social and economic *impasse.*

The mechanistic materialism of Descartes and Malebranche
ushered in a world in which there was no room for God or the idea of
community. All entities in nature, including human beings, were
viewed as objects. Thus 'God, deprived of the physical universe and
of the conscience of man, the only two instruments by which He had
been capable of communicating with man, departed from the world
where He could no longer speak to the person He had made in His
own image.'[47] Pascal's paradoxical position was summed up in his
idea of the wager on God's existence, an idea which Goldmann
considered to be the centrepiece of the *Pensées.* And here, too, lay
the continuity between Pascal and Marxism. For Marx and Lukács
had substituted for the wager on God's existence a wager on the
historical future and the possibility of a human community. For
Goldmann, Marxism, in spite of its debt to eighteenth-century
rationalism and therefore real opposition to Christianity, still had
room for the concept of faith. This did not involve an attempt to
smuggle transcendental values into Marxism. For 'Marxist faith is a
faith . . . in the future that we must make for ourselves by what we
do, so that this faith becomes a "wager" which we make that our
actions will, in fact, be successful. The transcendental element
present in this faith is not supernatural and does not take us outside
or beyond history; it merely takes us beyond the individual.'[48] Thus
Goldmann called Marxism a religion, but a religion of man and of
humanity. What Pascal shared with Marxism was the idea of the
antagonistic quality of all human reality and the aspiration to
synthesis and totality. But whereas in Hegel and Marx the historical
perspective showed the possibility of a resolution to the
antagonisms, in Pascal the lack of any such perspective rendered the
contradictions all the more acute.

5.   BLOCH

Horkheimer's theme of religion as the location of opposition to the
contemporary world was given a different and more extended
treatment by Ernst Bloch, whose work spans the five decades
1920–70. Bloch went back to the early Marx's comments on religion
as 'the sigh of the oppressed creature' and 'the feeling of a heartless

world' and took them further: religion, for Bloch, was no mere illusion and the taking seriously of some of Marx's statements might 'open the way to conversations between believers purged of ideology and unbelievers purged of taboo'.[49] Religious belief of some sort was a normal part of the human condition while there was still something for which to hope. Even under socialism there would be room for a socialist church to express the utopian aspirations of humankind. There was a strong continuity between Marxism and some forms of Christianity: Marxism was to make real the content of Christianity. In order to achieve this, Marxist atheism could not be simply negation. It had to be an active humanism that would bring to reality the 'hope treasures' of religion.

Naturally, when Bloch saw a continuity between Marxism and Christianity, he had in mind a specific form of Christianity. 'Religion', he wrote, 'is re-ligio, binding back. It binds its adherents back, first and foremost, to a mythical God of the Beginning, a Creator-God. So, rightly understood, adherence to the Exodus-figure called "I will be what I will be", and to the Christianity of the Son of Man and of the Eschaton, is no longer religion.'[50] Thus Marxist atheism was not a pure negation but an active humanism that aimed to include the 'hope treasures' of religion. What was needed was 'nothing less than a questioning that is present *within religion itself* – in other words, a religious critique of religion.'[51] To achieve this, Bloch presented his own reading of the Bible and of the development of Christianity. The Bible, for Bloch, was an extremely utopian document. In the Old Testament, the static creation myth of Jahweh is replaced by the God of the Exodus who led his people out of slavery into the promised land and who said not 'I am who I am' but 'I will be who I will be'. With the settlement in Canaan and the rise of a class society, the old ideas of God re-emerged, only to be opposed by the prophetic tradition and the idea of a Messiah who would create a new heaven and a new earth. The Exodus from Jahweh culminates in Jesus who reunites God with man in a revolutionary apocalypse that inaugurates an entirely new age. This vision was obscured by the sacrifice theology of Paul (here the difference between the evaluations of Bloch and Gramsci are striking) and the partial restoration by the Church of an authoritarian God. But true Christianity was kept alive in the heretical movements such as the Hussites, the Anabaptists and, above all, in Thomas Münzer, to whose life Bloch had early on devoted much study. Jesus himself was no mere political rebel against Roman authority. His social and political activity also contained a 'heretical' aspect which was irreducible to any social, political or moral doctrine. The heresy pointed to the unfulfilled dimension implied and anticipated in any such social or political doctrine and activity. Jesus was the arch-heretic of all time and 'the best thing in religion is that it produces heretics'.[52]

It would be difficult to overestimate the importance of eschatology for Bloch. He was particularly critical of liberal theology which banished eschatology from the Gospel, emphasised above all purity of heart and made the Kingdom of God into an ethical phenomenon, as in Bultmann's existential hermeneutics. On the contrary, according to Bloch, that classical text of Christian morality, the Sermon on the Mount, was not intended to be an ethical system of long duration: it only made sense in the context of an expectation of an imminent end to the world. Thus 'the Gospel is from this viewpoint not social, nor primarily moral. It is a gospel of eschatological salvation.'[53]

Bloch's criticism of religion from within religion had as little sympathy with the superficial reductionism of Kautsky as with the neo-bourgeois demythologising of Bultmann. Both sought to rob religion of its vital messianic and utopian elements. Bloch thus went further than Feuerbach and Marx. Feuerbach merely saw religion as the projection of actually existing man, of the abstractly stable human species. But 'the flatness of the "homo bourgeois", which Feuerbach absolutised, can definitely not accommodate the contents of religion, no more than the bourgeois has ever been the subject from which the wealth of divine images would come forth. Least of all can Feuerbach's statically extant subject accommodate the religious images that explode the status quo, the chiliastic ones of "Behold, I make all things new" and of the kingdom'.[54] Even Marx tended too easily to equate religion with the Church, but some of his early aphorisms were useful in that 'the critique of religion in the spirit and context of Marx's thought liberates from undiscriminating taboos far more than Marxism does.'[55]

This interpretation of 'true Christianity' leaves the way open for considerable affinity with Marxism:

True Marxism . . . takes true Christianity seriously – too seriously for just another grey and compromising dialogue. When Christians are really concerned for the emancipation of those who labour and are heavy-laden and when Marxists retain the depths of the Kingdom of Freedom as the real content of revolutionary consciousness on the road to becoming true substance, the alliance between revolution and Christianity founded in the Peasant Wars may live again – this time with success.[56]

Christianity, as the religion of total hope, had an important legacy for Marxism:

The place held in religions by the concept of God, the place filled with seeming reality, by the thing hypostatized as God, this place itself has not vanished with the disappearance of what seemed to fill it. For it always remains the place of projection at the focal point of radical utopian intentionality.[57]

The concrete Utopia of Marxism would always have room for elements inherited from religion:

Far from being a contradiction in terms concrete Utopia is the firmest of handholds, and by no means only where the propaganda and implementation of socialism is concerned. The whole *surplus force* of culture finds its salvation there, and these forces are becoming more and more relevant to us all the time – above all, the wealth of artistic allegories and religious symbols, whose day is not yet done when the ideology which bore them disappears.[58]

From the strictures of Marx on the early French utopian socialists, the word 'utopia' has always had an extremely pejorative connotation in Marxism. It was Bloch's great contribution to have attempted nevertheless to rescue the idea of utopia for Marxism.

Bloch's view of religion, and particularly his *Principle of Hope*, has had more influence on Christians (as we shall see in the next chapter) than on Marxists. For Bloch was a highly idiosyncratic Marxist who, many would claim, did not merit the label at all. He is certainly a difficult writer to pin down as his books are disorganised, syncretist and allusive. Occasionally he analyses some of the more social and ideological aspects of religion in a truly Marxist fashion, but more usually he is eclectic in drawing on varied sources to present an amalgam of Marxist and Christian eschatology. This is made possible by Bloch's curious version of Marxist materialism.

Firstly, he has not got much time for historical materialism as traditionally understood and tends to interpret it in a way that almost deprives it of any genuinely materialist basis at all. More importantly, Bloch subscribes wholeheartedly to an ontological dialectical materialism which he believes to be identical in Marx, Engels and Lenin. In particular, he has a sympathetic view of Engels's *Dialectics of Nature* as an attempt to give an account of the spiritual qualities of matter in that matter has some kind of an objective drive to self-completion. However interesting in itself, Bloch's account of matter is a speculative metaphysics far removed from Marxism.

6

Contemporary Marxism and Christianity in Europe and Latin America

1. INTRODUCTION

The discussion of Gramsci and the Frankfurt School in the previous chapter shows that Marxism in the 1930s, if not disintegrating, was at least becoming polymorphous and less easily tangible. The twin problems facing all Marxists as the twentieth century wore on was the non-occurrence of a proletarian revolution in the West and the phenomenon of Stalinism in the East. The general response was to revise the materialist conception of history that lay at the heart of Marxism and allot more importance to superstructural elements – culture, politics, ideas and ideology in general – than to strictly economic analyses. Gramsci is the most evident example of this trend. In addition, Gramsci was the last leading Marxist theorist to be also a prominent political activist. After the Second World War, Marxist theory in Europe and the United States was the product of intellectuals who mostly had no strong party affiliation. It was therefore not the product of political movements which saw religion as an obstacle to a given political programme. This new emphasis on the importance of cultural factors together with a lack of direct political struggle meant that a lot of Marxist theory looked more benignly on at least certain forms of religion.

This attitude was enhanced by the recent co-operation of many Marxists and Christians in resistance to Fascism. The polycentrism of Marxism inaugurated by the Sino-Soviet split and the distancing of European Communist Parties from Moscow meant that there was an increasing opportunity for 'dialogue' between Christianity and Marxism – particularly a Marxism that had taken account of the recently published writings of the young Marx, with their interest in philosophy and humanism.

Within the Christian Churches, too, a similar process could be

135

discerned. In the reformulations of Marxism, the crucial issue was the breakdown of the hard-and-fast distinction between base and superstructure and the emphasis on the latter at the expense of the former: in theology, too, the distinction between God and human beings, heaven and earth, had been radically reformulated. Under the impact of existentialism and humanism, theology underwent a substantial shift of focus and in the words of Bultmann: 'If we are asked how it might be possible to talk about God, we must reply that such talk is only possible insofar as it is talk about us.'[1] This change was most marked in sections of the Roman Catholic Church which moved very quickly from being the most conservative of major Christian institutions to producing some of the most interesting innovations. In his encyclical *Divini Redemptoris* of 1937, Pius XI had declared: 'Communism is intrinsically wrong and there can be no collaboration with it in any field on the part of those who want to save Christian civilization.'[2] John XXIII's *Pacem in Terris*, by contrast, while repudiating the philosophy of Communism, was less negative about the economic and social aspirations of Communists. 'Who can deny', he asked, 'the possible existence of good and commendable elements in these programmes, elements which do indeed conform to the dictates of right reason, and are the expression of men's lawful aspirations.'[3] For reasons of international politics it is only in the 1960s that Marx's thought made any serious impact in the West. The change in attitude was summed up in the title of Roger Garaudy's book *From Anathema to Dialogue*. As this dialogue progressed, some positions became rather blurred: a Christian theologian could write a book entitled *The Death of God* while a Marxist atheist was the author of *God is not Yet Dead*. Whether you were a Christian or Marxist seemed almost to take second place to the question of what *kind* of Christian or Marxist. And in non-European contexts, particularly Latin America, the common ground found in the fight for liberation appeared sometimes to obliterate all distinctions.

2.   SOVIET AND EAST EUROPEAN ATTITUDES

A. Official

However flexible their attitudes are in practice, the ideological evaluations of religion expressed by the Communist Parties of the

Soviet Union and Eastern Europe have remained starkly negative.
As we have seen, Lenin bequeathed a strongly anti-religious legacy
to his successors. The decree of 1918 separated Church and State,
and made all religious property public: but in general believers were
left free to practice their religion as long as they kept it private. In
1928 Stalin emended these regulations:

> the authorities became empowered to remove persons from
> executive positions in religious organisations; children were to
> be excluded from any activity connected with religious
> organisations; organisations were not permitted to initiate any
> activities of a social, cultural or welfare kind; religious
> functionaries were restricted to the geographical area in which
> their organisation was located.[4]

During the 1930s there was heavy pressure against any form of
religious activity. This attitude was revised during the war when
Stalin relied on nationalist rather than socialist sentiments to inspire
the population in the struggle against the invading Germans. This
nationalist crusade led to the rehabilitation of the Russian Orthodox
Church as part of the Russian national heritage. In 1959 under
Khrushchev a fresh anti-religious campaign was mounted, which
resulted in the closing of two-thirds of the Orthodox churches.

It was the Khrushchev era, too, which saw the promulgation of an
ideological counter-offensive in the shape of 'scientific atheism'.[5]
This was made a formal component of the Marxist–Leninist
world-view in 1954 when the two decrees of the Central Committee
pointed to the obsolescence of most atheist propaganda, instituted
compulsory courses on scientific atheism in all universities, and in
general demand a philosophical – rather than a purely ideological –
opposition to religion. A well-endowed Institute of Scientific
Atheism was established in 1963 to co-ordinate these efforts. Even
after the fall of Khrushchev, the Party authorities have taken
research into religious questions very seriously and devoted
considerable resources to pursuing them.

Although unremittingly hostile to all forms of religion – scientific
atheism being held to be an integral part of dialectical and historical
materialism – recent Soviet work on the subject has been more
nuanced. Much detailed work has been done, for example, on
primitive religion and there has been a lively debate on whether
there was (or could have been) religion in classless societies.

Research into these areas is intended, in the manner of late nineteenth-century rationalism, to discredit religion by uncovering its origins. Discussion of the origins of the major world religions, too, tends to be vague and schematic. Here the legacy of Lenin weighs heavily and Soviet historians find it difficult to go beyond the idea of religion as a reflection of class interest and to incorporate the notions of social protest to be found in Marx and Engels.

But the study of religion in Soviet society is necessarily partisan and it is contemporary society that is of most concern. The partisan commitment limits the kind of question that Soviet sociologists ask and the data they collect. This is, of course, a problem inherent in any sociology of religion: it is just more acute in the Soviet case. Nevertheless, given the importance attached to religious questions, Soviet scholars have had to move a little beyond the simple theses of dialectical materialism and develop a more sophisticated sociology and psychology of religion that are not a direct reflection of their official materialist philosophy. They point to aesthetic and emotional needs not satisfied by any purely 'scientific' account of the world: indeed, the recent promotion of secular ceremonies to rival the traditional religious rites of passage has proved far more successful in reducing religious practice than any classroom propaganda.[6] Soviet sociologists have also begun to broach some of the themes of alienation and humanism familiar to Western discussion and even go so far as to suggest that the continuance of religion may be the result of deficiencies still present in Soviet society. This has never, however, extended as far as sympathising with the relatively positive attitude taken to some forms of religion by their fellow-Communists in the West, such as Roger Garaudy, and all attempts at a Marxist–Christian 'dialogue' have been roundly condemned as involving a distortion of Marxism.

For the official view remains that religion is a survival from a past age without any real roots in present reality: since religion has its origin in exploitation and there is no exploitation in the Soviet Union, then all that is necessary to extirpate it is to make this clear by propaganda to which considerable efforts are devoted.[7] These generally involve appeals to science to show the falsity of the idea of the creation of the world by God, of miracles, and of the Biblical account of the origin of man. The effect of the persecution and propaganda has not been proportionate to the effort expended: the general result has merely been to enhance certain forms of religious activity at the expense of others. While the influence of the Russian

Orthodox Church has declined, the vitality of religious sects has been guaranteed by the social upheaval of recent decades and the militantly atheistic policies of the State. The Soviet Union contains an extremely wide spectrum of religious activity. Although notoriously difficult to measure, the general level of religiosity in the Soviet Union does not seem to be very different from that obtaining in Western Europe.[8]

The attitude of the Communist authorities in Eastern Europe has, on the whole, not been as uncompromising as in the Soviet Union. The power of the Catholic Church in Poland due to its links with nationalist sentiment and deep roots in the working class has made head-on opposition impossible. Although an atmosphere of confrontation has persisted in Czechoslovakia (with the brief exception of the years prior to 1968), both the East German and Hungarian regimes have moved from persecution at their foundation to an effort to establish a *modus vivendi* and even harness Church institutions for political ends.

B. Unofficial

The official Communist Parties of Eastern Europe and the Soviet Union have produced no interesting account of religion. Their Marxism has become, in the words of Leszek Kolakowski, 'a concept of institutional, rather than intellectual, content. . . . The word "Marxist" does not describe a man who believes in a specific world view whose content is defined. It refers to a man with a mental attitude characterised by a willingness to adopt institutionally approved opinions.'[9] Nevertheless, there have been several notable East European contributions from those thinking independently of the Party line, but still within a general Marxist perspective. These works were the product of the relatively liberal 1960s in Poland and Czechoslovakia. The most interesting are those of Leszek Kolakowski. In his *magnum opus*, *Christians Without a Church*, Kolakowski analysed in fascinating detail the seventeenth-century religious movements, particularly in Holland, which were either ill at ease inside the various Church structures or openly in rebellion against them. Kolakowski's declared aim was 'precisely to place these religious ideas and movements and to discover their role in the ensemble of the social institutions of the time and thus to treat them as manifestations of social conflicts.'[10] In so doing, Kolakowski saw as his principal opponents the phenomenologists such as Rudolf Otto or Max Scheler whose emphasis on the sacred as something wholly other precluded an account of religious phenomena by reference to anything else. Admitting that the phenomenological view would be correct if religious phenomena were being *reduced* to other phenomena, Kolakowski claimed to be maintaining their irreducibility while retaining a 'genetic' explanation based on a materialist conception of history.[11] The 'materialism' of Kolakowski's approach is, however, difficult to discern. His book consists of an effort to describe how religious needs 'are modified and variously determined, as regards their forms of expression and their satisfaction, by the simultaneous existence, in the same epoch, of other needs; and only the totality of these is a structure that is sufficiently autonomous to constitute a system of reference for detailed study in the human sciences.'[12] The emphasis on totality recalls the work of Goldmann (he and Kolakowski were close friends). But, for Kolakowski, Goldmann's *The Hidden God* attempted to establish too direct an isonomy between the religious conceptions of Jansenism and the class position of the *noblesse de robe* without paying sufficient attention to the confessional struggles *within* ecclesiastical organisations. Kolakowski does succeed impressively in linking various spiritualities to 'politics' in a wide sense – for example, in showing how the doctrines of Berulle represented an enhancement of the secular clergy and thus served to unify the French monarchy.[13] On the very last page of the book there is mention of Marx and the way in which all ideas have their origin in practical social activity. But this has very much the appearance of a *pro forma* addendum. Kolakowski is more interested in the way in which the differences between the Erasmian and the mystical currents in the seventeenth century display general antinomies which have been part of the Western intellectual tradition from St. Paul to Sartre. This theme is taken up in Kolakowski's essay *The Priest and the Jester* whose broad theme is that 'twentieth-century thinkers have done everything to keep alive in our minds the main questions that have troubled theologians over the years, though we phrase the questions somewhat differently.'[14] Contemporary philosophy merely presents the old themes of eschatology, revelation, theodicy, etc., in a different language. The central opposition is not between the religious and the secular but between open and closed minds which is to be found on either side of the former divide. Indeed, his exile from Poland was precipitated by his slide from a critique of organised Catholicism into an ever sharper rejection of the parallel theory and practice of Stalinism.[15]

Kolakowski eventually became completely disillusioned with Marxism. The difficulties of saying anything very interesting within the confines of orthodox Marxism are illustrated by the work of Adam Schaff. A member of the Central Committee in Poland, Schaff wrote a book entitled *Marxism and the Human Individual* which was indeed a landmark inside Poland for its thorough-going presentation of a Marxist humanism. But when dealing with religion, Schaff could go no further than quoting Feuerbach to the effect that 'man is to man the only God' and condemning those who 'in the name of Marxism deny the ideological significance of religious belief and of the struggle against it as a form of alienation'.[16] Religion, for Schaff, represented 'an ideology . . . that is connected with a straight choice between two alternatives: either God or man is the supreme being for men.'[17] And a sufficient refutation of such a view was, according to Schaff, to be found in the early writings of Engels.

Czechoslovakia in the 1960s was a more fruitful ground for serious Marxist analyses of religion. The Czechs enjoyed a tradition of open-minded discussion and, in any case, the attitude of Marxists there to Christianity was more urgent than in Poland. During the 1960s, while the 'Prague Spring' of 1968 was gestating, many Marxist intellectuals felt that 'socialism with a human face' would be impossible without coming to terms with the country's very varied Christian heritage: in the Hussite Reformation of the fifteenth century the union of progressive religion and progressive politics had left an indelible mark on the country's history. This more positive attitude on the part of Marxists was greatly encouraged by the understanding of, and even sympathy for, certain forms of Marxism evinced by such leading Czech theologians as Hromadka and Lochman.

Two contributions stand out. The first, Vitezslav Gardavsky's *God Is Not Yet Dead*, argues for a radical Marxism that goes to the roots of its own history and that these roots include Christianity. Gardavsky does not reject the type of materialist Marxist analysis which distances itself from religious concepts by finding, for example, in the Old Testament conceptions of Jahweh the reflection of a tribal society in the stage of transition from a nomadic to a settled form of life; but he is more interested in finding those elements in the Judaeo-Christian tradition which could contribute to an understanding of the modern age. For he is convinced that

'Christianity as a religious movement can be altered to fit in with socialism, with the tasks it has set itself, and its aims'.[18]

In order to demonstrate this possible incorporation of Christianity, Gardavsky deals in turn with typical figures: Jacob, Jesus, Augustine, Aquinas and Pascal. In the story of Jacob, with all its vicissitudes and betrayals, Gardavsky sees 'the first action to have any sort of historical status, it is the first authentic human action'.[19] With Jacob the idea of choice and personal identity enters human history and, as opposed to the classical ideas of a predestined system and cosmic harmony, finds its full flowering in Marx who, as a Jew, was 'more capable than virtually anyone before him of reading the prophecies given in the Bible'.[20] Jesus, too, lies in this tradition. Gardavsky has little time for the view that Jesus was really the first Communist and that Marxism is simply a secularised version of Christianity. What strikes Gardavsky in early Christianity is its emphasis on eschatology, even apocalypse, and the present necessity for collective choice. Jesus, in this view, is the prime example of successful subjectivity. In this view, he writes, 'man is a creature who evolves by fighting and by answering the call of the present with a free decision.'[21] Gardavsky is evidently over-impressed by Bultmann's existentialist interpretation of the Gospels.

Where does all this leave Marxist materialism? Gardavsky admits that socialism, both in its early formulation and in its historical forms, has been infected by bourgeois anti-clerical and Enlightenment rationalism which was merely the use of instrumental reason for the greater glory of the bourgeoisie. The present task of Marxist materialism, according to Gardavsky, is to make 'a searching investigation of everything which attempted, in conditions which were historically inevitable, to establish an order which would give a firm basis to man's existence on earth.'[22] The early Marx understood this. It would therefore be wrong to suppose that the roots of religion lay in the antagonism of economic interests and would be eliminated with the disappearance of such antagonisms. Religion also feeds on the conflict between the interests of citizens and the power of the State. On this view, remarks Gardavsky gloomily, with an eye on contemporary Communist society, 'it is virtually certain that we will go on living in social conditions which foster religion for a long time to come.'[23] He nevertheless clings to a belief in a reformed communism which will make real the illusory hopes placed in God. 'That is why', he concludes his book, 'we do not believe in God, although it is absurd.'[24]

The work of Gardavsky is that of a wide-ranging philosopher. Machovec's *A Marxist Looks at Jesus* is much more precise – a sort of contemporary replacement for Kautsky's *Foundations of Christianity*. But whereas Kautsky's aim was to undermine and demolish, Machovec's intentions are constructive. With their view that 'Christianity began with a dreamer and ended with a well-fed clergy',[25] Engels and Kautsky had concentrated too much on 'explaining away' by reference to economic forces. Even Marx is insufficient, for

> Marx developed his 'atheism' as a critique of the conventional nineteenth-century representations of God, and should these change, then the genuine Marxist would have to revise his critique. Twentieth-century theologians have worked out new and more dynamic models for thinking about God, so that often we Marxists do not know whether we are still atheists or not in their regard.[26]

Earlier Marxism provides no models or clear indications for tackling many contemporary problems which Machovec lists as the place of spiritual aspirations in a sated consumer society, the trampling on human dignity in the world of industry, the painful moral conflicts of means and ends, and the better understanding of other intellectual traditions.[27] Without rejecting the necessity to look for the socio-economic roots of ideas, modern Marxism would have to ask 'which of these ideas offers positive and true knowledge about man's being and existence as well as inspiring ideals, models and norms of value without which even the best-organised, affluent and technically perfect society would remain impoverished and indeed barbarous.'[28]

Like Gardavsky, Machovec takes Bultmann as pre-eminent in his critique of religious matters. Although he rejects the manner in which Kautsky 'reduced the entire content of Christianity to social interests' and portrayed Jesus as a 'politically active dissident and a social revolutionary',[29] Machovec does insist on a rigid distinction between the Jesus of history and the picture of Christ constructed in later preaching, and the reduction of the latter to the former. At the same time, Machovec draws interesting parallels between the situation of present-day Marxists in Communist countries and that of the early Christians: his book was written soon after the re-imposition of authoritarian Communism in 1968. There is the obvious similarity between the way in which the early Christians had to come to terms with the non-appearance of the second coming and the disillusionment of Marxists with the advent of 'true communism' seeming as distant as ever. Marxism has no models for failure, disappointment and tarnished ideals whereas the history of Christianity is rife with such experience and ways of coping with them. More interestingly, Machovec recognises that whereas many Biblical stories, such as the Good Samaritan, seemed to the early socialists to be merely reactionary forms of individualist charity, the taking over of these enterprises by the State has made them more relevant. Age-old human egoism, Pharisaism and cowardice have reappeared in new disguises. Thus if the Marxist of 150 years ago opened the Bible at all, after a few pages he would be saying to himself: 'Heaven, animals, paradise, sin, Eve with nothing on – this is all tedious mythology, a fairy story, an old wives' tale.' But today, after his experiences in established socialist society, the Marxist can read the same pages of the Bible and, without finding reasons why he ought immediately to become a Christian, approve of the question 'Where is your brother Abel?' and find it highly relevant and interesting. He sees more in the Bible, is more understanding and less critical, less put off by the 'mythological' element.[30]

It should be added that the efforts of such as Kolakowski, Gardavsky and Machovec have not found any echo in the Communist authorities. All three were deprived of their teaching posts shortly after the 'springtime' of 1968.

3. WESTERN EUROPEAN MARXISM

In Western Europe, the developing Marxist–Christian dialogue tended to centre around the existence of relatively strong Communist Parties. In West Germany there was no Communist Party and the developing interest of Christian thinkers there in Marxism had to look abroad for its interlocutors. Between 1965 and 1967 a group of German-speaking theologians and scientists calling themselves the *Paulusgesellschaft* held three successive meetings with Marxists at Salzburg, Chiemsee and Marienbad. The debates, which revolved around the idea of humanism, were chiefly concerned with opening up some sort of dialogue with revisionist

Marxists in Eastern Europe;[31] and it is significant that the Warsaw Pact invasion of Czechoslovakia in 1968 precluded any further such meetings. Nevertheless, the influence of Marxism on German theology was profound. The theology of hope associated with Jürgen Moltmann and the political theology of Johannes Metz set out to challenge existing reality by anticipating and to some extent creating a new reality. They owe a great debt to Bloch and such Frankfurt School authors as Adorno, Marcuse and Habermas.

In France, Spain and Italy, by contrast, the attitude of the Communist Parties to religion was a more practical problem. The Communist Parties of Western Europe, forced into some sort of compromise with the capitalist societies in which they were operating, evolved a more conciliatory approach to religion than their Eastern counterparts. Already in 1945, the Italian Communist Party had accepted, in its Constitution, that religious belief was no bar to Party membership. In 1962 the PCI went further and accepted, at its Tenth Congress, the view that 'we have to understand that the aspiration for a socialist society can not only find a place among men who have a religious faith but that it can also find a stimulus in the religious conscience itself confronted with the dramatic problems of the contemporary world.'[32] Indeed, its General Secretary, Palmiro Togliatti, declared soon afterward that religious belief would find a place in a future Communist society not merely as a legacy from the past but as a positive force for constructing the future. Even the less adventurous French Communist Party went as far as to say: 'Increasingly numerous are the Christians who conclude that a society based on the exploitation of man and subject to the law of profit is incompatible with the demands of their faith; they commit themselves to fight for a socialist France and find themselves beside the Communists.'[33]

The leading theoretical exponent of this view during the 1960s was the French Marxist, Roger Garaudy. Following the tradition of Bloch and Goldmann, Garaudy – together with the Italian Marxists Lombardo-Radice and Luporini – has tried, in his critical approach to Christianity, to embody in his Marxism its critical insights. Garaudy distinguished in Marx himself two attitudes towards religion. The first – encapsulated in a specific interpretation of the phrase 'opium of the people' – saw religion as an illusion which distracted believers from improving their material life. The other strand in Marx was the view of religion as 'the expression of real suffering and the protest against real suffering'.[34] This second view (which Garaudy took up in direct opposition to Soviet commentators) could be used to rescue Marxism from the danger of a one-dimensional approach. For Christianity asked questions of abiding importance and provided a symbolic language to express the deepest of human aspirations, together with a radical judgement on the insufficiency – to date at least – of all human achievements. Although Garaudy's approach was ultimately reductionist in that he believed some form of Marxism to contain the meaning of history, he was concerned to play down atheism as an essential component and to emphasise the possible contribution of Christianity to a common humanism which had room for concepts such as creativity, love and transcendance. If Marxism *was* atheistic, then this was due not to any materialist dogma, but to its humanism which could only be successful in the future if that future were viewed as an entirely human responsibility rather than – as in Christianity – in some way guaranteed by God. In this, he was followed by the Czech writers Gardavsky and Machovec.

Garaudy eventually abandoned Marxism: the line between his Marxist humanism and some form of religious belief was never very distinct. The rise of neo-structuralist Marxism, however, with its declared anti-humanism seemed to leave little scope for anything but the categorisation of religion as an ideology. Certainly Althusser's talk of the dissolution of man and his attack on the idea of the subject do contradict many Christian conceptions.[35] However, his strong separation of science from ideology does leave space for religion as the latter. This recalls the room left for religion by neo-Kantian versions of Marxist science.[36] And Althusser is more definite than most Marxists in his assertion of the continuing need for religion as a mass ideology in future communist society.[37] Some Christians have seen structuralism in general as little more than the ideology of an advanced industrial society reflecting in its own analysis the elimination of the subject achieved by the progress of bureaucracy and technology: and Althusser's neo-structuralist reading of Marx could appear to be a peculiarly subtle intellectual justification of the French Communist Party's accommodation to its Stalinist past and its current revolutionary impotence. Others, however, have welcomed his approach and tried to apply it in their research. The Althusserian distinction between 'domination' and 'determination' has enabled some of his followers to account for the power of religion in feudal society. Under capitalism, on this account, the economy is both dominant and determining as the laws of the market force the property-less worker to sell his or her labour-power; under feudalism, however, the relative independence of the peasantry required a dominant politico-religious ethos to ensure their subordination.[38] These accounts are, however, exceptionally vague both in their conflation of politics and religion and in their indifference as to what people believed and how many actually believed it. This disregard for empirical history and any form of subjectivity is also evident in Fernando Belo's *A Materialist Reading of the Gospel of Mark*,[39] the *ne plus ultra* of Althusserian Marxist analysis in the field of religion. The declared aim of Belo's book is to show 'the possibility of analyzing the Christian phenomenon in the epistemological field of historical materialism'.[40] In order to achieve this he deploys an array of Althusserian concepts even more abstract than those of their originator. Belo then analyses the Old Testament into two distinctive systems: a priestly system revolving around concepts of pollution and a deuteronomistic, prophetic system concerned with ideas of debt. He then describes Palestine in the first century AD as an instance of a sub-asiatic mode of production. The bulk of the book is a structuralist reading of Mark virtually impenetrable to those without a degree in semiotics. Although occasionally stimulating and insightful, it is difficult to see what is Marxist or even materialist about much of Belo's exegesis. He deplores the absence of sociological analysis of early Christianity in what he calls 'bourgeois' exegesis, but he fails to provide any himself. Indeed, he stands materialism, as ordinarily understood, on its head by declaring that

> classical exegesis, because its attention is so much focused on the real, historical 'referent' of the text being analysed, goes astray in its reading and quite often ends up by causing the materiality of the text to disappear from view. For that kind of exegesis, the *history* (not the narrative) is the important thing.[41]

What really interests Belo are the narrative codes of the New Testament which he discusses with great subtlety: when it comes to properly Marxist concepts such as the Asiatic mode of production, state monopoly capitalism or the class struggle, Belo takes them completely on trust without any indication of the theoretical or empirical difficulties that they notoriously contain. In the interaction between Marxism and structural linguistics, it is Marxism which has been dissolved.[42]

4. MARXISM AND CHRISTIANITY IN LATIN AMERICA

In considering the liberation theology of Latin America, we move from a critique of Christianity offered by Marxists to a reformulation of Christianity by Christians who are either Marxists themselves or strongly influenced by the Marxist tradition. In the early 1970s, the idea of theology based on the materialist conception of history was only tentatively advanced by a few. By the end of the decade, however, there were a growing number of Christians who not only professed themselves to be Marxists but also considered their Marxism to be an indispensable part of their Christianity.

In its origin in the early 1960s, liberation theology was mainly a clerical movement of younger theologians whose studies in Europe had led them to abandon traditional Thomism in favour of biblical and patristic sources and the 'salvation history' contained therein. They were also influenced, on their own continent, by such works as *Pedagogy of the Oppressed* by the Brazilian educator Paolo Freire and the various polemics of Ivan Illich from the Intercultural Centre for Documentation at Cueurnavaca in Mexico. The Second Vatican Council (1961–5) appeared to give official blessing to aspirations for Church renewal – a process which reached its Latin American high point in 1968 when the Second Conference of Latin American bishops meeting at Medellin in Columbia proclaimed its 'option for the poor'. The countries who have made the biggest contribution to liberation theology are Argentina, Uruguay, Chile, Peru and Brazil – which has more Catholics than any other country in the world. And it will come as no surprise that, in such a continent-wide movement, there are very diverse currents. Liberation theology is supported by a significant – though definitely minoritarian – part of the episcopate, including such notable figures as Helder Camara, Archbishop of Recife in Brazil. Its theologians vary from the Columbian Camillo Torres, who felt he could best fulfil his priestly vocation by joining the guerillas, was killed by the security forces, and has become something of a martyr of the Left, to the decidedly more nuanced writings of the Peruvian Jesuit Gustavo Guttierez whose *Theology of Liberation* is the best selling of liberation theology books – the most magisterial being the multi-volume works of Juan Luis Segundo. What unites all these currents is the use of apparently Marxist categories to achieve critical self-renewal.

Lenin is reported as saying that 'only Communism and Catholicism offered two diverse, complete and inconfusible conceptions of human life'.[43] But he reckoned without the experience of Latin America which is the only continent to have been both Christian and colonised. Christian Europe was never colonised and other colonised continents have not, on the whole, been Christian. After centuries of domination and oppression, first by Spain and later by the United States, the increased industrialisation and urbanisation produced, in the 1930s, populist movements demanding democratic control over social and economic policies. The failure of these movements in post-war Latin America and the growing influence of multi-national corporations allied to repressive and unrepresentative ruling groups led to greater radicalisation of opposition, a radicalisation helped both by the success of the Cuban revolution and by the decline in power and cohesion of the traditional Communist Parties.

From the point of view of Latin America, therefore, much if not all European theology of the last five decades has been unconsciously compromised by its involvement with political and social oppression.

> It would be no exaggeration to say [writes one powerful advocate of this view] that in many respects it [modern European theology] is really a theological ideology in that many facets of it remain unseen by virtue of its origins, just as we are unable to see the further side of the moon simply because we are inhabitants of planet earth.[44]

Living in an exploited and dependent continent where the violence implicit in much of the domination is sanctioned, and often practised, by the established order, Latin American liberation theologians are more radical than even the most 'progressive' theologies produced in the West. For they reject the secularising theology which accepts the autonomy of modern profane society since they regard this acceptance as little more than an uncritical acquiescence in what, seen from Latin America, is an essentially oppressive system. Even the political theology emanating from Germany is criticised for being too abstract and, in effect, reformist as it refuses to opt for socialism on the grounds that an eschatological perspective necessarily relativises all political options. There is a striking parallel here with Trotsky's theory of permanent revolution, according to which the very backwardness of Russia and therefore the lack of a strong bourgeois ethos meant that it could bypass any prolonged period of capitalism and move rapidly towards socialism. Similarly, the very under-development of Latin America provides a revolutionary transformation not open to the more staid societies of Europe, both East and West.

Latin American theology has therefore attempted to integrate into its reflection the whole tradition of historical materialism and develop a theology which is both critical and materialist. This has involved a move away from the focus on humanism which dominated both Western theology from 1930 to 1960 and also the Marxist–Christian dialogue in post-war Eastern Europe. In the decades preceding the mid-1960s, progressive theology had defined itself in terms of the tradition of existential philosophy from Pascal through Kierkegaard to Heidegger and Sartre. This existential theology, typified by Bultmann and Tillich, concentrated on the salvation of the individual human being and embodied an ethics which concentrated on absolute respect for the human person – a point of view which East European Marxists, faced with the oppressive bureaucracies of state socialism, obviously found attractive. But from the Latin American perspective such an outlook tended to oscillate between very general notions of humanity and specific individuals, both of which poles seemed increasingly to be idealist and abstract. Individuals could only be treated as real-life persons through the mediation of the social and the political, to which an interpretation of Christianity as a historical doctrine could give due weight. The general influence of structuralism made appeals to essential human nature seem old-fashioned and tame. Talk about 'man as such' was on the wane as an unreal intellectual concept to be replaced by reference to identity in terms of sex, class, race and language. This rejection of traditional humanism was typified by Sartre's revision of his earlier views and his attempts to come to terms with Marxism which he declared to be 'the philosophy of our time'.[45] What Aristotle had been to the twelfth and thirteenth centuries, Marx was to many contemporary theologians. The Marxist hypothesis seemed to be the most comprehensive approach to the human sciences and thus a necessary preliminary for a contemporary theology. And by the time this realisation took place, Marxist humanism was itself on the defensive in face of more structuralist versions. Indeed, the Althusserian reading of Marx can claim a longer lasting influence in Latin America than elsewhere. This is partly due to two factors. Firstly, the time when Marxism began to have a profound impact on theology was the same time that Althusser's ideas were at their most popular in the Latin countries of Europe. Secondly, this interpretation, with its talk of 'relatively autonomous levels', etc., explicitly left room (of a sort) for religious belief. The much vaunted 'scientificity' of Althusser also made it seem more neutral than other forms of Marxism. The essential passivity of this type of approach was less appreciated.

This rejection of traditional humanism was particularly appropriate for Latin American theology. The idea of there being a 'third way' between capitalism and socialism, an idea propounded by the Christian Democratic parties, had proved incapable of seriously modifying the gross inequalities of Latin American society and challenging the ravages of capitalism. Given the blatancy of this exploitation, the dialogue between Marxists and Christians took on a different tone from that in Europe: whereas in Europe the dialogue was about general and ultimate questions, the pressing challenges of Latin America forced the participants to concentrate on more particular and penultimate problems. Particularly in Latin America,

> current political theology is opting for a knowledge of historical reality with the same care and attention that scholastic theology paid to the most subtle metaphysical distinctions and that existentialist theology paid to the analysis of depth psychology. Gospel message and political happening serve as principles of mutual interpretation.[46]

In Europe, two almost self-contained conceptual systems confronted each other and, on comparison between them, conclusions were drawn concerning the possibility of co-operation; in Latin America, common experience of the practical problems of confronting oppression and exploitation came first and the theoretical reflexion on them came second. The words of Kautsky have been taken to heart: 'a man who has learnt to live in the feelings and aspirations of the proletariat, fighting by their side, may lay claim to an ability to understand many things about the beginnings of Christianity more easily than scholars who have viewed the proletariat only from afar.'[47]

This emphasis on practice and experience is one of the main aspects of Marxism that Latin American Christians have used to evaluate and transform their religious heritage. As a leading exponent has put it:

Perhaps one of the deepest coincidences between a non-dogmatic Marxism and an authentically Biblical Christianity lies precisely in this, that both have an absolutely peculiar relation to truth. Both of them demand that their truth be 'verified', that it 'become true', that it be fulfilled. They demand to be confirmed by the facts. They conceive of truth as truth in the facts and it is precisely in this that they stand opposed to all forms of idealism, metaphysics or ideology that understand truth as something 'in itself', outside the facts, in a 'separate realm'.[48]

Here the impact of Marx's *Theses on Feuerbach* cannot be over-estimated. From the Latin American point of view, much previous Western theology of the 'death of God' variety, with its concentration on humanism and the individual, derived its inspiration from Feuerbach and thus seemed static and ultimately conservative compared to the practical, revolutionary emphasis of Marx. The liberation theologians are convinced that basic revolutionary change is necessary. And their presupposition is that 'the socioanalytical tools, the historical horizon of interpretation, the insight into the dynamics of the social process, and the revolutionary ethos and programme which Marxism has either received and appropriated or itself created are, however corrected or reinterpreted, indispensable for revolutionary change.'[49]

It is as well to stress that the liberation theologians do not wish to demonstrate any straightforward congruence between Marxism and Christianity. An example of such an approach would be two books by the Mexican theologian Miranda entitled *Marx and the Bible* and *Marx against the Marxists*. In the first work, Miranda attempts to document a convergence of views between the Bible and Marx and thus finds in the former the roots of Marx's own approach. This is achieved by emphasising the moral aspects of Marx's thought and finding affinities and parallels in the Bible in terms of rather broad concepts such as justice, egotism, love, etc. The conclusion is that 'Marx belonged to the category of the prophets of Israel, and . . . both his messianism and his passion for justice originated in the Bible', for 'both Marx and the biblical writers believe that man can cease being selfish and merciless and self-serving and can find his greatest fulness in loving his neighbour.'[50] In his latest work, subtitled 'The Christian Humanism of Karl Marx', Miranda emphasises 'the explicit, normative humanism'[51] of Marx and arrives at the surprising deduction that 'if Marx's fundamental and thorough-going criticism of capitalism centres around the fact that capitalism does not respect human being as persons, as real subjects and agents, then this analysis turns out to be eminently Christian.'[52] This idea of the assimilation of Marxism and Christianity on the basis of an alleged common moral stance, is explicitly rejected by liberation theology. Theirs is a much more critical enterprise – the reinterpretation of traditional Christian ideas through a rigorous application of the Marxist materialist conception of history which is more fruitful than Western Christian commentators on Marx have realised.[53] The gospel of love may be the general framework of aspiration underlying all human activity: but what the gospel will require in practice – for example, class strife and violence – will be decided by theoretical analysis of a Marxist type. Thus there is no specifically *Christian* politics or social theory.

The most general impact of Marxism on liberation theology is the self-critical, self-reflexive attitude which they both share. Thus the first target of liberation theology self-criticism is the involvement of the Latin American Church in the social and political structures that have compounded the domination and oppression of the mass of the people. For 'an awareness of the need for self-liberation is essential to a correct understanding of the liberation process. It is not a matter of "struggling for others", which suggests paternalism and reformist objectives, but rather of becoming aware of oneself as not completely fulfilled and as living in an alienated society.'[54] This self-critical attitude rules out any dogmatic interpretation of the Christian faith. The immobility of dogma inevitably serves to sanctify the present order of things, whereas Christian faith is inherently critical and subversive.

More specifically, liberation theology has re-evaluated the Old Testament to which, as Ernst Bloch pointed out, all Christian rebels have appealed. As opposed to Pascal, who contrasted the carnality of the Old Testament with the spirituality of the New, liberation theology sees the earthy realism of the Old Testament – and particularly the Exodus – as a paradigm of political liberation. According to Guttierez, 'the liberation of Israel is a political action. It is the breaking away from a situation of despoliation and misery and the beginning of the construction of a just and fraternal society.'[55] The Exodus from Egypt, a country which was the home of a sacred monarchy, reinforces the idea that faith desacralises creation: the Exodus is 'the desacralisation of social praxis which from that time on will be the work of man'.[56] Talking of the Exodus in words that echo the master/slave dialectic of Hegel, Jean Cardonnel states: 'The concrete experience of liberation is the only way to discover the fact of creation. It is the only deeply lived experience of oppression that prompts man to work toward his radical liberation, in which process he can come to discover that the world is a creation.'[57]

Similarly in its interpretation of the Gospel narratives, liberation theology is concerned to discover themes that find in Jesus's political messianism suggestive symbols and signposts rather than specific examples to imitate. Unlike such commentators as Engels or Kautsky, they are not concerned to link Jesus directly with the contemporary revolutionary movement of the Zealots. The picture of Jesus as an armed guerrilla fighter is not essential for liberation theology. It is clear that Jesus was engaged in active opposition to political authority. But the main point is that, for Jesus, the liberation of the Jewish people was only part of a universal revolution with more profound and permanent consequences than could be encompassed by the political liberation of a single people.

More generally, liberation theology, under the impact of Marxist approaches, wishes to relativise the concepts in which the Bible is expressed and accord them no more permanent authority than it does to biblical cosmology. It seeks to give a social and political dimension to traditional Christian concepts which tend to have become 'privatised'. The injunction to love your enemy, for example, no longer involves a vague universal good will: 'Love does not mean that oppressors are no longer enemies, nor does it eliminate the radicalness of the combat against them. 'Love of enemies' does not ease tensions; rather it challenges the whole system and becomes a subversive formula.'[58] Returning to the Marxist tradition which saw early Christianity as the religion of the oppressed, 'poverty' is not something spiritual or individual, but implies solidarity with the poor and a protest *against* poverty. And salvation is viewed, at least in the first instance, as liberation from specific social and political oppression. What is clearly evident in all these changes of perspective, is the influence of the Marxist criticism of any individual morality divorced from the social and economic framework.

Liberation theologians are not to be confused with advocates of a 'secular theology' which is seen by them as little more than the ideology of and advanced industrial society where a private faith conforms with society as it is. Unlike the secular theologians, liberation theology rejects the present order of things but in a revolutionary, not an escapist, manner. Its 'liberation' is one which takes root in a close analysis of the present. Class struggle and violence are not *advocated*: they are recognised as being present facts. In its emphasis on the practical problems of oppression and exploitation, liberation theology echoes the words of the young Marx: 'Self-understanding . . . by an age of its struggles and wishes. This is a task for the world and for us. It can only be the result of united forces. What is at stake is a confession, nothing more. To get its sins forgiven, humanity only needs to describe them as they are.'[59]

In a famous statement, Che Guevara declared:

Christians must definitely decide for revolution, particularly in our continent, where the Christian faith is so important among the masses of the people. When Christians will dare to give a total revolutionary testimony, the Latin American revolution will be invincible, because until now Christians have allowed their doctrine to be instrumentalised by reactionaries'.[60]

In response to this call, many Christians in Latin America have indeed developed a distinctly revolutionary testimony. Their efforts have been dismissed as simply persuasive but insubstantial rhetoric in which, in the words of a recent commentator, 'happy-sounding metaphors are stretched across biblical and Marxist categories, in which the *anawim* becomes the proletariat, liberation becomes redemption politicised, alienation is original sin, and even, I have heard, the priesthood is metamorphosed into Leninist revolutionary leadership.'[61] But this is to mistake the *genre*: much liberation theology is poetry and celebrates the life and work of Christ in *chansons de geste* which parallel the Old Testament psalmist's *chansons de geste* about God.[62] This poetic tinge – itself, of course, often culled from current liturgical practice – has enabled a realisation of alienation and oppression (and therefore resistance to it) to take place from within religious consciousness among people who would be quite untouched by the rational tones of a pure Marxist discourse. Indeed, this form of Christianity has succeeded in reintroducing into Marxism the utopian element by giving a real framework for the judgement of Marcuse: 'What is denounced as "utopian" is no longer that which has "no place" and cannot have any place in the historical universe, but rather that which is blocked from coming about through the power of established societies.'[63]

These theologians wish to use Marx to go beyond Marx, many of whose views they consider to be too narrow and one-dimensional, reflecting a bourgeois mentality inside a closed capitalist system.[64] Of course, many Christians have thought some liberation theology – particularly the later works of Girardi and the Chilean-inspired Christians for Socialism movement – to be too Marxist to be Christian.[65] But it is at least obvious that Marxism contains certain views that some versions of (thereby impoverished) Christianity have ceased to propagate: of human beings as essentially social, of solidarity with the poor and outcast, of taking history seriously, and of looking towards the future. And liberation theology has been concerned to return these dimensions to Christianity. It raises the central problem of whether – to turn the matter round – this incorporation of Marxism is thereby to impoverish *that* tradition – one of the questions to which the last chapter is devoted.

Conclusion: Marxism and Religion

What are we to make of the Marxist accounts of religion rehearsed in the previous chapters? What is, or should be, the relationship of Marxism to religion? Before I try to sketch the framework of an answer, one obvious preliminary question to pose is whether Marxism is not itself some sort of religion. Certainly a whole range of commentators have asserted that Marx himself was a religious thinker and have characterised Marxism in religious terms. Of course, I am well aware that the question itself is obscure or, at the very least, conceptually complex. What sort of religion is being referred to here and what do we mean by 'religion' anyway? Equally, what sort of Marxism is being referred to here and is there some describable essence or core of Marx's thought and that of his followers? In a very vague sense, there is obviously some connexion, if not continuity, between Marx and the Judaeo-Christian tradition. Marx was, after all, a Jew and his Jewishness, it might be thought, must have had some sort of effect on this thought. Equally, Marx was deeply imbued with the cultural heritage of Western Europe – a heritage which had itself been informed by Christianity for many centuries. To take only the most obvious example, Hegel's whole system can be seen as an attempt to adapt Protestant Christianity to the *Zeitgeist*. And inasfar as Marx is viewed as a disciple of Hegel, the filiation of ideas is clear.

Nevertheless, what I do wish to contest is the overly facile and conceptually unrigorous assimilation of Marxism and religion. Karl Popper, for example, affirms the religious character of Marx's thought on the basis of its being what he calls an 'oracular philosophy'.[1] Berdiaev tells us that

> if communism is opposed to all religion, it is less in the name of the social system that it embodies than because it is itself a religion. For it wishes to be a religion fit to replace Christianity, it claims to answer the religious aspirations of the human sort and give a meaning to life. Communism sees itself as universal, it wishes to control all existence and not simply some of its aspects.[2]

Again, Pareto, with a psychological reductionism typical of so many of these approaches, calls socialism a 'lay religion', a non-rational faith of the lower classes. And, finally, Schumpeter declares categorically:

> Marxism is a religion. To the believer it presents, first, a system of ultimate ends that embody the meaning of life and are absolute standards by which to judge events and actions; and secondly a guide to those ends which implies a plan of salvation and the indication of the evil from which mankind, or a chosen section of mankind, is to be saved.[3]

This sort of judgement is often coloured by political or religious prejudice: the ecclesiastically minded present Marxism as an *ersatz*-religion attempting to usurp the place of true religion; the anti-ecclesiastical wish to place Marxism in the same category as religion, which is seen as irrational, based on myth, and the enemy of civilised progress. It should be noted in passing that the equation of Marxism and religion is occasionally made even by Marxists who wish to incorporate into their Marxism the element of aspirational faith.[4]

All the above quoted characterisations of Marx and Marxism tend to be rather impressionistic. A fuller version of Schumpeter which is also conceptually more rigorous is that of Robert Tucker in his *Philosophy and Myth in Karl Marx*. Tucker finds parallels between Marxism and post-Augustinian Christianity in at least four respects. Firstly they both aspire to a total account of the world: 'Like medieval Christianity, Marx's system undertakes to provide an integrated, all-inclusive view of reality, an organization of all significant knowledge in an interconnected whole, a frame of reference with which all possible questions of importance are answered or answerable.'[5] Secondly, both Marxism and Christianity view all experience as historical – a story with a beginning, middle and end. Thirdly, the main theme of this story is that of salvation or redemption in Christianity to which, according to Tucker, the Marxian idea of the revolutionary regeneration of humanity is strongly analogous. Finally, both systems contain the idea of the unity of theory and practice where the faith/works complex of mediaeval Christianity parallels Marx's revolutionary praxis.

Tucker's view relies almost exclusively on Marx's early writings and therefore neglects the possibility of any break – or even development – in Marx's thought, as well as Marx's savage repudiation of the many equations of socialism and religion made in his own time.[6] Moreover, Tucker's approach amounts to characterising almost any form of totalitarianism (if Marxism be such) – or even any 'ism' at all – as religious. But a satisfactory analysis of the relation of Marxism to religion is only forthcoming, if at all, through the use of rather more rigorous definitions which are necessarily prescriptive and therefore essentially contestable. It is from this point of view that I want to deny that Marx was a religious thinker and that it is appropriate to regard Marxism as a religion. For such a characterisation of Marxism as religious tends to do an injustice, through conceptual wooliness, both to Marxism and to religion. To Marxism, because it does not take seriously either its own self-description or the clear implications of its science of society. To religion because it tends to rob it of its essential transcendence by subjecting it to currently fashionable secularising trends. Of course, this whole area tends to be bedevilled by problems of definition and the word 'religion' is being used loosely in my discussion to refer to what the Marxists under discussion had in mind when *they* were referring to religion – of which the model would be some sort of mainstream Christianity.[7] If the conception of religion is broadened, as in much anthropological literature of Durkheimian inspiration, then the equation of Marxism and religion becomes too vague to be useful; though it should still be noted that, even on the most functionalist account of things, there are certain functions of religion that Marxism is simply not equipped to fulfil.[8] So let us now turn to the slightly more tractable question of what might be meant by 'Marxism' in this context.

There is one sense in which there are obviously close parallels between Marxism and religion – the sense in which both terms can be descriptions of mass movements. As such they share traits that almost any mass movement that persists for a considerable length of time will exhibit. The Communist Party and the Catholic Church, for example, are both characterised by the same sort of hierarchical organisation, the same attachment to sacred texts, the same penchant for dogma, and the same keen attention to heresy. But looked at rather as a body of ideas and attitudes, most versions of Marxism clearly resist assimilation to religion. Let us consider three versions. Firstly, Marxism is seen by some of its exponents as simply a science of society, a description of how society works. This view

became the dominant interpretation of Marxism before the First
World War and was well expressed by Kautsky at the end of his
book on ethics:

> Neither can social democracy as the organisation of the proletariat
> in its class struggle do without the moral ideal, without moral
> revulsion against exploitation and class domination. But this ideal
> can gain no assistance from scientific socialism. . . . Of course, in
> socialism the researcher is also a fighter. . . . Thus, for example,
> in a Marx the working of a moral ideal breaks through in his
> scientific research but he is always at pains, and rightly so, to
> banish it from his work, in as far as it is possible. . . . Science has
> only to do with the knowledge of necessity.[9]

On this view – also favoured by many of the theologians of liberation
– Marxism is simply an instrument of analysis with no pretension to
answer many of the questions raised by religion. And it would be
extremely difficult to regard this rather jejune version of Marxism as
a religion – any more than it would be easy to regard Durkheim's or
Weber's analyses as such.[10]

But there is a second version of Marxism that is more ambitious
than a simple theory of society. Here Marxism is indeed well on the
way to becoming a total view of the world, a *Weltanschauung*. This
version of Marxism begins with Engels's *Anti-Dühring*, is
extensively worked at in the official Soviet doctrine of dialectical
materialism, and contains a metaphysical doctrine about what exists
– only matter in one form or another. The objects of religious
discourse do not exist and to believe that they do is simply
erroneous. The judgements passed in dialectical materialism are not
functional but ontological. They are rooted in the tradition of British
empiricism or French positivism which sees religious statements as
either false or meaningless. The simple and uncompromising
materialism of this version of Marxism is clearly incompatible with
religious belief but, paradoxically, is precisely the kind of Marxism
that those who describe Marxism as a religion have most in mind.

But these versions – Marxism as a theory of society or as dialectical
materialism – contrast with the general approach of Marx himself
who was much more in line with the views of Nietzsche or Freud,
where religion was viewed as a symptom with meaning that needed
deciphering through some kind of 'genealogy'. In such a Marxism
the concepts of alienation and emancipation play a central role and

the account of Marxism as a secularised form of the Judaeo-Christian tradition gains in plausibility.[11] Marxism obviously contains the idea that history has a purpose that is being relentlessly worked out and a powerful vision of future harmony to contrast with present discord. Marx's thought has an eschatological dimension which has strong religious roots. But a conception of the world can have a religious origin without itself being religious. While it may be just about possible to count Feuerbach among the theologians, to put Marx there as well is to disregard his trenchant criticism for the whole Feuerbachian approach. Nor will it do to say that Marxism's anti-religious stance is merely a product of local circumstances and not of its essence. It is, of course, true that Marx's account of religious alienation is born out of the extreme Lutheranism of his time, that Engels's views bear the stamp of the grim Pietism rife in the Wuppertal of his boyhood, and that even Lenin's vitriolic remarks are understandable in the context of the virtually total subordination to Tsarist autocracy of the contemporary Russian Orthodox Church. But the Marxist critique of religion goes beyond mere historical contingency. It is possible to claim that Marxism inherits major themes from Christianity, but the type of inheritance implies, here as in most cases, the death of the testator. Marxism may, in some sense and in some aspects, be a secularised religion, but it remains secularised and it should be treated in its own categories and not re-translated back into religious ones.

If, then, Marxism can be legitimately counterposed to religion, how valid is its account thereof? Before attempting a general evaluation of the Marxist critique of religion, it may be useful to attempt to bring out the specificity of the Marxist approach by comparing it with that of the other two great founding fathers of sociology: Durkheim and Weber.

There are several striking similarities between the Marxist approach and that of Durkheim. This is not surprising, given that both Marx and Durkheim attempted to synthesise the German philosophical tradition with French politics and classical political economy – with Durkheim more influenced by his native French positivism and Marx by his Hegelian background. Durkheim saw history as a progressive evolution and was sympathetic to socialism. Like Marx, he admired Saint Simon and sought an interpretation of society that would deal with the problems created by the impact of capitalism. Durkheim, too, held to a unity of theory and practice (albeit in a positivist framework) and was even more determinist than Marx on his application of the formula that social being determines consciousness.

But this same social being was viewed very differently by Durkheim and Marx. While locating, like Marx, the source of religion in the social structure, Durkheim saw religion as always a source of social integration. Marx saw religion as sometimes, indeed usually, such a source but he was much more interested in tracing the origins of social conflict. Durkheim's attitude can, therefore, seem more bland, with no analysis of exploitative economic relations, no account of the class and group conflict to be found in Marx who was interested in the relationship of human beings to their environment rather than treating the social structure as a given. Durkheim foresaw no violent revolution: modern society, he thought, could – eventually – cope with the problems of anomie and disintegration. He saw the form of religion and the form of society as being, in some sense, identical, whereas Marx viewed religion as a transformation, indeed a deformation, of reality. Thus for Marx religion was an alienating force to be transcended in the near future rather than understood as a constant source of social integration. Durkheim therefore attributed much more importance to religion than did Marx and to talk of Durkheim as a reductionist is possibly misleading. In his most considered comment on historical materialism, he said:

In showing that religion is something essentially social, we do not mean to say that it confines itself to translating into another languge the material forms of society and its immediate vital necessities. It is true that we take it as evident that social life depends upon its material foundation and bears its mark, just as the mental life of an individual depends upon his nervous system and in fact his whole organism. But collective consciousness is something more than a mere epiphenomenon of its morphological basis, just as individual consciousness is something more than a simple efflorescence of the nervous system. In order that the former may appear, a synthesis sui generis of particular consciousness is required. Now this synthesis has the effect of disengaging a whole world of sentiments, ideas and images which, once born, obey laws all their own. They attract each other, repel each other, unite, divide themselves, and multiply, though these combinations are not commanded and necessitated by the condition of the underlying reality. The life thus brought into being even enjoys so great an independence that it sometimes indulges in manifestations with no purpose or utility of any sort, for the mere pleasure of affirming itself. We have shown that this is often precisely the case with ritual activity and mythological thought.[12]

These comments of Durkheim refer to the Marxism of his own day, most of which stressed economic determinism in a rather crude manner.[13] In response to the political events of this century, many Marxists have been inclined to abandon the 'economistic' version of Marxism, of which Karl Kautsky would be a prime example, and give more weight to superstructural factors, including religion. Such revisions of Marxism have often been cast in a neo-Hegelian form, with an emphasis on subject rather than structure which is far removed from Durkheim. But certain recent neo-structuralist (and heavily revisionist) versions of Marxism, on the other hand, do bear a striking resemblance to Durkheim's position[14] – for example, Poulantzas's view of the state as a symbolic expression of the unity of the social formation. This is not surprising as Durkheim has obviously been a profound influence on the development of structuralism. The appeal of versions of Marxism strongly influenced by structuralism was the product of the long post-war capitalist boom when western societies seemed by and large to be well-ordered and consensual. Paradoxically, the Durkheimian approach is well suited both to primitive societies and to very modern societies such as the USA where the civil religion of 'faith in faith' does indeed serve to promote social integration[15] and the same analysis could sometimes be applied to Communism itself in established socialist societies. Marxism, by contrast, is at its strongest in societies which are divided religiously and where there is marked group conflict – situations for which Marxism can at least offer some explanation but which are intractable on Durkheimian principles.

A more direct competitor to Marx has often been seen in Weber. For it is commonly assumed that Weber was writing in more or less direct opposition to Marx and that, in emphasising and investigating in detail the influence of religion and ideas in general, he was denying Marx's materialism and even replacing it by an idealist interpretation of history. Talcott Parsons, for example, says that Weber aimed to provide an 'anti-Marxian'[16] interpretation of modern capitalism and its genesis. Of course, it should be remembered that when Weber described his sociology of religion as an 'empirical refutation of historical materialism',[17] the historical materialism that he (like Durkheim) was referring to was presumably that of contemporary Marxists who were much more inclined, under the influence of the later Engels, to see in religion simply the passive reflection or effect of material circumstances.[18] If even Marx, when faced with such 'disciples', was irritated enough to declare himself no Marxist,[19] any talk of direct opposition of Marx to Weber is rendered problematic.

Nevertheless, there *are* obvious areas of disagreement. Marx offered few detailed analyses of religion to be compared with those of Weber. The relationship of Calvinism to capitalism is an obvious example which will be discussed below. Usually Marx's remarks are delivered *en passant* as, for example, in his apparent view that the social basis of early Christianity consisted in migrant outcasts and slaves[20] – which can be contrasted (unfavourably) with Weber's account of the early Christians as urban artisans and journeymen. And certainly there is in Weber a very close attention to the different religious conceptions of various social strata, as opposed to Marx's tendency to see religion as a lower class phenomenon. More broadly, Marx had a much more confident view of historical progress. Marx detected a logic to history, a rational scheme to historical development whose culmination in the unalienated society of socialism allowed him to make a much clearer judgement about the illusoriness of various ideologies on the grounds that they represented sectional class interests as against the soon-to-predominate interests of the proletariat as the representative of society as a whole. Weber, on the other hand, with his principled neo-Kantian distinction between fact and values, could find no overall meaning to history and had to confine himself to the various and conflicting views of historical actors.

One consequence of this difference was that Weber inclined to give a greater autonomy to religion than did Marx. He emphatically rejected the view that 'the specific nature of a religion is a simple "function" of the social stratum which appears as its characteristic bearer, or that it represents the stratum's "ideology", or that it is a "reflection" of the stratum's material or ideal interest-situation.'[21] He claimed, on the contrary, that 'however incisive the social influences, economically and politically determined, may have been upon a religious ethic in a particular case, it receives its stamp primarily from religious sources and, first of all, from the content of its annunciation and its promise.'[22] Specifically, by emphasising both the religious needs and the search for salvational meaning among marginal groups and also the role of religious specialists in self-consciously elaborating religious ideas, Weber attempted to show that these often went far beyond the mere articulation of class interests.

There is, on the other hand, a strong case for saying that, far from opposing Marx, Weber assumed him. Thus Schumpeter could say that, as far as the sociology of religion was concerned, 'the whole of Max Weber's facts and arguments fits perfectly into Marx's system.'[23] Weber was happy to locate different religious conceptions in different social strata – as in his connection of this-worldly religion with privileged classes and salvation religion with underprivileged classes.[24] And his studies of Chinese and Indian religion give strong emphasis to property and production relations. Since Weber had more respect for religion than did Marx, he was more interested in its detailed content, its internal differentiation, the sociology of its various specialists, and the ideological and psychological variables that mediated religious doctrine and economic practice. As far as modern society is concerned, Weber sometimes comes very near to describing religion as an alienation in terms that recall the young Marx: Weber's concept of 'disenchantment' was borrowed from Schiller, who was also a strong influence on Marx's early writings. This affinity with Marx is more characteristic of the later Weber: his editors have detected 'a definite drift of emphasis in his intellectual biography towards Marx.'[25] But even in his early work on the Protestant ethic, which some have taken as an intended refutation of Marx, Weber's position is ambivalent.

> It is, of course [he writes] not my aim to substitute for a one-sided materialistic an equally one-sided spiritualistic causal interpretation of culture and of history. Each is equally possible, but each, if it does not serve as the preparation, but as the conclusion of an investigation, accomplishes equally little in the interest of historical truth.[26]

The key concept that forms a bridge between Weber and Marx is that of 'elective affinity'. Thus, as Karl Lowith has put it, 'the spirit of capitalism exists for Weber only in so far as there is a general tendency towards a rational conduct of life, borne along by the bourgeois stratum of society, which establishes an elective affinity between the capitalist economy on one side and the Protestant ethic on the other.'[27] For Weber is concerned to show that elements of ideas which begin as purely religious are sifted out or 'elected' according to the affinity they have with other ideal or material interests. Weber's account of this process is sometimes very near that of Marx, who would have agreed with Weber's formulation that 'ideas are discredited in the face of history unless they point in the direction of conduct that various interests promote.'[28] The crucial difference lies in the importance that Weber attached to ideal, as well as material, interests, and in the view that these ideal interests often had their origin in particular religious conceptions that had only the most tenuous connection with the economic organisation of society.

These comparisons of Marxist approaches with those of Durkheim and Weber show once again how difficult it is to isolate a distinctively Marxist doctrine. Although traditionally historical materialism has allotted an extremely meagre place to religion, there have recently been attempts to be more accommodating. The subtlest defender of Marx's base/superstructure metaphor has recently proposed a 'restricted' form of the doctrine which

> does not say that the principal features of spiritual existence are materially or economically explained. It requires of spiritual phenomena only that they do not disrupt the material and economic sequence, and also that they do not so contribute to that sequence that it cannot be conceived as possessing the autonomy any historical materialism must assign to it.[29]

Just as many theologians began to talk of the death of God and abandon distinctions between earth and heaven, so many Marxist theorists have lost confidence in the classical base-superstructure metaphor and rigorous formulations of materialism. Nevertheless, at the very least Marxism combines two aspects: a sociology of religion which regards religion as a dependent variable – dependent on social and economic relations which involve class conflict; and, secondly, a view of religion as an 'alienation' due to disappear with the advent of a socialist society. The first is descriptive and the second is evaluative, though, as always in Marxism, they are intimately connected. Let us deal with each of them in turn.

On the more descriptive side, is it true that religion is a dependent variable? Prescinding, for the moment, from questions of definition, let us look briefly at three areas where Marxist interpretations are well to the fore: Calvinism, early Methodism, and millenarian movements. The relationship of Calvinism to capitalism is, in many ways, the *locus classicus* of the Marxist theory of religion. As emerges from the previous discussion of Marx and Weber, however, it is difficult to see whether there is any basic disagreement between them. Or rather, if there is fundamental disagreement, it seems to hinge on something more than simple descriptions of historical causation. The case of the impact of Methodism on British society in the eighteenth and early nineteenth centuries appears to be an instance of where the Marxist view of religion as caused by social deprivation has considerable support: it offers a promising example of the thesis that sects are both more 'really religious' and a lower-class phenomenon. Here there are two views with a distinctively Marxist flavour. E. P. Thompson in his *Making of the English Working Class* interprets Methodism as a compensation for failed revolutionary initiative, claiming that, in the period 1790 to 1830, 'religious revivalism took over just at the point where "political" or temporal aspirations met with defeat.'[30] However, this retrospective 'opium of the people' thesis has been strongly challenged on empirical grounds. It is directly contradicted by Hobsbawm's view[31] that political radicalism and religious revival are contemporaneous. Kiernan, on the other hand, argues that one of the chief effects of the Methodist revival was to disarm rebellion by itself becoming part of the established order. The upper classes, when faced with novel religious impulses 'move from hostility to acceptance only when an external shock comes to emphasise the dangers of internal discontent. Jacobinism, which abolished the Christian calendar in France, helped to establish the Victorian Sabbath in England.'[32] According to Kiernan, around 1800 the Evangelical revival began to be regarded by influential members of the establishment, and particularly Wilberforce, as a possible support of order and stability and thus, in this case at least, there is support for the Marxian view that religion serves, through inculcation by the ruling class, as an opium of the people and therefore an instrument of continued class domination. For in so far as society is viewed as class divided and religion as a source of social stability, then it follows that religion is an instrument of class domination. The millenarian movements, however, cannot easily be fitted into such a scheme. Analyses of Marxist inspiration, such as those of Hobsbawm and Worsley,[33] tend to see these movements as prototypes or precursors of political revolutionary movements, following the classic accounts of Münzer and the Anabaptists by Engels in his *Peasant War in Germany*. In modern societies, at any rate, millenarian movements seem to dissuade their adherents from engaging in any political activity rather than leading them towards it. Moreover, the approach of Hobsbawm and Worsley simply assumes that religion is an ideology concealing social and economic interests and thus, with Engels, undervalues the importance that doctrine and ritual may take. Their evolutionary optimism leads them, to suppose that such movements will rapidly disappear under the impact of the modernising process as their hidden (political) rationality appears.

All this suggests that Marxism, at least from a sociological point of view, has indeed made a strong contribution to our understanding of religion and society by stressing the strong support religion receives from social or economic interests. But Marxism has larger ambitions than the purely descriptive. On the face of it, we could agree with the modest Marxist description of religion as a highly dependent variable but this would not, of itself, enable us to judge of its social worth – let alone its truth. In the case, for example, of Halévy's thesis about Methodism's being an antidote to revolution, this might be regarded as in Methodism's favour – indeed Halévy did so regard it; as again, in the study of millenarian movements, Cohn's judgement of them is almost the exact opposite of Hobsbawm and Worsley, though his sociological approach is similar. Clearly, if religion were always an instrument of class domination, this might be grounds for an adverse judgement. But this is evidently not so: religion can also be a protest against domination and exploitation, 'the soul of soulless circumstances', etc. But it does not follow, for the Marxist, that there could be good religion and bad religion – just as there could be good politics or bad politics or good literature or bad literature according to its social role. For Marxism is committed to the view that all religion – unlike all politics or all literature – is an alienation, a symptom of social malformation. This in turn leads into some notion of secularisation – the possibility or inevitability of a non-religious society which is thereby more human.

This concept of secularisation has aroused extensive debate among sociologists of religion. Marx is clearly strongly committed to a strong version of it. He was much influenced by the climate of opinion in the mid-nineteenth century which suggested that religion was disappearing – and rightly so – under the impact of science both natural and social. This simplistic view was already under attack by the end of the nineteenth century when the *Zeitgeist* had changed radically – as exemplified by the work of Durkheim.[34] The mention of Durkheim immediately indicates that the whole concept of secularisation is strongly contested in that its viability depends crucially upon the broad approach adopted and the definition of religion employed. Even on as narrow a definition of religion as involving belief in supernatural beings and of religious practice as involvement in ecclesiastical organisations, the empirical evidence is by no means one-sided: it has to take into account the increasing prevalence of cults, particularly among the young, the revival of religion in the USA from the 1950s onwards, and its extraordinary resilience in the USSR. This empirical approach also depends on the assumption of a 'golden age' or religion, usually the Middle Ages. However, as Keith Thomas has said in his classic work, 'not enough justice has been done to the volume of apathy, heterodoxy and agnosticism which existed long before the onset of industrialism. . . . The hold of organised religion upon the people was never so complete as to leave no room for rival systems of belief.'[35] And even the idea that primitive human beings were particularly religious has been questioned by contemporary anthropologists.[36]

More fundamentally, definitions of religion reveal metaphysical choices. The definitions of Yinger, for example, make secularisation virtually impossible. The more nuanced approaches of Luckmann and Berger, working in the Durkheimian tradition suggest the emergence of a new form of religion rather than its complete disappearance.[37] Although it is too extreme to say, with David Martin, that secularisation is 'less a scientific concept than a tool of counter-religious ideologies',[38] it is clear that it is not a value-neutral concept. And the same is true of Marxism as a particular version of the secularisation thesis. Marxism holds there is a correlation between the advance of socialism and the decline of religion. Since socialism is the creation of the working class, it is there that irreligion should increasingly be concentrated. Even if we can discount the multi-faceted phenomenon of 'Christian socialism' as a passing stage, such a view encounters two empirical difficulties. Firstly, the irreligion of much of the western European working class is due more to the influence of bourgeois anti-clericalism and bourgeois aggressive positivism. Secondly, the working class had never originally adhered *en masse* to Christianity which had, in nineteenth-century England at least, been much more a bourgeois affair. More generally, the advent of Marxian socialism, in the West, at any rate, seems as distant a prospect as it did in Marx's day. The social and cultural integration of the working class has meant the diffusion of bourgeois culture rather than its supercession by a working class (and, in Marx's view, therefore irreligious) culture.

More fundamentally still, it might be claimed that Marxism is not radical enough in its approach to the human condition. For the Marxist picture of the centrality of production relations, and therefore of class, can be questioned. Race and (more importantly) gender have come to be seen by many as even more basic. On such a view, the emergence of black or feminist theology could render Marxist attitudes to religion distinctly beside the point. 'To be radical', wrote Marx, 'is to grasp the matter by the root. But for man the root is man himself.' For Pascal, religion was worthy of respect 'because it has known humankind well'. How well has Marxism known humankind? Marxism has often been called a Christian heresy and to be heretical is to choose or emphasise one aspect at the expense of others. Marx's heresy may consist in generalising from the function of religion in mid-nineteenth century Western Europe to the function of religion in all societies and in reducing the significance of religion to that of the economic conflicts it was held to reflect. As befitted a Rhineland intellectual, Marx conserved a strong element of enlightenment rationalism in his view of the world. This led him, and his followers, to underestimate the cognitive importance of non-rational modes of discourse. But the religious mode, like the artistic, can refresh parts that more rational modes cannot reach. Such a criticism of Marxism would not concentrate on its atheism, but on its inadequate grasp of human nature – and this not in the banal sense that socialist projects neglect some supposedly ineradicable individual self-interest. On the contrary, the criticism would be that Marxism is too narrow, too exclusive, too shortsighted in its conception of human potential. Consider the following questions that Roger Garaudy put to himself while still a Marxist:

> How could I possibly speak of a universal project for humanity and of a meaning that must be attributed to its history when millions of humans are excluded from its past, when so many

slaves and soldiers have lived and died without their lives and deaths being meaningful? How could I reconcile myself to the thought that people in the future, too, will sacrifice their lives for this new world if I were not convinced that all these are included in this new reality and so survive that they live and are resurrected in it? Either my ideal of future socialism is an abstract idea which promises to the elect of the future a victory possibly gained through the millennia-long annihilation of the masses, or things so happen that my whole action is founded on a belief in the resurrection of the dead.[39]

Marxism, in other words, addresses itself to the living, to the victors, to those who have won through: Christianity addresses itself, by preference, to the defeated, the maimed and even to the dead.

Finally, there is too facile an assumption of the disappearance of religion under communism. There is a strong parallel between the Marxist view of the transparency of human relations under communism and the Christian tradition of the disappearance of religious symbols and images in the Kingdom of God. Thus Christianity is, or should be, inherently iconoclastic. When we see through a glass darkly, the mediation of symbols and image is necessary – though always tending to lapse into anthropomorphic idolatry. Their role will disappear when we know as we are known. A common objection against Marxism is that its account of how a socialist society would function is far too vague. While this accusation is fair enough in Marxism's own terms, from a religious point of view, the opposite applies. Horkheimer drew attention to the parallel between the refusal of a description of Communism by Marx and the refusal of the Jews to name God.[40] But Marx and Marxists have *not* been as abstemious as the Jews: inherent to Marxism is the claim that the fundamental questions of meaning (the why? questions) can be solved by a reorganisation of the relations of production. But if socialism is to have a future, then it will have to go beyond any society describable in Marxist terms. As Robert Heilbroner has put it:

The ethos of a socialist socio-economic formation is . . . likely to be 'sacred' rather than 'profane', morally accountable rather than amorally expedient, fraught with spiritual significance rather than pragmatic options. . . . The ideological image of socialism, as a new socio-economic formation, seems therefore to resemble that of a religious society.[41]

Of course both Marxism and Christianity have institutionalised themselves in the past and preserve a certain nostalgia for this past in spite of its obvious failures. But their vitality lies in their strength as oppositional movements. But Marxism's whole *raison d'être*, as indicated above, lies in worldly success. Failure there is liable to be ultimately dispiriting, whereas for most religions it would serve more as a salutory (literally) warning. In Marxism's view, reason and reality must ultimately coincide. But if we take seriously Weber's observation that 'the experience of the irrationality of the world has been the driving force of all religious evolution',[42] then, however dispiriting it may be in the short term, few would dispute that there is a better future for religion than for Marxism.

Notes and References

1. Marx

1. See, for example, V. Lenin, 'Socialism and religion', *Collected Works* (Moscow, 1972) vol. 10, pp. 83f. For a more recent negative view, see B. Turner, *Religion and Social Theory* (London, 1983) pp. 76f.
2. Cp. E. Bloch, *Atheism in Christianity* (New York, 1972) pp. 58ff. and M. Bertrand, *Le statut de la religion chez Marx et Engels* (Paris, 1979) pp. 45ff.
3. See, for example, P. Frostin, *Materialismus, Ideologie, Religion* (Munich, 1978) particularly pp. 147ff.
4. Cf. J.-Y. Calvez, *La pensée de Karl Marx* (Paris, 1956) p. 22.
5. The question of whether Marx's views as a whole could be considered religious will be dealt with in the conclusion, pp. 157ff. below.
6. The characterisation of Marx's brother-in-law, Edgar von Westphalen, quoted in O. Maenchen-Helfen and B. Nicolaievsky, *Karl Marx*, 2nd edn (Frankfurt, 1963) p. 5.
7. Heinrich Marx to Karl Marx, in K. Marx and F. Engels, *Collected Works* (London, 1975ff.) vol. 1, p. 647.
8. For an extended commentary which attributes much more importance to these essays, see A. Van Leeuwen, *Critique of Heaven* (London, 1972) pp. 26ff.
9. For Hegel's views on religion, see further R. Solomon, *In the Spirit of Hegel* (New York, 1983) ch. 10.
10. K. Marx, *Selected Writings*, ed. D. McLellan (Oxford, 1977) p. 8.
11. Further on the Young Hegelians, see D. McLellan, *The Young Hegelians and Karl Marx* (London, 1969); *The Young Hegelians: An Anthology*, ed. L. Stepelevich (Cambridge, 1983).
12. K. Marx, F. Engels, *Collected Works* (London, 1975ff.), vol. 5, p. 141.
13. K. Marx, *Selected Writings*, pp. 12f.
14. See further M. Rose, *Marx's Lost Aesthetic* (Cambridge, 1984) pp. 60ff.
15. K. Marx, F. Engels, *Collected Works*, vol. 1, p. 200.
16. Ibid., p. 189.
17. Ibid., pp. 394f.
18. On Bauer and Feuerbach *op. cit.*, see D. McLellan, *The Young Hegelians and Karl Marx*, pp. 48ff., 85ff., and K. Clarkson and D. Hawkins, 'Marx on religion: the influence of Bruno Bauer and Ludwig Feuerbach on his thought and its implication for the Christian–Marxist dialogue', *Scottish Journal of Theology*, vol. 31 (Dec. 1978).
19. K. Marx, F. Engels, *Collected Works*, vol. 1, p. 395.
20. K. Marx, *Selected Writings*, pp. 43f.
21. 'Man, even when he proclaims himself an atheist through the intermediary of the state, i.e. when he proclaims the state to be atheist, still retains his religious prejudice, just because he recognizes himself

only by a detour and by the medium of something else. Religion is precisely the recognition of man by detour through an intermediary. The state is the intermediary between man and his freedom. As Christ is the intermediary onto whom man unburdens all his divinity, all his religious bonds, so the state is the mediator onto which he transfers all his Godlessness and all his human liberty'. (Ibid., p. 45.)

22. Ibid., p. 47.
23. 'What makes the members of the political state religious is the dualism between their individual life and their species-life, between life in civil society and political life, their belief that life in the state is the true life even though it leaves untouched their individuality. Religion is here the spirit of civil society, the expression of separation and distance of man from man. What makes a political democracy Christian is the fact that in it man, not only a single man but every man, counts as a sovereign being; but it is man as he appears uncultivated and unsocial, man in his accidental existence, man as he comes and goes, man as he is corrupted by the whole organization of our society, lost to himself, sold, given over to the domination of inhuman conditions and elements – in a word, man who is no longer a real species-being. The fantasy, dream, and postulate of Christianity, the sovereignty of man, but of man as an alien being separate from actual man, is present in democracy as a tangible reality and is its secular motto'. (Ibid., p. 50.)
24. Ibid., p. 56.
25. Cf. K. Marx, *Selected Writings*, pp. 59ff.
26. K. Marx, F. Engels, *Werke* (Berlin, 1965) vol. 1, p. 418. (The expression is toned down in *Collected Works*, vol. 1, p. 400.)
27. See in particular the careful account of J. Carlebach, *Karl Marx and the Radical Critique of Judaism* (London, 1976) ch. 18.
28. Cp. his remark in *The Holy Family*: 'Feuerbach . . . was the first to complete the criticism of religion', *Collected Works*, vol. 4, p. 135.
29. K. Marx, *Selected Writings*, p. 62. It is interesting to note that Marx's most famous description of religion is also his least original: parallels between religion and opium were widespread in contemporary writing. See D. McLellan, *The Young Hegelians and Karl Marx*, pp. 78f., and W. Post, *Kritik der Religion bei Karl Marx* (Munich, 1969) pp. 167ff.
30. Cf., for example, M. Bertrand, *Le statut de la religion chez Marx et Engels* (Paris, 1979) pp. 50ff.
31. K. Marx, *Selected Writings*, p. 63.
32. Ibid., p. 69.
33. 'Protestantism by turning laymen into priests emancipated the lay popes, the princes, together with their clergy, the privileged and the philistines. Similarly philosophy, by turning the priestly Germans into men, will emancipate the people. But just as emancipation did not stop with the princes, so it will not stop with the secularization of goods involved in the spoliation of the church that was above all practised by hypocritical Prussia. The peasants' war, the most radical event in German history, failed then because of theology. Today, when theology itself has failed, the most unfree event in German history, our *status quo*, will be wrecked on philosophy'. (Ibid.)

34. Ibid.
35. Ibid., pp. 72f.
36. See, for example, C. Wackenheim, *La faillite de la religion d'après Karl Marx* (Paris, 1963) p. 200.
37. E. Olssen, 'Marx and the Resurrection', *Journal of the History of Ideas* (1968) p. 136.
38. I say 'attributed' since, as Krishan Kumar has pointed out to me, what Sieyès actually said the Third Estate should be was 'something' – a much more modest claim.
39. K. Marx, *Selected Writings*, pp. 76ff.
40. Ibid., pp. 78f.
41. Ibid., p. 85.
42. Ibid., p. 90.
43. 'A being that does not have its nature outside itself is not a natural being and has no part in the natural world. A being that has no object outside itself is not an objective being. . . . A non-objective being is a non-being. Imagine a being which is neither itself an object nor has an object. . . . Such a being would be the only being, there would be no being outside it, it would exist solitary and alone. . . . But a non-objective being is an unreal, non-sensuous being that is only thought of, i.e. an imaginary being, a being of abstraction . . . atheism is humanism mediated with itself through the supersession of religion, and communism is humanism mediated with itself through the supersession of private property. Only through the supersession of this mediation, which is, however, a necessary pre-condition, does positive humanism that begins with itself come into being'. (Ibid., p. 104, 108.)
44. Ibid., p. 95.
45. Ibid., p. 95.
46. Ibid.
47. Ibid., p. 89.
48. Ibid., p. 157.
49. 'In direct contrast to German philosophy which descends from heaven to earth, here we ascend from earth to heaven. That is to say, we do not set out from what men say, imagine, conceive, nor from men as narrated, thought of, imagined, conceived, in order to arrive at men in the flesh. We set out from real, active men, and on the basis of their real life-process we demonstrate the development of the ideological reflexes and echoes of this life-process. The phantoms formed in the human brain are also, necessarily, sublimates of their material life-process, which is empirically verifiable and bound to material premisses. Morality, religion, metaphysics, all the rest of ideology and their corresponding forms of consciousness, thus no longer retain the semblance of independence. They have no history, no development; but men, developing their material production and their material intercourse, alter, along with this their real existence, their thinking and the products of their thinking. Life is not determined by consciousness, but consciousness by life. (Ibid., p. 164.)
50. K. Marx, F. Engels, *Collected Works*, p. 154.
51. K. Marx, *Selected Writings*, pp. 384ff.

52. Ibid., pp. 384ff.
53. K. Marx, *Capital*, vol. 1 (Harmondsworth, 1976) p. 176.
54. K. Marx, F. Engels, *Collected Works*, vol. 5, p. 44.
55. Ibid., p. 45.
56. Ibid., p. 56.
57. Ibid., pp. 281ff.
58. Ibid., p. 159.
59. Ibid., p. 56.
60. For Marx's antipathy towards the German clergy who tended to support workers' demands, see his letter to Engels, in *Werke*, vol. 32, p. 371.
61. This makes the reported remark of Marx that 'the religion of the workers is godless because it seeks to restore the divinity of man' unlikely to be authentic. See further, H. Desroches, *Socialismes et sociologie religieuse* (Paris, 1965) p. 201.
62. K. Marx, F. Engels, *Collected Works*, vol. 3, p. 399.
63. K. Marx, F. Engels, *Collected Works*, vol. 6, p. 45.
64. Ibid., p. 46.
65. Further on the *Circular* and its background, see H. Desroches, *Socialismes et sociologie religieuse*, pp. 298ff.
66. K. Marx, F. Engels, *Collected Works*, vol. 6, p. 231.
67. This latter point is expanded in *The Holy Family*, cf. K. Marx, F. Engels, *Collected Works*, vol. 4, pp. 172ff.
68. K. Marx, *Selected Writings*, p. 239.
69. Ibid., p. 236.
70. Ibid., p. 236.
71. Ibid., p. 237.
72. Ibid., p. 436.
73. Ibid.
74. Ibid., p. 509.
75. Ibid.
76. K. Marx, *Capital*, vol. 1 (Harmondsworth, 1976) p. 493.
77. Ibid., p. 494.
78. Ibid.
79. K. Marx, F. Engels, *Collected Works*, vol. 5, p. 154.
80. K. Marx, *Capital*, vol. 1, p. 494.
81. K. Marx, F. Engels, *Collected Works*, vol. 5, pp. 235f.
82. K. Marx, *Capital*, vol. 1, p. 375.
83. Ibid., p. 351.
84. Ibid., p. 92.
85. K. Marx, 'Anti-Church Movement', in K. Marx, F. Engels, *On Religion* (New York, 1964) p. 129.
86. K. Marx, *Capital*, vol. 1, p. 92.
87. Ibid., p. 173.
88. Cf. K. Marx, F. Engels, *Collected Works*, vol. 1, p. 189. See also his explanation of the domination of priests in Ancient Egyptian society by the necessity of using astronomy to predict the rise and fall of the Nile: *Capital*, vol. 1, p. 649.
89. K. Marx, F. Engels, *On Religion*, p. 94.

90. K. Marx, F. Engels, *Collected Works*, vol. 5, p. 189.
91. K. Marx, F. Engels, *Collected Works*, vol. 6, p. 631. It should be noted that this is from the minutes of a report that Marx gave to the German Workers Educational Association in London. But the minutes are so precise here that there is no reason to doubt their accuracy. Marx quotes as his authority Friedrich Danmer on whom he was quick elsewhere to pour scorn. See *Capital*, vol. 1, p. 400 and *On Religion*, pp. 90ff.
92. K. Marx, F. Engels, *Collected Works*, vol. 5, p. 176.
93. K. Marx, *Capital*, vol. 1, p. 176.
94. Cf. N. Poulantzas, *Political Power and Social Classes* (London, 1973) Part 2.
95. Cf. B. Turner, *Religion and Social Theory* (London, 1983) pp. 137f.
96. K. Marx, *Capital*, vol. 1, p. 907.
97. Cf. K. Marx, *Theories of Surplus Value*, vol. 3 (Moscow, 1968) pp. 527ff.
98. Cf. K. Marx, *Selected Writings*, p. 69.
99. K. Marx, *Capital*, vol. 1, p. 387.
100. Ibid.
101. K. Marx, *Capital*, vol. 3 (London, 1976) p. 592.
102. K. Marx, F. Engels, *Selected Works* (Moscow, 1962) vol. 1, p. 519.
103. Ibid.
104. K. Marx, F. Engels, *Selected Works*, vol. 2, p. 323.
105. Ibid., p. 333f.
106. Ibid., p. 351.
107. Cf. K. Marx, *On Colonialism and Modernization*, ed. S. Avineri (New York, 1968) p. 427.
108. See further T. Ling, *Karl Marx and Religion* (London, 1980) ch. 7.
109. K. Marx, *On Religion*, p. 94.
110. K. Marx, F. Engels, *Collected Works*, vol. 5, p. 56.
111. See Marx's comments on the Paris Commune in *Selected Writings*, pp. 542ff.
112. Cf. K. Marx, *Selected Writings*, pp. 121f.
113. K. Marx, *Capital*, vol. 1, p. 173.
114. Cf. G. Cohen, *Karl Marx's Theory of History: A Defence* (Oxford, 1978) pp. 326ff.

2. Engels

1. For further detail on Pietism see the very critical history of A. Ritschl, *Geschichte des Pietismus*, 3 vols. (Berlin, 1880–86). Also E. Troeltsch, *The Social Teaching of the Christian Churches*, vol. 2 (New York, 1956) pp. 686ff., 714ff.
2. Cf. F. Engels, 'Letters from Wuppertal', *Collected Works*, vol. 2, p. 10.
3. Ibid., p. 14.
4. Ibid., p. 17.
5. F. Engels to F. Graeber, 9 April 1839, *Collected Works*, vol. 2, p. 423.
6. F. Engels to F. Graeber, 23 April 1839, *Collected Works*, vol. 2, p. 426.
7. F. Engels to F. Graeber, 15 June 1839, *Collected Works*, vol. 2, p. 454.
8. F. Engels to F. Graeber, 26 July 1839, *Collected Works*, vol. 2, p. 461.

9. F. Engels to W. Graeber, 8 October 1839, *Collected Works*, vol. 2, p. 471.
10. F. Engels to W. Graeber, 20 November 1839, *Collected Works*, vol. 2, p. 486.
11. F. Engels to F. Graeber, 21 January 1840, *Collected Works*, vol. 2, p. 489.
12. Cf. D. Riazanov, Introduction to K. Marx, F. Engels, *Gesamtausgabe* (Berlin, 1927ff.) Pt I, vol. 2, pp. LXXX f.
13. Cf. F. Engels, 'The progress of social reform on the Continent', *Collected Works*, vol. 3, p. 404.
14. F. Engels to W. Graeber, 15 June 1839, *Collected Works*, vol. 2, p. 456.
15. F. Engels, 'The progress of social reform on the Continent', *Collected Works*, vol. 3, p. 406.
16. F. Engels, *Anti-Dühring* (Moscow, 1954) p. 438.
17. Ibid.
18. F. Engels, 'Ludwig Feuerbach and the end of Classical German Philosophy' in K. Marx and F. Engels, *On Religion* (Moscow, 1957) p. 225. This account is in sharp contrast to Engels's view in *Anti-Dühring*, pp. 191f., where, trying to fit the whole of human intellectual development into a single 'Hegelian' triad, he claims that animist conceptions were preceded by a materialist view of the world.
19. Cf. E. Tylor, *Primitive Culture*, 7th edn (New York, 1924) esp. ch. 11.
20. F. Engels, 'Ludwig Feuerbach, etc.', p. 261.
21. K. Marx and F. Engels, *Selected Correspondence* (Moscow, 1965) p. 423.
22. C. Lévi-Strauss, *Structural Anthropology* (New York, 1963) p. 337.
23. Cf. K. Marx and F. Engels, *Collected Works*, vol. 5, p. 44.
24. Cf. F. Engels, *The Origin of the Family, State and Private Property*, ed. E. Leacock (New York, 1973) p. 117.
25. F. Engels, 'Ludwig Feuerbach, etc.', p. 226.
26. Ibid., pp. 225f.
27. Ibid., p. 261.
28. Ibid., pp. 261f.
29. F. Engels, 'The history of early Christianity', in K. Marx and F. Engels, *On Religion*, p. 331.
30. For example, his strange remarks on comparative philology in *Anti-Dühring*, p. 438.
31. F. Engels, *The Origin of the Family*, etc., p. 154.
32. F. Engels, 'Bruno Bauer and early Christianity', *MER*, p. 194.
33. Ibid.
34. F. Engels, *The Peasant War in Germany* (London, 1969) p. 197.
35. F. Engels, 'Ludwig Feuerbach, etc.', *MER*, p. 240.
36. F. Engels, *Anti-Dühring*, p. 439. Compare Marx's much more specific linking of Christianity's 'abstractness' to the growth of commodity producing society: *Capital* (London, 1954) vol. 1, p. 79.
37. F. Engels, 'Bruno Bauer and early Christianity', *MER*, p. 252.
38. F. Engels, 'On the history of early Christianity', *MER*, p. 331.
39. F. Engels, 'Bruno Bauer and early Christianity', *MER*, pp. 201, 203; cf. also *MER*, pp. 330f.
40. Cf. F. Engels, 'Bruno Bauer and early Christianity', *MER*, p. 197. Bauer's most striking formulations of the link between the levelling effect of Roman power and the rise of Christianity are to be found in

Kritik der evangelischen Geschichte der Synoptiker (Leipzig, 1841/2), vol. 2, p. 46 and vol. 3, p. 309f. For further comment see D. McLellan, *The Young Hegelians and Karl Marx*, 2nd ed. (London, 1980) pp. 55ff., and Z. Rosen, *Bruno Bauer and Karl Marx* (The Hague, 1977) pt I, chs 6 and 8.

41. Cf. Bruno Bauer, *Christus und die Cäsaren. Der Ursprung des Christentums aus dem römischen Griechentum* (Berlin, 1877).
42. F. Engels, 'On the history of early Christianity', *MER*, pp. 321, 343.
43. See F. Engels, 'The Book of Revelation', *MER*, pp. 204ff.
44. F. Engels, 'Bruno Bauer and early Christianity', *MER*, p. 195.
45. Ibid., p. 206.
46. Cf. A. Schweitzer, *The Quest of the Historical Jesus*, 3rd edn (London, 1954) pp. 157ff. Contrast the better use made of Bauer by Mehring in his 'Moderne Evangelienkritik', *Gesammelte Schriften*, vol. 13 (Berlin, 1961).
47. See for example, W. D. Davies, *Christian Origins and Judaism* (London, 1962) and R. M. Wilson, *Gnosis and the New Testament* (New York, 1968).
48. F. Engels, 'Bruno Bauer and early Christianity', *MER*, p. 205.
49. Ibid., p. 211.
50. Cf. J. Court, *Myth and History in the Book of Revelation* (London, 1979).
51. F. Engels and K. Kautsky, 28 July 1894, in *Aus der Frühzeit des Marxismus. Engels Briefwechsel mit Kautsky* (Prague, 1935) p. 371. Also, 'Bruno Bauer and early Christianity', *MER*, p. 208 and D. Riazanov's comments in MEGA.
52. F. Engels, 'Ludwig Feuerbach, etc.', p. 238f.
53. Cf. Engels, ibid.
54. F. Engels, *Anti-Dühring*, p. 476.
55. F. Engels, 'Ludwig Feuerbach, etc.', p. 199.
56. F. Engels, *Anti-Dühring*, p. 145.
57. F. Engels, 'On the history of early Christianity', *MER*, p. 330. See also Engels to Kautsky, 28 July 1894 in *Aus der Frühzeit des Marxismus. Engels Briefwechsel mit Kautsky* (Prague, 1935) p. 371, where this is somewhat qualified.
58. F. Engels, 'On the history of early Christianity', *MER*, p. 201.
59. G. Theissen, *The First Followers of Jesus. A Sociological Analysis of the Earliest Christianity* (London, 1978) p. 46.
60. R. Grant, *Early Christianity and Society* (London, 1978) p. 11. See also pp. 79ff.
61. 'Ludwig Feuerbach, etc.' in K. Marx and F. Engels, *On Religion*, p. 262.
62. 'The condition of England', *Collected Works*, vol. 3, p. 461. Here Engels seems to view the Middle Ages as better, at least in its religion, than later centuries as the strength of mediaeval faith reinforced humanity's self-image: the later waning of faith left less substance for humanity.
63. F. Engels, 'Socialism: utopian and scientific', in *On Religion*, p. 297.
64. Ibid., p. 298.
65. F. Engels, 'Juristic socialism', *On Religion*, p. 268.
66. Cf. F. Engels, 'Ludwig Feuerbach, etc.', p. 262.
67. Compare 'Ludwig Feuerbach, etc.', p. 262 and *The Peasant War in Germany* (London, 1969) p. 45.
68. Cf. F. Engels, *The Peasant War in Germany* (London, 1969) p. 47.

69. Cf. ibid., p. 29.
70. *Aus der Frühzeit des Marxismus. Engels Briefwechsel mit Kautsky* (Prague, 1935) p. 249.
71. Contrast, however, Engels's earlier equation of Mercantilism with 'Catholic candour', Protestantism only coming to the fore with eighteenth-century capitalism: 'Outlines of a critique of political economy', *Collected Works*, vol. 3, p. 422.
72. F. Engels, *The Peasant War in Germany*, p. 7.
73. W. Zimmermann, *Der grosse deutsche Bauernkrieg*, 5th edn (Berlin, 1979) pp. 8f.
74. See the excellent discussion in A. Friesen, *Reformation and Utopia* (Wiesbaden, 1974) pp. 114ff.
75. Compare Engels's much less secular view of Münzer in 'The progress of social reform on the Continent', *Collected Works*, vol. 3, p. 400.
76. F. Engels, *The Peasant War in Germany*, p. 7.
77. Ibid., p. 47.
78. F. Engels, *Dialectics of Nature* (Moscow, 1972) p. 20.
79. Cf. K. Marx, *Capital* (Moscow, 1956) vol. 1, pp. 192, 592f.
80. F. Engels, *The Peasant War in Germany*, p. 52.
81. F. Engels, 'Socialism: utopian and scientific', *On Religion*, p. 298.
82. See, for example, P. Anderson, *Lineages of the Absolutist State* (London, 1974) pp. 15ff.
83. Cp. P. Noyes, *Organisation and Revolution; Working Class Associations in the German Revolutions of 1848/49* (Princeton, 1966).
84. An interesting modern parallel is the interpretation of the Cargo Cults, as embryonic forms of political protest. For a view which has similarities to Engels's position see P. Worsley, *The Trumpet Shall Sound* (London, 1968).
85. L. Krieger, Introduction to F. Engels, *The German Revolutions* (Chicago, 1967) pp. XLIff.
86. F. Engels, 'Socialism: utopian and scientific', *On Religion*, p. 298.
87. F. Engels, 'Ludwig Feuerbach, etc.', p. 264.
88. F. Engels, 'Socialism: utopian and scientific', *On Religion*, p. 298.
89. Ibid.
90. See e.g. M. Hill, *A Sociology of Religion* (New York, 1973) chs 5 and 6, and the literature there quoted. Also the discussion on pp. 164ff.
91. As, for example, G. Elton, *Reformation Europe 1517–1559* (London, 1963) pp. 305ff.; C. George and K. George, *The Protestant Mind of the English Reformation* (Princeton, 1961) pp. 160ff.
92. F. Engels, 'Socialism: utopian and scientific', *On Religion*, p. 299.
93. H. Trevor-Roper, *Historical Essays* (London, 1957) p. 197.
94. C. Hill, *The World Turned Upside Down* (Harmondsworth, 1972) and the literature quoted there.
95. F. Engels, 'Socialism: utopian and scientific', *On Religion*, p. 301.
96. Ibid.
97. Cf. ibid., pp. 289ff.
98. Cf. ibid., p. 302.
99. Cf. C. Macpherson, *The Political Theory of Possessive Individualism* (Oxford, 1962) esp. pp. 79ff.

100. F. Engels, 'Juristic socialism', *On Religion*, p. 268.
101. F. Engels, 'Socialism: utopian and scientific', *On Religion*, p. 302.
102. Ibid.
103. F. Engels, 'Ludwig Feuerbach, etc.', p. 264.
104. F. Engels, 'Socialism: utopian and scientific', *On Religion*, p. 302.
105. Cf. F. Engels, 'Ludwig Feuerbach, etc.', pp. 306ff.
106. F. Engels, 'Ludwig Feuerbach, etc.', p. 237.
107. Cf. ibid., p. 239.
108. See J. Ehrard and P. Vallaneix (eds) *Les Fêtes de la Révolution* (Paris, 1977) pp. 457ff.
109. Cf. K. Marx, F. Engels, *Selected Correspondence* (Moscow, 1965) pp. 417ff.
110. F. Engels, 'Ludwig Feuerbach, etc.', p. 24.
111. F. Engels, 'On the history of early Christianity', *On Religion*, p. 314.
112. F. Engels, 'The Book of Revelation', *On Religion*, pp. 204f. See also 'Letters from London', *Collected Works*, vol. 3, pp. 379f.
113. F. Engels, Introduction to Marx's *Class Struggle in France*, in K. Marx, F. Engels, *Selected Works* (Moscow, 1962) vol. 1, p. 137.
114. Cf. F. Engels, 'On the history of early Christianity', *On Religion*, p. 313.
115. F. Engels, 'The condition of England', *Collected Works*, vol. 3, pp. 462f.
116. F. Engels, 'Friedrich Wilhelm IV, King of Prussia', *Collected Works*, vol. 3, p. 463.
117. F. Engels, 'The condition of England', *Collected Works*, vol. 3, p. 463.
118. F. Engels, 'The progress of social reform on the Continent', *Collected Works*, vol. 3, p. 399.
119. F. Engels, 'The condition of England', *Collected Works*, vol. 3, p. 472.
120. F. Engels, 'Socialism: utopian and scientific', *On Religion*, pp. 291f.
121. Ibid., p. 310.
122. Ibid.
123. F. Engels, 'Letters from London', *Collected Works*, vol. 3, p. 385.
124. F. Engels, 'The condition of the working class in England', *Collected Works*, vol. 4, p. 421.
125. See, for example, A. Gilbert, *Religion and Society in Industrial England* (London, 1978) pt I.
126. F. Engels, 'The condition of the working class in England', *Collected Works*, vol. 4, p. 526.
127. F. Engels, '"Young Germany" in Switzerland', *Collected Works*, vol. 4, p. 653.
128. F. Engels, 'Emigrant literature', *On Religion*, p. 141.
129. Cf. F. Engels, *Collected Works*, vol. 12, pp. 510f.
130. For a particularly striking example of Engels's teleological approach, see F. Engels, 'The condition of the working class in England', *Collected Works*, vol. 4, p. 526.
131. F. Engels, *The Origin of the Family, Private Property and the State*, p. 258.
132. F. Engels, 'Ludwig Feuerbach, etc.', p. 261.
133. See p. 36.
134. F. Engels, *Anti-Dühring*, p. 480.
135. F. Engels, *Dialectics of Nature* (Moscow, 1972) p. 218.
136. Ibid., p. 181.

137. F. Engels, *Anti-Dühring*, p. 438.
138. Ibid.
139. Ibid., pp. 439f.
140. See, for example, recent studies of French religious practice of which the pioneer is G. Le Bras, *Etudes de sociologie religieuse*, 2 vols (Paris, 1955f.).
141. See R. Zaehner, *Christian Materialism and Dialectical Christianity* (Oxford, 1971) pp. 31ff.; L. Althusser, *For Marx* (London, 1970) pp. 238ff.

3. German Social Democracy

1. F. Engels, *Anti-Dühring* (Moscow, 1954) p. 14.
2. It is instructive, as indicating the general decline, to compare Engels's comparatively subtle treatment of the Reformation of his *Peasant War* with Bernstein's mechanistic account of 1895 in his *Cromwell and Communism* (London, 1930).
3. *Protokoll über die Verhandlungen des Parteitages zu Hannover* (Berlin, 1899) p. 148. See also the contempt for Hegel expressed in H. Cunow, *Die Ursprung der Religion* (Berlin, 1913) pp. 10ff.
4. On Christian Socialism in Germany around the turn of the century, see particularly, J. Bentley, *Between Marx and Christ* (London, 1982) ch. 2.
5. See the survey of religious feeling of SPD members reported in H. Rolfes, *Jesus und das Proletariat* (Düsseldorf, 1982) pp. 126ff.
6. J. Dietzgen, 'The religion of Social Democracy', *Philosophical Essays* (Chicago, 1912) p. 90.
7. Ibid., p. 113.
8. Ibid., p. 91.
9. Ibid., p. 126.
10. Ibid.
11. Cf. J. Dietzgen, *op. cit.*, p. 90.
12. Quoted in C. Read, *Religion, Revolution and the Russian Intelligentsia* (London, 1979) p. 81.
13. A. Bebel and K. Witthoff, *Christentum und Sozialismus* (Berlin, 1901) pp. 10, 16, quoted in H. Rolfes, *op. cit.*, pp. 81ff.
14. A. Bebel, *Society of the Future* (Moscow, 1971) p. 88.
15. Ibid., p. 89.
16. Ibid.
17. P. Lafargue, 'Die Ursachen des Gottesglaubens', *Die Neue Zeit* (1905/6) vol. 24, pt I, p. 508.
18. Cf. P. Lafargue, *op. cit.*, pp. 517ff.
19. K. Kautsky, *Thomas More and His Utopia* (London, 1979) p. 72.
20. Ibid., p. 73.
21. Cf. K. Kautsky, *Foundations of Christianity* (London, 1978) pp. 129, 178.
22. Cf. p. 76.
23. Cf. K. Kautsky, 'Über Religion', *Die Neue Zeit*, vol. I, no. 6 (1913) p. 184.

24. K. Kautsky, 'Über Religion', *Die Neue Zeit*, vol. I, no. 10 (Dec. 1913) p. 354.
25. Cf. D. McKown, *The Classical Marxist Critique of Religion* (The Hague, 1975) pp. 131ff.
26. See, from a Marxist point of view, A. Drews, *Die Christusmythe* (Jena, 1909) and, especially, the work of a Lutheran pastor strongly influenced by historical materialism: A. Kalthoff, *Die Entstehung des Christentums* (Jena, 1904).
27. K. Kautsky, *Foundations of Christianity* (London, 1975) p. 10.
28. Ibid., p. 15.
29. Ibid., p. 14. For the more promising view that only a committed socialist can understand early Christianity, see the passage quoted p. 151.
30. K. Kautsky, *Foundations of Christianity*, p. 31.
31. Ibid., p. 38.
32. Ibid., p. 179.
33. Ibid., pp. 200f.
34. Ibid., p. 201.
35. Cf., for example, J. Bright, *A History of Israel*, 2nd edn (London, 1972) pp. 95ff. and the literature quoted.
36. Cf. Kautsky, *Foundations of Christianity*, p. 201.
37. For a different account, see M. Weber's *Ancient Judaism* which emphasises the social isolation of the prophets. This in turn is contested by H. Hahn, *The Old Testament in Modern Research* (Philadelphia, 1966).
38. K. Kautsky, *Foundations of Christianity*, p. 262.
39. Cf. ibid., p. 273.
40. Ibid., p. 323.
41. Ibid., p. 364.
42. Ibid., p. 370.
43. Ibid., p. 379.
44. Ibid., p. 378.
45. E. Troeltsch, *The Social Teaching of the Christian Church* (London, 1931) vol. 1, pp. 28ff.
46. K. Kautsky, *op. cit.*, p. 363. It is worth noting, in mitigation, that the most recent Marxist work to deal with this period – G. E. M. de Ste. Croix's *Class Struggles in the Ancient World* – while admirable in so many other respects, is more prejudiced and less informative on early Christianity than is Kautsky.
47. Cf. Adler's review 'Karl Kautsky's Urchristentum', *Der Kampf*, vol. 2 (1908) pp. 183ff.
48. K. Kautsky, *Foundations of Christianity*, p. 40.
49. The best modern defence of this view is S. G. F. Brandon, *Jesus and the Zealots* (Manchester, 1967). For a thorough critique, see M. Hengel, *Christ and Power* (Philadelphia, 1977).
50. M. Hengel, *Property and Riches in the Early Church* (Fortress Press, 1974) p. 60, pp. 20ff. For further evidence on the social bases of early Christianity see A. Malherbe, *Social Aspects of Early Christianity* (University Press, Louisiana State, 1977) pp. 66ff. and G. Theissen, *Studien zur Soziologie des Urchristentums*, 2nd edn (Tübingen, 1983).

51. Schweitzer's *Quest of the Historical Jesus* (A and C, Black, London, 1910), which emphasises this point, had been published two years earlier.
52. K. Kautsky, *Foundations of Christianity*, p. 171.
53. K. Kautsky, *Thomas More and His Utopia*, p. 79.
54. Ibid., pp. 34ff.
55. K. Kautsky, *Die Vorläüfer des neueren Sozialismus*, vol. 2 (Stuttgart, 1894).
56. Cf. K. Kautsky, *Die Materialistische Geschichtsauffassung* (Berlin, 1927) p. 827.
57. See the commentary in A. Friesen, *Reformation and Utopia* (Wiesbaden, 1974).
58. Cf. E. Bernstein, *Cromwell and Communism* (London, 1930) pp. 165ff.
59. Cf. S. Andreski, *Elements of Comparative Sociology* (London, 1964) pp. 192ff.
60. K. Kautsky, *Foundations of Christianity* (London, 1978) p. 171.
61. Ibid., p. 471.
62. Cf. E. Troelsch, *The Social Teaching of the Christian* (London, 1931) vol. 1, p. 36.
63. H. Cunow, *Ursprung der Religion und des Gottesglaubens* (Berlin, 1913) p. 4.
64. Ibid., p. 14.
65. Ibid., p. 17.
66. Ibid.
67. Ibid., p. 19.
68. Ibid., p. 105.
69. Ibid., p. 164.
70. See K. Kautsky, 'Über Religion', *Die Neue Zeit*, vol. I, no. 6, 1913, p. 184.
71. M. Adler, *Kant und der Marxismus* (Berlin, 1925) p. 162, quoted in *Austromarxism*, ed. T. Bottomore and P. Goode (Oxford, 1978) p. 65.
72. K. Marx, *Selected Writings* (Oxford, 1977) p. 236.
73. O. Bauer, *Sozialdemokratie, Religion und Kirche* (Vienna, 1927) p. 19.
74. Ibid.
75. Ibid., p. 21.
76. Ibid., p. 28.
77. Ibid., pp. 27f.
78. Ibid., p. 34.
79. Ibid., p. 35. See also the rather more positive assessment of Max Adler's 'religion of the philosophers' on p. 28.
80. See further P. Zulehner, *Kirche und Austromarxismus* (Vienna, 1967) pp. 157ff.
81. Cf. E. Bernstein, *Evolutionary Socialism* (New York, 1961) pp. 222ff., and P. Angel, *Edward Bernstein et l'évolution du socialisme allemand* (Paris, 1961) pp. 193ff.
82. M. Adler, *Kant und der Marxismus* (Berlin, 1925) p. 190, quoted in *Austromarxism*, ed. T. Bottomore and P. Goode, p. 68.
83. M. Adler, ibid.
84. Cf. M. Adler, *Marx und Engels als Denker* (Berlin, 1970) pp. 137ff. and 140.
85. Ibid., p. 207.

86. Cf. M. Adler, *Lehrbuch der materialistischen Geschichtsauffassung* (Vienna, 1930) p. 108.
87. M. Adler, *Das Soziologische in Kants Erkenntniskritik* (Vienna, 1924) p. 454.
88. M. Adler, 'Über den kritischen Begriff der Religion', in *Festschrift fur Wilhelm Jerusalem* (Vienna, 1915), p. 18.
89. M. Adler, *Das Soziologische in Kants Erkenniskritik*, p. 346.
90. Ibid., p. 397.
91. Cf. M. Adler (1924) *op. cit.*, pp. 400, 405.
92. Ibid., p. 408.
93. Ibid., p. 445.
94. Ibid., p. 447.
95. Ibid., p. 449.
96. Ibid., pp. 450f.
97. Ibid., p. 451.
98. Ibid., p. 452.
99. Ibid., p. 469.
100. Ibid., p. 472.
101. Ibid., p. 395.
102. M. Adler, 'Über den kritischen Begriff der Religion', *op. cit.*, p. 43.
103. Ibid., p. 44.
104. Cf. M. Adler, *Marx und Engels als Denker* (Berlin, 1970) pp. 206f.

4. Soviet Marxism

1. On the earlier period, see further: R. Pipes, *Russia under the Old Regime* (London, 1974) ch. 9. For the early twentieth century, see E. Simon, 'Church, State and Society', in *Russia Enters the Twentieth Century 1894–1917*, ed. G. Katkov *et al.* (London, 1971).
2. See, for example, the opening section of G. Plekhanov, *The Development of the Monist View of History.*
3. G. Plekhanov, *Our Differences*, in *Selected Philosophical Works*, vol. 1 (London, 1929) p. 21.
4. See, for example, G. Plekhanov, *Fundamental Problems of Marxism* (London, 1929) p. 21.
5. Cf. G. Plekhanov, *Our Differences*, pp. 17, 46.
6. See, for example, G. Plekhanov, *Fundamental Problems of Marxism*, sections 2 and 3.
7. Ibid., p. 7.
8. Ibid., p. 10.
9. G. Plekhanov, 'Notes to Engels's book on Feuerbach', *Collected Works*, vol. 1, p. 505.
10. Ibid.
11. E. Seligman, *The Economic Interpretation of History* (New York, 1902).
12. G. Plekhanov, *Fundamental Problems*, p. 34.
13. G. Plekhanov, *The Development of the Monist View of History* (London, 1947) p. 206.
14. Ibid., p. 209.

15. V. Lenin, *The State and Revolution*, *Collected Works*, vol. 25, p. 420.
16. V. Lenin to M. Gorki, November 1913, *Collected Works*, vol. 35, p. 128.
17. Ibid., p. 129.
18. V. Lenin, 'Political agitation and the class point of view', *Collected Works*, vol. 5, p. 338.
19. V. Lenin, 'Socialism and religion', *Collected Works*, vol. 10, pp. 83f.
20. Ibid., p. 84.
21. Ibid., p. 85.
22. Cf. D. McLellan, *Marxism After Marx* (London, 1980) pp. 102ff.
23. V. Lenin, 'To the rural poor', *Collected Works*, vol. 6, p. 402.
24. V. Lenin, 'A draft programme of our party', *Collected Works*, vol. 4, p. 243.
25. V. Lenin, 'The Third Congress', *Collected Works*, vol. 8, p. 448.
26. V. Lenin, 'Socialism and religion', *Collected Works*, vol. 10, p. 85.
27. Ibid., pp. 85f.
28. Ibid., p. 86.
29. Ibid.
30. On these thinkers, whose work unfortunately lies outside the scope of the present work, see further the excellent study by C. Read, *Religion, Revolution and the Russian Intelligentsia 1900–1912* (London, 1979), ch. 3.
31. Further on the background, see D. Joravsky, *Soviet Marxism and Natural Science* (London, 1961) pp. 24ff.
32. Further on *Materialism and Empiriocriticism* see G. Wetter, *Dialectical Materialism* (London, 1958) pp. 116ff.; A. James Gregor, *A Survey of Marxism* (New York, 1965) ch. 3.
33. V. Lenin, *Materialism and Empiriocriticism* (Moscow, 1970) p. 29.
34. Ibid., pp. 333f.
35. Ibid., p. 330.
36. Ibid.
37. Cf. D. McKown, *The Classical Marxist Critique of Religion* (The Hague, 1965) pp. 114ff.
38. Cf. V. Lenin, 'Conspectus of Feuerbach's book *Lectures on the Essence of Religion*', *Collected Works*, vol. 38, pp. 61ff.
39. Quoted in G. Wetter, *Dialectical Materialism* (London, 1960) p. 91. See also T. Masaryk, *The Spirit of Russia* (London, 1955) vol. 2, pp. 358f., and especially G. Kline, *Religious and Anti-Religious Thought in Russia* (Chicago, 1968) ch. 4.
40. Quoted in C. Read, *op. cit.*, p. 84.
41. Quoted in C. Read, *op. cit.*, p. 84f.
42. Quoted in J. Hecker, *Religion and Communism* (London, 1933) p. 186.
43. Ibid., p. 188.
44. See V. Lenin, 'The faction of supporters of Otzovism and God-building', *Collected Works*, vol. 16, pp. 29ff.
45. Quoted in B. Bociurkiw, 'Lenin and religion', in L. Schapiro and R. P. Reddaway (eds) *Lenin: The man, the theorist, the leader* (London, 1967) pp. 122f.
46. V. Lenin, 'Leo Tolstoy as Mirror of the Russian Revolution', *Collected Works*, vol. 15, p. 205.
47. V. Lenin, 'The Attitude of the Workers' Party to religion', *Collected*

Works, vol. 15, p. 409. See also Plekhanov's slightly more subtle attack on the God-builders in *Materialismus Militans: A Reply to Mr. Bogdanov* (Moscow, 1973).

48. V. Lenin, 'The Attitude of the Workers Party to Religion', *op. cit.*, pp. 405f.
49. Lenin to Gorki, November 1913, *Collected Works*, vol. 35, p. 127.
50. Ibid., p. 121.
51. Ibid., p. 128.
52. Ibid., p. 129.
53. Cf. B. Bociurkiw, 'Lenin on Religion', *op. cit.*, p. 128.
54. V. Lenin, 'Conspectus of Hegel's book *The Science of Logic*', *Collected Works*, vol. 38, p. 171.
55. V. Lenin, *Collected Works*, vol. 29, p. 134.
56. For a critical view from one of Lenin's collaborators, see: A. Balabanoff, *Impressions of Lenin* (Ann Arbor, 1968) pp. 48ff.
57. V. Lenin, 'On the significance of militant materialism', *Collected Works*, vol. 33, p. 228.
58. Ibid., p. 229.
59. Ibid., p. 233.
60. Ibid., p. 234.
61. *Basic Writings of Trotsky*, ed. I. Howe (London, 1964) p. 375.
62. L. Trotsky, *Where is Britain Going?* (London, 1926) pp. 46f.
63. L. Trotsky, 'The tasks of communist education', in *Problems of Everyday Life and Other Writings on Culture and Science*, ed. G. Novack (New York, 1973), p. 112.
64. Ibid., p. 118.
65. L. Trotsky, 'Culture and Socialism', pp. 247f.
66. L. Trotsky, *Literature and Revolution* (Ann Arbor, 1960) p. 39.
67. L. Trotsky, 'The tasks of communist education', *Culture and Revolution*, p. 113.
68. L. Trotsky, 'Leninism and Workers' Clubs', *Culture and Revolution*, p. 309.
69. *Basic Writings of Trotsky*, *op. cit.*, p. 373.
70. L. Trotsky, 'Leninism and Workers' Clubs', *Culture and Revolution*, p. 313.
71. L. Trotsky, 'Vodka, the Church and the Cinema', *Culture and Revolution*, p. 35.
72. N. Bukharin, *Historical Materialism* (New York, 1925) p. 169.
73. Ibid., p. 170.
74. Ibid., p. 177.
75. Ibid., p. 179.
76. Ibid., p. 180.
77. On Bogdanov's thought in general, see: G. Wetter, *Dialectical Materialism* (London, 1958) pp. 92ff.; K. Jensen, *Beyond Marx and Mach* (Dordrecht, 1978); D. Lecourt, 'Bogdanov, miroir de l'intelligentsia soviétique', in A. Bogdanov, *La science, l'art et la classe ouvrière* (Paris, 1977).
78. Quoted in K. Jensen, *op. cit.*, p. 37.
79. A. Bogdanov, 'L'Héritage artistique', in A. Bogdanov, *op. cit.*, p. 243.

80. Ibid., p. 249.
81. Ibid., p. 250.
82. Ibid.
83. Ibid., p. 254.
84. Ibid., p. 255.
85. *A History of the Communist Party of the Soviet Union (Short Course)* (Moscow, n.d.) p. 130.
86. For the more recent Soviet treatment of religion, see ch. 6, pp. 136ff.

5. Gramsci and the Frankfurt School

1. A. Gramsci, *Selections from the Prison Notebooks*, ed. Q. Hoare and G. Nowell Smith (London, 1971) p. 326.
2. Ibid., p. 344.
3. Ibid., p. 419.
4. A. Gramsci, *Quaderni del Carcere*, ed. V. Gerratana (Turin, 1975ff.) vol. 2, p. 1397.
5. A. Gramsci, *Selections from the Prison Notebooks*, p. 328.
6. Ibid., p. 405.
7. A. Gramsci, *Quaderni del Carcere*, vol. 2, p. 1389.
8. A. Gramsci, 'Il Partito Comunista', *Ordine Nuovo 1919–1920* (Turin, 1954) p. 154.
9. A. Gramsci, *Quaderni del Carcere*, vol. 2, p. 882.
10. Ibid., p. 1388.
11. Ibid.
12. A. Gramsci, *Quaderni del Carcere*, vol. 1, p. 669.
13. A. Gramsci, *Selections from the Prison Notebooks*, p. 331.
14. Ibid., pp. 17ff.
15. A. Gramsci, *Quaderni del Carcere*, vol. 1, p. 649.
16. Ibid., p. 648.
17. A. Gramsci, *Selections from the Prison Notebooks*, p. 170.
18. A. Gramsci, *Quaderni del Carcere*, vol. 3, p. 1914.
19. A. Gramsci, *Quaderni del Carcere*, vol. 2, p. 1389.
20. Ibid.
21. A. Gramsci, *Selections from the Prison Notebooks*, p. 332.
22. Ibid., p. 395.
23. A. Gramsci, *Quaderni del Carcere*, vol. 2, pp. 1380f.
24. A. Gramsci, *Selections from the Prison Notebooks*, p. 397.
25. Ibid.
26. Ibid., p. 132.
27. Ibid., p. 133.
28. A. Gramsci, *Quaderni del Carcere*, vol. 3, p. 1862.
29. M. Horkheimer, *Critical Theory* (New York, 1972) p. 129.
30. Cf. M. Horkheimer, *Kritische Theorie*, ed. A. Schmidt, 2nd edn (Frankfurt, 1969) vol. 2, p. 227. See further C. Davis, *Theology and Political Society* (Cambridge, 1980) pp. 133ff.
31. Cf. M. Horkheimer, *Critique of Instrumental Reason* (New York, 1974)

pp. 46ff., and the commentary in J. Carlebach, *Karl Marx and the Radical Critique of Judaism* (London, 1978) pp. 234ff.

32. M. Horkheimer, *Critical Theory* (New York, 1972) p. 131.
33. Cf. S. Buck-Morss, *The Origin of Negative Dialectics* (Hassocks, 1977) p. 141.
34. W. Benjamin, *Illuminations: Essays and Reflections*, ed. H. Arendt (New York, 1968) p. 255.
35. See further R. Siebert, *The Critical Theory of Religion. The Frankfurt School* (Berlin, 1985) pp. 355ff.
36. M. Lowy, 'Revolution against "Progress": Walter Benjamin's Romantic Anarchism', *New Left Review* (Nov./Dec., 1985) p. 58.
37. F. Borkenau, *Der Übergang vom Feudalen zum Bürgerlichen Weltbild* (Paris, 1934) p. 158. The passages translated are taken from *Sociology and Religion*, ed. N. Birnbaum and F. Zenger (Englewood Cliffs, 1969) p. 285.
38. F. Borkenau, *op. cit.*, p. 159.
39. *Zeitschrisht für Sozialforschung*, vol. 1 (1932) p. 174, quoted in J. Bentley, *Between Marx and Christ*, p. 56. See also R. Siebert, *The Critical Theory of Religion. The Frankfurt School*, pp. 146ff.
40. E. Fromm, *The Dogma of Christ and Other Essays* (New York, 1967) p. 45.
41. Ibid., p. 63.
42. Ibid., p. 56.
43. L. Goldmann, *The Hidden God* (London, 1964) p. 69.
44. Ibid., p. 284.
45. B. Pascal, *Pensées*, ed. L. Brunschvicg (Paris, 1976) p. 94.
46. Ibid., p. 120.
47. Ibid., p. 31.
48. Ibid., p. 90.
49. E. Bloch, *Atheism in Christianity* (New York, 1972) pp. 62ff. These themes are worked out most fully in Bloch's *magnum opus*, the shapelessly eclectic *Principle of Hope*, 3 vols. (Oxford, 1986).
50. E. Bloch, *Atheism in Christianity*, p. 9. This rejection of the traditional idea of creation is strikingly parallel to Gramsci on the same theme.
51. Ibid., p. 112.
52. E. Bloch, *Atheism in Christianity*.
53. Ibid.
54. E. Bloch, *Man on his Own* (New York, 1973) pp. 209ff.
55. E. Bloch, *Atheism in Christianity*, p. 62.
56. Ibid., p. 272.
57. E. Bloch, *Man on his Own*, pp. 160ff.
58. E. Bloch, *Atheism in Christianity*, p. 269.

6. Contemporary Marxism and Christianity in Europe and Latin America

1. R. Bultmann, *Glauben und Verstehen* (Tubingen, 1966) vol. 1, p. 33.
2. *The Papal Encyclicals*, ed. A. Freemantle (New York, 1956) p. 261.
3. *Pacem in Terris* (Catholic Truth Society, London, 1963) p. 47.
4. C. Lane, *Religion in the Soviet Union* (London, 1978) pp. 27ff.

5. See here, and for the following, the excellently documented study of James Thrower, *Marxist-Leninist 'Scientific Atheism' and the study of religion and atheism in the USSR* (Amsterdam, 1983).

6. Cp. D. Powell, *Antireligious Propaganda in the Soviet Union* (Cambridge, Mass., 1975) pp. 79ff.

7. Figures for propaganda are available in F. Skoda, *Die Sowjetrussische Philosophische Religionskritik Heute* (Freiburg, 1968) p. 11.

8. See C. Lane, *Religion in the Soviet Union* (London, 1978) pp. 222ff.

9. L. Kolakowski, *Towards a Marxist Humanism* (New York, 1968) p. 174.

10. L. Kolakowski, *Chrétiens sans église* (Paris, 1965) p. 45.

11. Cf. L. Kolakowski, *Towards a Marxist Humanism*, pp. 49ff.

12. Ibid., p. 50.

13. Ibid., pp. 389ff.

14. Ibid., p. 9.

15. Cf. G. Schwan, *Leszek Kolakowski. Eine Marxistische Philosophie der Freiheit* (Stuttgart, 1971) pp. 33ff.

16. A. Schaff, *Marxism and the Human Individual* (New York, 1970) p. 111.

17. Ibid.

18. V. Gardavsky, *God is Not Yet Dead* (Harmondsworth, 1973) p. 15.

19. Ibid., p. 31.

20. Ibid., p. 33.

21. Ibid., p. 51.

22. Ibid., p. 76.

23. Ibid., p. 172.

24. Ibid., p. 218.

25. M. Machovec, *A Marxist Looks at Jesus* (London, 1976) p. 31.

26. Ibid., p. 21.

27. Cf. M. Machovec, *op. cit.*, p. 29.

28. Ibid., p. 35.

29. Ibid., p. 217.

30. Ibid., p. 30.

31. Cf. pp. 139ff.

32. See J. Bonino, *Marxists and Christians* (London, 1976) p. 54 for references.

33. G. Marchais and G. Hourdin, *Communistes et chrétiens* (Paris, 1976) p. 52.

34. K. Marx, 'Introduction to a critique of Hegel's *Philosophy of Right*', *Selected Writings* (Oxford, 1977) p. 64.

35. And many non-traditional ones as well. For a convincing critique of Althusser on subjectivity, see D. Turner, *Marxism and Christianity* (Oxford, 1983) pp. 187ff.

36. See pp. 79ff., above.

37. See L. Althusser, *Pour Marx* (Paris, 1965) pp. 238ff.

38. See N. Poulantzas, *Political Power and Social Classes* (London, 1973) and B. Hindess and P. Hirst, *Pre-Capitalist Economic Formations* (London, 1975).

39. See also M. Clevenot, *Approaches matérialistes de la Bible* (Paris, 1978).

40. F. Belo, *A Materialist Reading of the Gospel of Mark* (Maryknoll, 1981) p. 297.

41. Ibid., pp. 95f.
42. Cf. P. Anderson, *On the Tracks of Historical Materialism* (London, 1983) ch. 2.
43. V. Lenin, quoted in J. Hellman, 'French "Left-Catholics" and Communism in the Nineteen-thirties', *Church History*, vol. 45 (1976) p. 507.
44. E. Dussel, 'Domination–Liberation: a new approach', *Concilium* (June, 1974) p. 49.
45. Jean-Paul Sartre, *Search for a Method* (New York, 1968) p. 30.
46. A. Fierro, *The Militant Gospel* (London, 1977) p. 106.
47. K. Kautsky, *Foundations of Christianity* (London, n.d.) p. 10.
48. J. Bonino, *Christians and Marxists: The Mutual Challenge to Revolution* (London, 1976) p. 18.
49. Ibid., p. 8.
50. J. Miranda, *Marx and the Bible* (New York, 1974) pp. 16, 292.
51. J. Miranda, *Marx against the Marxists* (London, 1980) p. xi.
52. Ibid.
53. See the comments of A. Fierro on Calvez and Gollwitzer in *The Militant Gospel* (Maryknoll, 1977) p. 116.
54. G. Guttierez, *A Theology of Liberation* (New York, 1973) p. 146.
55. Ibid., p. 155.
56. Ibid., p. 159.
57. J. Cardonnel, *Dieu est mort en Jésus-Christ* (Bordeaux, 1968) p. 123.
58. G. Gutierrez, *op. cit.*, p. 276.
59. K. Marx, 'A correspondence of 1843', *Selected Writings*, ed. D. McLellan (Oxford, 1977) p. 38.
60. Quoted in J. Bonino, *Christians and Marxists* (London, 1976) p. 27.
61. D. Turner, *Marxism and Christianity* (Oxford, 1983) p. 211.
62. Cf. A. Fierro, *The Militant Gospel*, p. 172.
63. H. Marcuse, *An Essay on Liberation* (Harmondsworth, 1972) p. 13.
64. Cf. J. Bonino, *Christians and Marxists*, p. 73.
65. For particularly sharp critiques from this point of view see G. Fessard, *Chrétiens marxistes et théologie de la libération* (Paris, 1978) and A. Senke, *Marxismus als atheistische Weltanschauung* (Paderborn, 1983) ch. 6.

Conclusion: Marxism and Religion

1. K. Popper, *The Open Society and Its Enemies*, 4th edn (London, 1962) vol. 2, p. 224.
2. N. Berdiaev, *Les sources et le sens du communisme russe* (Paris, 1951) p. 316.
3. J. Schumpeter, *Capitalism, Socialism and Democracy*, 4th edn (London, 1954) p. 5.
4. See, for example, L. Goldmann, *The Hidden God* (London, 1964) p. 90.
5. R. Tucker, *Philosophy and Myth in Karl Marx* (Cambridge, 1961) p. 22.
6. See, in particular, K. Marx and F. Engels, 'Circular against Kriege', *Collected Works* (London, 1975ff) vol. 6, pp. 46ff.
7. See, for example, the clear discussion by R. Horton, 'A definition of

religion, and its uses', *Journal of the Royal Anthropological Institute*, vol. 90 (1960).

8. See further, p. 170.
9. K. Kautsky, *Ethik and materialistische Geschichtsauffassung* (Stuttgart, 1906) p. 141.
10. For the most thorough recent attempt so to de-limit Marx, see P. Frostin, *Materialismus, Ideologie, Religion* (Munich, 1978).
11. See, for example, the splendid first chapter of Kolakowski's *Main Currents of Marxism* (Oxford, 1978) vol. 1.
12. E. Durkheim, *The Elementary Forms of the Religious Life* (London, 1915) pp. 423f.
13. See, particularly, A. Cuvillier, 'Marx et Durkheim', *Cahiers Internationaux de Sociologie* (1948) pp. 84ff.
14. See S. Strawbridge, 'Althusser's theory of ideology and Durkheim's account of religion: an examination of some striking parallels', *Sociological Review*, vol. 30 (1982) pp. 125ff.
15. See R. Bellah, *Beyond Belief* (New York, 1970).
16. T. Parsons, *The Structure of Social Action* (New York, 1949) p. 505.
17. Quoted in R. Aron, *The Main Currents of Sociological Thought* (London, 1968) vol. 2, p. 262.
18. See K. Lowith, *Max Weber and Karl Marx* (London, 1980) p. 100.
19. K. Marx, F. Engels, *Werke* (Berlin, 1957ff.) vol. 35, p. 388.
20. K. Marx, *The German Ideology* (Moscow, 1968) pp. 143, 188f.
21. *From Max Weber: Essays in Sociology*, ed. H. Gerth and C. Wright Mills (London, 1948) pp. 269f.
22. Ibid. See also the discussion of Weber on Indian religion, and the differences this demonstrates from Marx's approach, in T. Ling, *Karl Marx and Religion* (London, 1980) ch. 6.
23. J. Schumpeter, *Capitalism, Socialism, and Democracy* (London, 1954) p. 11.
24. Cf. M. Weber, *Economy and Society* (New York, 1968) ch. 6, sections 5 and 6.
25. *From Max Weber*, etc., p. 63.
26. M. Weber, *The Protestant Ethic and the Spirit of Capitalism*, ed. T. Parsons (New York, 1958) p. 183.
27. K. Lowith, *Max Weber and Karl Marx* (London, 1980) p. 102.
28. *From Max Weber*, etc. p. 63.
29. G. Cohen, 'Restrictive and inclusive historical materialism', in *Marx en perspective*, ed. B. Chavance (Paris, 1985) p. 59.
30. E. P. Thompson, *The Making of the English Working Class* (Harmondsworth, 1968) p. 428.
31. Cf. E. Hobsbawm, 'Methodism and the threat of revolution in Britain', *History Today* (vol. 8, 1952) pp. 115ff.
32. V. Kiernan, 'Evangelicalism and the French Revolution', *Past and Present*, vol. 1 (Feb. 1952) p. 44.
33. Cf. E. Hobsbawm, *Primitive Rebels* (Manchester, 1959); P. Worsley, *The Trumpet Shall Sound* (London, 1957).
34. R. Nisbet, *The Sociological Tradition* (New York, 1986) pp. 221ff.
35. K. Thomas, *Religion and the Decline of Magic* (London, 1971) p. 173.

36. See, for example, M. Douglas, *Natural Symbols – Explorations in Cosmology* (London, 1973) ch. 1.

37. See the brief but incisive discussion in N. Gottwald, *The Tribes of Jahweh* (Maryknoll, 1979) pt 10.

38. D. Martin, 'Towards eliminating the concept of secularization', *Penguin Survey of the Social Sciences, 1965*, ed. J. Gould (Harmondsworth, 1965) p. 169. On the superficiality of much talk about secularization from the point of view of European intellectual history, see H. Blumenberg, *The Legitimacy of the Modern Age* (Cambridge, Mass., 1983).

39. R. Garaudy, 'Glaube und Revolution', in *Marxisten und die Sache Jesu*, ed. I. Fetscher and M. Machovec (Mainz, 1974) p. 43. See further the pursuance of this theme in C. Lenhardt, 'Anamnesic Solidarity: the proletariat and its *Manes*,' *Telos*, vol. 25 (1975).

40. See M. Jay, *The Dialectical Imagination* (London, 1973) pp. 56, 262.

41. R. Heilbroner, *Marxism: For and Against* (London, 1980) pp. 167f.

42. M. Weber, 'Politics as a vocation', in *From Max Weber*, ed. Gerth and Mills (London, 1948) p. 123.

Select Critical Bibliography

The following is largely a list of books and articles I have consulted. I have added some comments on the items, thinking it helpful to the potential reader to have some indication, albeit subjective, of their content beyond their bare titles.

General

ASSMANN, H. and MATE, R., *Sobre la religion* (ed. Sigueme, Salamanca, 1975). The fullest collection of post-Marx writings from Bebel to Mao Zedong.

BENT, ANS J. VAN DER, *The Christian Marxist Dialogue. An annotated bibliography, 1959–1969* (World Council of Churches, Geneva, 1969). A useful resource document.

BENZ, E., *Buddhism or Communism?* (Allen & Unwin, London, 1966). An examination of their present political relationship in Asia.

BIRNBAUM, N., 'Conflicting interpretations of the rise of capitalism: Marx and Weber', *British Journal of Sociology*, June 1953. A brief but insightful discussion of this broad topic.

BIRNBAUM, N., 'Beyond Marx in the sociology of religion', in C. Glock and P. Hammond (eds), *Beyond the Classics?: Essays in the scientific study of religion* (Harper & Row, New York, 1973). A long essay, providing probably the best introduction to the topic.

CENTRE D'ETUDES ET DE RECHERCHES MARXISTES (ed.), *Philosophie et religion* (Editions Sociales, Paris, 1974). A general collection of articles by French Marxists.

CHATTOPADHYAYA, D., *Indian Atheism. A Marxist approach* (PPH, New Delhi, 1980). A thorough discussion of both Hindu and Buddhist religions from a resolutely Marxist standpoint.

DEBRAY, R., *Critique of Political Reason* (Verso, London, 1983). Contains, in Part Two, some remarkable parallels between early Christianity, Islam, and institutionalised Marxism.

DESROCHE, H., *Marxisme et religions* (Presses Universitaires de France, Paris, 1962). A short but extremely stimulating discussion of the continuities and discontinuities between Marxism and Christianity.

FESSARD, G., 'Is Marx's thought relevant to the Christian?', in *Marx and the Western World*, ed. N. Lobkowicz (University of Notre Dame Press, Notre Dame, 1967). A view of Marx and Marxism as a perversion of Christian values.

GOLLWITZER, H., *The Christian Faith and the Marxist Critique of Religion*, tr. D. Cairns (St Andrew's Press, Edinburgh, 1970). An excellent introduction from an evangelical viewpoint.

GOTTWALD, N., *The Tribes of Jahweh* (SCM, London, 1980). See Chapter 50 for a brief but telling discussion of Marxian cultural materialism.

HILL, M., *A Sociology of Religion* (Basil Books, New York, 1973). Good introductory background to the Marx–Weber debate.

HOFFMAN, JOHN, 'A relationship of a new kind: Marxism as a transcendental atheism', *New Blackfriars* (1986). A challenging small article in which Marxist transcendence renders God redundant.

LING, T., *Buddha, Marx and God*, 2nd edn (Macmillan, London, 1979). A wide-ranging discussion of the relation of Buddhism to Marxism in the perspective of comparative religion.

LOWITH, K., *Von Hegel zu Nietzsche, Der revolutionare Bruch im Denken des 19 Jahrhunderts. Marx und Kierkegaard* (Europa, Zurich, 1953). Classic discussion placing Marx in the context of the history of ideas.

MARSHALL, G., *Presbyteries and Profits: Calvinism and the development of Capitalism in Scotland, 1560–1707* (Oxford University Press, 1980). A detailed piece of research tending to support Weber's thesis.

MACINTYRE, A., *Marxism and Christianity* (Penguin, Harmondsworth, 1971). Mainly a general exposition of Marx but also contains insightful comments on Christianity.

MCFADDEN, C., *Christianity Confronts Communism* (Franciscan Herald Press, Chicago, 1982). A sustained attack on Marxism/Communism by an Augustinian priest.

MCGOVERN, A., *Marxism: An American Christian Perspective* (Orbis, New York, 1980). An enthusiastic account of the possibilities inherent in Marxism by an American Jesuit.

MCKOWN, D. B., *The Classical Marxist Critique of Religion: Marx, Engels, Lenin, Kautsky* (Nijhoff, The Hague, 1975). A thorough, thoughtful, descriptive/analytical account.

SMART, NINIAN; CLAYTON, JOHN, *et al.*, *Nineteenth-Century Religious Thought in the West*, vol. III (Cambridge University Press, Cambridge, 1985). Excellent essays on, e.g., Muller, Weber, Troeltsch – good background for understanding the emerging Marxist critique.

TURNER, B., *Religion and Social Theory* (Heinemann, London, 1983). Contains several pertinent observations on Marx and Marxism, particularly in Chapters 3, 7 and 8.

TURNER, D., *Marxism and Christianity* (Blackwell, Oxford, 1983). A difficult, sharp, extremely stimulating book. More about ideology and morality than about Christianity.

VERRET, M., *Les Marxistes et la religion* (Editions Sociales, Paris, 1965). A meditative discussion, with a strong historico-literary background, by a French Communist.

WETTER, G., 'Über die Trennbarkeit von Marxismus als Weltanschauung und Marxismus als Instrument gesellschaftspolitischer Analyse', *Informationisdienst des katholischen Arbeitskreises fur Zeitgeschichtlichen Fragen*, vol. 10 (1980). An incisive questioning of the use of Marxism purely as an analytical tool.

Chapter 1

BERTRAND, M., *Le statut de la religion chez Marx et Engels* (Editions Sociales, Paris, 1979). A measured treatment by a French Communist.

BIELER, A., *Chrétiens et Socialistes avant Marx* (Labov et Fides, Geneva, 1982). A detailed treatment which provides good background to Marx.

BOCHMUEHL, KLAUS ERICH, *Leiblichkeit und Gesellschaft. Studien zur Religionskritik und Anthropologie im Fruhwerk von Ludwig Feuerbach und Karl Marx* (Forschungen zur Systematischen Theologie und Religionsphilosophie Bd. VII, Gottingen, 1961). A detailed, fundamental study of the similarities and differences between Feuerbach and Marx on religion by an evangelical theologian.

CALVEZ, J.-Y., *La pensée de Karl Marx* (Seuil, Paris, 1956). A thorough exposition of Marx by a French Jesuit with pertinent remarks about religion, particularly in the last section.

CARLEBACH, J., *Karl Marx and the Radical Critique of Judaism* (Routledge & Kegan Paul, London, 1978). Contains detailed discussions of Marx (Ch. 8) and Horkheimer (Ch. 11).

CHADWICK, O., *The Secularization of the European Mind in the Nineteenth Century* (Cambridge University Press, Cambridge, 1975). Chapter 3 contains an excellent discussion of Marx within the context of the title.

CLARKSON, K. and HAWKINS, D., 'Marx on Religion: The influence of Bruno Bauer and Ludwig Feuerbach on his thought and its linguistic implications for the Christian–Marxist Dialogue', *Scottish Journal of Theology*, vol. 31 (December 1978). Emphasises particularly the influence of Bauer.

COMSTOCK, R., 'The Marxist critique of religion: a persisting ambiguity', *Journal of the American Academy of Religion*, vol. 44 (1976). A stimulating original article concentrating on the ambiguities in Marx's critique of Feuerbach.

COTTIER, G., *L'athéisme du jeune Marx* (Vrin, Paris, 1969). An examination of the Hegelian origins of Marx's atheism as an explanation for its deficiencies.

DELAKAT, F., 'Vom Wesen des Geldes. Theologische Analyse eines Grundbegriffes in Karl Marx: "Das Kapital"', *Marxismusstudien, Schriften der Studiengemeinschaft der Ev. Akademien*, 3 (Tubingen, J. C. B. Mohr, 1954). Finds theological motifs in Marx's concept of money.

FACKENHEIM, E., *The Religious Dimension in Hegel's Thought* (Indiana University Press, Bloomington, 1967). A rigorous, profound and difficult discussion.

FROSTIN, PER, *Materialismus, Ideologie, Religion. Die materialistische Religionskritik bei Karl Marx* (Gleerup, München, 1978). A very thorough discussion: champions a late, 'scientific' Marx as an ally of progressive religion.

JACOBSON, N., 'Marxism and religious naturalism', *Journal of Religion*, vol. 29 (1949). Incisive article claiming that Marx's conceptions are a variety of religious naturalism.

LASH, N., *A Matter of Hope. A theologian's reflections on the thought of Karl*

Marx (Darton, Longman and Todd, London, 1981). The best book on the subject: sympathetic, well-informed and philosophically very acute.

LEEUWEN, A. TH. VAN, *Critique of Heaven* (Lutterworth, London, 1972). A detailed, rather heavy, philosophical account of the development of Marx's view up to the end of 1843.

LEEUWEN, A. TH. VAN, *Critique of Earth* (Lutterworth, London, 1974). A companion volume to the above. Deals at great length with Marx's 1843/44 writings.

LING, T., *Karl Marx and Religion in Europe and India* (Macmillan, London, 1980). Rather episodic. Good sections on the early Marx and on comparing Marx and Weber on Indian religion.

LOBKOWICZ, N., 'Karl Marx's attitude toward religion', *The Review of Politics*, vol. 26 (1964). Concentrates on the atheism of Marx in his early writings.

MARX, K. and ENGELS, F., *On Religion* (Foreign Languages Publishing House, Moscow, 1951). Contains all their major comments.

MARX, K. and ENGELS, F., *On Religion*, intro. by Reinhold Niebuhr (Scholars Press, Chicago, California, 1982). Same texts and translations as the Moscow edition.

MARX, K., *On Religion*, ed. S. Padover (McGraw-Hill, New York, 1974). The fullest-available in English with a somewhat hostile commentary.

MARX, K., *Marx e la religione*, ed. O. Todisco (Città Nuova, Rome, 1975). The fullest collection.

MASTERSON, P., *Atheism and Alienation. A study of the philosophical sources of contemporary atheism* (Gill and Macmillan, Dublin, 1971). Chapters 3, 4 and 5 contain short, balanced discussions of Hegel, Feuerbach and Marx.

MIRANDA, J., *Marx against the Marxists* (Orbis, Maryknoll, 1980). Portrays Marx's thought (but not that of his followers) as a continuation of early Christianity.

NGUYEN, NGOC VU, *Ideologie et religion d'après Marx et Engels* (Aubier Montaigne, Paris, 1975). An exposition which is, in parts, very stimulating.

PLAMENATZ, J., *Karl Marx's Philosophy of Man* (Oxford University Press, Oxford, 1975). Chapter 9 contains a careful analytical discussion of Marx's (and Engels's) views on religion.

POST, WERNER, *Kritik der Religion bei Karl Marx* (Kosel Verlag, München, 1969). A thorough and sympathetic treatment concentrating on the early writings.

REDING, M., *Der politische Atheismus*, 2. Aufl. (Styria, Graz-Wien-Koln, 1958). Argues that Marx's atheism is contingently dependent on the context of his times.

TODISCO, O., *Marx tra Dio e L'Uomo* (Città de vita, Florence, 1974). A sympathetic relativizing of Marx's atheism.

TUCKER, R., *Philosophy and Myth in Karl Marx* (Cambridge University Press, Cambridge, 1961). Stresses, in the first few chapters, the 'religious' aspects of Marx's thought.

WACKENHEIM, C., *La faillite de la religion d'après Karl Marx* (Presses Universités de France, Paris, 1963). Concentrates on Marx's pre-1848 writings. The most thorough exposition available.

Chapter 2

BIDET, J., 'Engels et la religion', in *Philosophie et religion* (Editions Sociales, Paris, 1974). Finds more merit in Engels than most have.

DESROCHES, H., *Socialismes et sociologie religieuse* (Cajas, Paris, 1965). See Chapters 2 and 5 for insightful remarks on Engels.

FRIESEN, A., *Reformation and Utopia, The Marxist interpretation of the Reformation and its antecedents* (Steiner, Wiesbaden, 1974). A wide-ranging and scholarly work, particularly good on Engels and Kautsky.

KOCH, H.-G., *The Abolition of God. Materialist atheism and Christian religion* (SCM, London, 1961). Chapters 3 and 4 contain evaluations of Engels and Lenin from an evangelical standpoint.

SEEGER, R., *Friedrich Engels. Die religiose Entwicklung des Spatpietisten und Fruhsozialisten* (Klinz, Halle, 1935). A detailed account of Engels's early break with Pietism.

ZAEHNER, R., *Christian Materialism and Dialectical Christianity* (Oxford University Press, Oxford, 1971). Attempts to find some convergence between Engels's dialectical materialism and the thought of Teihard de Chardin.

See also the books by Bertrand, Nguyen and Plamenatz listed under Chapter 1.

Chapter 3

ADLER, M., *Das Soziologische in Kants Erkenntniskritik* (Vienna, 1924). The major work in which Adler expounds his Kantian religious views.

ADLER, M., 'Über den kritischen Begriff der Religion', *Festschrift fur Wilhelm Jerusalem* (Vienna, 1915). A summary of Adler's neo-Kantian approach to religion.

BAUER, O., *Sozialdemokratie, Religion und Kirche* (Vienna, 1927). Discusses the relationship of religion and socialism in the context of the politics of Austria in the 1920s.

BEBEL, A., *Society of the Future* (Progress, Moscow, 1971). Chapter 4 contains Bebel's views on the future of religion.

BENTLEY, J., *Between Marx and Christ* (Verso, London, 1982). An interesting account of Christian–Marxist relations in the German-speaking world over the last century.

BERNSTEIN, E., *Cromwell and Communism* (Spokesman, Nottingham, 1980). A sometimes rather simplistic Marxist account of the English Civil War and the accompanying religious ideas.

CUNOW, H., *Die Ursprung der Religion und des Gottesglaubens* (Berlin, 1913). The first extended Marxist discussion of the origin of religion.

HEINTEL, PETER, *System und Ideologie. Der Austromarxismus im Spiegel der Philosophie Max Adlers* (Oldenbourg, Vienna, 1967). See particularly Chapter 9 for Adler on religion.

KAUTSKY, K., *Foundations of Christianity* (Orbach and Chambers, London, n.d.). The classic Marxist treatment. Dated but still interesting.

KAUTSKY, K., *Die Vorlaufer des neueren Sozialismus,* vol. 2 (Stuttgart, 1984). Contains Kautsky's views on the Reformation.

KAUTSKY, K., *Thomas More and His Utopia* (Lawrence and Wishart, London, 1979). A Marxist account of the Renaissance.

LESER, NORBERT, *Zwischen Reformismus und Bolschewismus. Der Austromarxismus als Theorie und Praxis* (Europa Verlag, Vienna, 1968). The most thorough work on Austro-Marxism in general.

PFARBIGAN, A., *Max Adler. Eine Politische Biographie* (Campus Verlag, Frankfurt/Main, 1982). Contains some good discussion of Adler's religious views.

ROLFES, H., *Jesus und das Proletariat* (Dusseldorf, 1982). A detailed account of the picture of Jesus held among German Marxists from Engels to the present day.

SORG, RICHARD, *Marxismus und Protestantismus in Deutschland* (Pahl-Rugenskin, Koln, 1974). Study of Marx-reception in Evangelical Church 1848–1948.

THEISSEN, G., *The First Followers of Jesus: a Sociological analysis of the first followers of Jesus* (SCM, London, 1978). A well-informed account against which to judge the assertions of Engels and Kautsky.

ZULEHNER, PAUL, *Kirche und Austromarxismus* (Herder, Vienna, 1967). Good on the historical/political background to the Austromarxists' writings.

Chapter 4

BEESTON, T., *Discretion and Valour* (Fortress Press, Philadelphia, 1974; 2nd edn, Collins, London, 1982). An account of religious life in Russia and Eastern Europe.

BERDIAEV, N., *Les Sources et le sens du communisme russe* (Gallimard, Paris, 1951). The classic account of Russian Marxism as a pseudo-religion – see particularly Chapter 7.

BOCIURKIW, B., 'Lenin and religion', in *Lenin: The man, the theorist, the leader,* ed. L. Schapiro and R. Reddaway (Pall Mall, London, 1967). A thorough, if hostile, account.

BOCIURKIW, B. and STRONG, J., *Religion and Atheism in the USSR and Eastern Europe* (Macmillan, London, 1975). Twenty scholarly essays on relatively specific aspects.

BORDEAUX, M., *Opium of the People. The Christian religion in the USSR* (Mowbrays, Oxford, 1977). A historical account imbued by a thorough-going anti-communism.

BRAKER, HANS, 'Die religionsphilosophische Diskussion in der Sowjetunion. Zur heutigen Auseinandersetzung des Marxismus-Leninismus mit dem Christentum', in *Marxismusstudien,* 5 (Folge hrsg. von Ulrich Duchrow, Tubingen, 1969). A useful discussion of post-war Soviet attitudes to religion.

ELLIS, J., *The Russian Orthodox Church: a contemporary history* (Croom Helm, London, 1986). An up-to-date and thorough account of relationships with the Communist authorities over the last two decades.

HECKER, J., *Religion and Communism: a study of religion and atheism in Soviet Russia* (Chapman and Hall, London, 1933). A pioneering study containing original material.

KLINE, G., *Religious and Anti-Religious Thought in Russia* (University of Chicago Press, Chicago, 1968). Good background for the debates between Lenin and his followers.

LABICA, G., 'Lenine et la religion', in *Philosophie et religion* (Editions Sociales, Paris, 1974). An informed and interesting elaboration of Lenin's views.

LANE, C., *Christian Religion in the Soviet Union: a sociological study* (Allen & Unwin, London, 1978). A well-informed and up-to-date study.

LENIN, V., *On Religion* (Martin Lawrence, London, n.d.). A small book containing most of what Lenin wrote on the matter.

PLEKHANOV, G., *Materialismus Militans: A reply to Mr Bogdanov* (Progress, Moscow, 1973). The first letter contains a succinct polemic against the God-builders.

POWELL, D., *Anti-religious Propaganda in the Soviet Union* (MIT Press, Cambridge, Mass., 1975). A thorough and well-documented study of this topic.

READ, C., *Religion, Revolution and the Russian Intelligentsia, 1900–1912* (Macmillan, London, 1979). Discusses Berdaev, Bulgakov and Lunacharsky.

SKODA, F., *Die Sowjetrussische philosophische Religionskritik heute* (Herder, Freiburg, 1968). Contains a lot of interesting statistical information.

THROWER, J., *Marxist–Leninist 'Scientific Atheism' and the Study of Religion and Atheism in the USSR* (Mouton, Amsterdam, 1983). A lengthy and thorough account based on primary sources.

WETTER, G., *Dialectical Materialism* (Routledge & Kegan Paul, London, 1960). The fullest treatment of this boring topic: but see sections on the God-builders and Bogdanov in Chapter 4.

Chapter 5

BLOCH, E., *Atheism in Christianity* (Herder & Herder, New York, 1972). Typically eclectic: contains Bloch's main ideas in a relatively accessible form.

BLOCH, E., *The Principle of Hope*, 3 vols (Blackwell, Oxford, 1986). His maddeningly unorganised and highly seminal *magnum opus*.

BORKENAU, F., *Der Ubergang vom feudalen zum burgerlichen Weltbild* (Alcan, Paris, 1934). A detailed discussion of the rise of capitalism (and Protestantism) by a leading member of the Frankfurt School.

COX, H., 'Ernst Bloch and "The Pull of the Future"', *New Theology No. 5*, ed. M. E. Marty and D. G. Peerman (New York, 1968) pp. 191–203. A good short introduction.

DAVIS, C., *Theology and Political Society* (Cambridge University Press, Cambridge, 1980). An important book which develops a critical theology in dialogue with Habermas.

FROMM, E., *The Dogma of Christ and Other Essays*, trans. J. L. Adams, 1953

(Holt, Rinehart & Winston, New York, 1963). An interesting attempt to mix psycho-analysis with Marxism in the interpretation of early Christianity.

GOLDMANN, L., *The Hidden God* (Routledge & Kegan Paul, London, 1964). The classic Marxist discussion of Pascal. A great book.

GRAMSCI, A., *Selections from the Prison Notebooks*, ed. Q. Hoare and P. Nowell Smith (Lawrence & Wishart, London, 1976). See particularly Part III for Gramsci's main comments.

HORKHEIMER, M., *Die Sehnsucht nach dem ganz Anderen* (Furche, Hamburg, 1970). Develops his 'negative' theology at greatest length.

LENHARDT, C., 'Anamnesic solidarity: the proletariat and its *Manes*', *Telos*, vol. 25 (1975). A remarkable article taking up Benjamin's ideas on redemptive memory.

LOWY, M., 'Revolution against "Progress": Walter Benjamin's romantic anarchism', *New Left Review*, Nov./Dec. (1985). A stimulating discussion of Benjamin's revolutionary messianism.

PORTELLI, H., *Gramsci et la question religieuse* (Anthropos, Paris, 1974). Splendidly thorough and informative.

SIEBERT, R., *The Critical Theory of Religion. The Frankfurt School* (Mouton, Berlin, 1965). A long, difficult and tortuous book which nevertheless comprises the most extensive discussion of the allusive remarks of Adorno, Benjamin, and Horkheimer.

See also the book by Carlebach (Chapter 1).

Chapter 6

A. Marxist–Christian Dialogue

APTHEKER, H. (ed.), *Marxism and Christianity* (Humanities Press, New York, 1968). Eleven heterogeneous contributions to this symposium sponsored by the American Institute for Marxist studies.

BENT, A., VAN DER, *The Christian–Marxist Dialogue. An annotated bibliography, 1959–1969* (Geneva, 1969). A useful tool for research.

DEAN, THOMAS, *Post-Theistic Thinking. The Marxist–Christian dialogue in radical perspective* (Temple University Press, Philadelphia, 1975). Attempts to re-think both Marxism and Christianity on the basis of a radical metaphysics which borrows from existentialism.

FETSCHER, I. and MACHOVEC, M., eds., *Marxisten und die Sache Jesu* (Kaiser, München, 1974). Leading European Marxists discuss their conceptions of Jesus.

GIRARDI, G., *Marxism and Christianity* (Gill & Macmillan, Dublin, 1968). A sympathetic discussion by a leading Catholic.

HEBBLETHWAITE, P., *The Christian–Marxist Dialogue and Beyond* (Darton, Longman and Todd, London, 1977). A short, measured, well-informed account.

KELLNER, ERICH (Hrsg.), *Christentum und Marxismus – heute* (Europa Verlag, Vienna, 1966). A substantial contribution to the Christian–Marxist dialogue organised by the Paulus-Gesellschaft.

KLUGMANN, J. (ed.), *Dialogue of Christianity and Marxism* (Lawrence & Wishart, London, 1968). Fourteen brief contributions which originally appeared in *Marxism Today*.

KLUGMANN, J. and OESTREICHER, P. (eds) *What Kind of Revolution? A Christian–Communist dialogue* (Panther, London, 1968). Ten essays by prominent Christians and Marxists.

LOCHMAN, J. M., *Christus oder Prometheus? Die Kernfrage des christlich-marxistischen Dialogs und die Christologie* (Hamburg, 1972). A good discussion by a leading Czech theologian.

LOCHMAN, J. M., 'Marxism, Liberalism and religion, an East European perspective', in *Marxism and Radical Religion*, ed. J. C. Raine and T. Dean (Philadelphia, 1970) pp. 11–25. The dialogue viewed from the practical difficulties of the Czech situation.

MARCHAIS, G. and HOURDIN, G. (eds) *Communistes et Chrétiens* (Desclée, Paris, 1976). A document of the contemporary political debate in France.

MOJZES, P. (ed.), *Varieties of Christian–Marxist Dialogue* (Ecumenical Press, Philadelphia, 1978). A very ecumenical collection, and probably the most interesting.

OGLETREE, THOMAS, *Openings for Marxist–Christian Dialogue* (Abingdon Press, Nashville, 1969). Four essays by Christians sympathetic to the dialogue.

STOHR, M. (ed.) *Disputation zwischen Christen und Marxisten* (Kaiser, München, 1968). A series of articles by Czeck Marxists and West German Protestants.

TOWERS, B. and DYSON, A. (eds) *Evolution, Marxism and Christianity* (Garnstone Press, London, 1967). Various contributions, some of which aim at a rapprochement between Marx and Teilhard.

VREE, DALE, *On Synthesizing Marxism and Christianity* (Wiley, New York, 1976). Examines protagonists on both sides of this synthesis and concludes that Marxism and Christianity are disjunctive belief systems.

Chapter 6

B. Liberation Theology

BELO, F., *A Materialist Reading of the Gospel of Mark* (Orbis, Maryknoll, 1981). An unremittingly structuralist essay: only for those well versed in semiotics.

BONINO, J. M., *Doing Theology in a Revolutionary Situation* (Fortress, Philadelphia, 1935). A good short introduction to liberation theology.

FESSARD, G., *Chrétiens marxistes et théologie de la libération* (Lethielleux, Paris, 1978). A strong attack on Girardi and the Christians for Socialism movement.

FIERRO, A., *The Militant Gospel* (Orbis Books, Maryknoll, 1977). The best general account of the contribution that Marxism can make to a 'liberation' view of Christianity.

GIRARDI, G., *Marxism and Christianity* (Gill and Macmillan, Dublin, 1968).

An influential contribution to the 'dialogue' by one of the leading Catholic protagonists.

GUTIERREZ, G., *A Theology of Liberation* (SCM, London, 1974). The classic text of liberation theology.

HADJOR, K. and WREN, B. (eds) 'Christian faith and Third World Liberation', *Third World Book Review*, vol. 1, nos. 4 and 5 (1985). An excellent overview of contemporary literature on the subject.

MIRANDA, J., *Marx and the Bible. A critique of the philosophy of oppression* (Orbis, New York, 1974). Finds a remarkable convergence between Marx and the Bible.

SEGUNDO, J. L., *Faith and Ideologies*, vol. 1 (Orbis, Maryknoll, 1984). A massive and rather heavy work by a Uruguayan theologian. Chapters 7, 8 and 9 deal explicitly with Marxism.

SENKE, A., *Marxismus als atheistische Weltanschauung* (Patmos, Paderborn, 1983). A thoughtful and detailed discussion claiming a strong incompatibility between Marxism and Christianity. See Chapter 6 for liberation theology in this context.

Chapter 6

C. Miscellaneous

ADELMANN, F., *From Dialogue to Epilogue. Marxism and Catholicism Tomorrow* (Nijhoff, The Hague, 1968). A short philosophical discussion of the bases of coexistence.

D'ARCY, M., *Communism and Christianity* (Penguin, Harmondsworth, 1956). Contrasts Christianity favourably with Orthodox Communism.

GARAUDY, R., *From Anathema to Dialogue: The Challenge of Marxist–Christian Cooperation* (Collins, London, 1967). Classic statement by a leading Marxist in the wake of Vatican II.

GARAUDY, R., *Marxism in the Twentieth Century* (Collins, London, 1970). Chapter 4 contains the best summation of Garaudy's view while he was still a Marxist.

GARDAVSKY, V., *God is Not Yet Dead* (Penguin, Harmondsworth, 1973). A thought-provoking examination of the Christian tradition by a Czech Marxist.

GONZALES-RUIZ, J., *The New Creation: Marxist and Christian?* (Orbis, Maryknoll, 1976). A positive answer to this question by a Spanish theologian.

GROSS, D., 'Symposium on religion and politics', *Telos*, vol. 58 (Winter 1983/84). Twenty-one contributions across a wide range of contemporary issues.

KEE, A. (ed.) *A Reader in Political Theology* (SCM, London, 1974). Short readable contributions by many hands on Marxism, liberation and revolution.

KOLAKOWSKI, L., *Chrétiens sans église* (Gallimard, Paris, 1965). A *magnum opus* studying religious dissidence in seventeenth-century Europe.

KOLAKOWSKI, L., *Towards a Marxist Humanism* (Grove Press, New York, 1968). The first essay – 'The Priest and the Jester' – is stimulating on the abiding nature of theological questions.

LISCHER, R., *Marx and Teilhard. Two ways to the New Humanity* (Orbis, Maryknoll, 1979). Compares the two in a broad historical synthesis which is a bit nearer Teilhard than Marx.

LOCHMAN, J., *Encountering Marx* (Christian Journals Ltd, Belfast, 1977). A short sympathetic assessment of Marxism by a leading Czech theologian.

MACHOVEC, M., *A Marxist Looks at Jesus* (Darton, Longman and Todd, London, 1976). A sympathetic discussion of the New Testament picture of Jesus.

NORRIS, RUSSELL, *God, Marx and the Future* (Fortress, Philadelphia, 1974). A sympathetic Christian commentary on Garaudy.

OUDENRIJN, F., *Kritische Theologie als Kritik der Theologie: Theorie und Praxis bei Karl Marx* (Kaiser, München, 1972). A radicalising of Metz's political theology by one of his disciples.

PARSONS, HOWARD, *Marxism, Christianity and Human Values* (Gruner, Amsterdam, 1981). An evaluation from a Communist Party perspective.

SWEEZY, P. and MAGDOFF, H. (eds) 'Religion and the Left', *Monthly Review*, vol. 36, no. 3 (1984). An excellent collection, well illustrative of contemporary American debates.

WEST, C., *Communism, and the Theologians* (Macmillan, New York, 1958). Discusses the opinions about Communism of such theologians as Hromadka, Tillich, Berdiaev, Niebuhr and Barth.

Index